D1523097

Kant on Evil, Self-Deception, and Moral Reform

KANT ON EVIL,
SELF-DECEPTION,
AND MORAL REFORM

Laura Papish

OXFORD
UNIVERSITY PRESS

Oxford University Press is a department of the University of Oxford. It furthers
the University's objective of excellence in research, scholarship, and education
by publishing worldwide. Oxford is a registered trade mark of Oxford University
Press in the UK and certain other countries.

Published in the United States of America by Oxford University Press
198 Madison Avenue, New York, NY 10016, United States of America.

Library of Congress Cataloging-in-Publication Data
Names: Papish, Laura, author.
Title: Kant on evil, self-deception, and moral reform / Laura Papish.
Description: New York : Oxford University Press, 2018. |
Includes bibliographical references and index.
Identifiers: LCCN 2017045790 (print) | LCCN 2018006491 (ebook) |
ISBN 9780190692131 (online course) | ISBN 9780190692117 (updf) |
ISBN 9780190692124 (epub) | ISBN 9780190692100 (cloth : alk. paper)
Subjects: LCSH: Kant, Immanuel, 1724–1804. | Good and evil. | Self-deception.
Classification: LCC B2798 (ebook) | LCC B2798 .P165 2018 (print) | DDC 170.92—dc23
LC record available at https://lccn.loc.gov/2017045790

9 8 7 6 5 4 3 2 1

Printed by Sheridan Books, Inc., United States of America

To the memory of my father, Richard P. Papish

CONTENTS

ACKNOWLEDGMENTS

There are many people who have helped make this book a reality. To start, I want to thank Lucy Randall, Hannah Doyle, and the rest of the staff at Oxford University Press who helped at various stages of production. I want to give special thanks to Lucy, since without her enthusiasm at the very beginning of my work on this manuscript, the project would never have gotten off the ground. I owe a similar debt of gratitude to my colleagues in the Department of Philosophy at George Washington University (GW). I wish to thank Gail Weiss, who was chair upon my hire and who continued to advocate and look out for me during my career. I also wish to thank Tad Zawidzki, my current chair, as he has enabled me—through research and travel support, a flexible teaching schedule, and overall good vibes—to both complete this manuscript and secure a much-needed set of course releases to help me recover from completing it. In addition, I owe an enormous debt to David DeGrazia, who has served as my mentor throughout my time at GW. David has offered invaluable advice both on publishing in general and on how to develop this particular book project, and at crucial junctures he has helped me navigate the publishing process and my reviewer feedback. I feel incredibly lucky to have him as a mentor, since without his encouragement and guidance I would have never had the confidence to try to write a book. I also want to thank GW and the John Templeton Foundation for financial support. In 2015, GW granted me a University Facilitating Fund award, which proved especially helpful to my research that summer. Through the Templeton Foundation, I was able to participate in Christian Miller's 2013 Character Project Summer Seminar, and without this opportunity I would not have been able to do the research that informed much of Chapter 2.

There are many more people who played distant and near roles in the development of this book. I want to note my gratitude to John Russon, my undergraduate professor, whose excellence as a teacher and passion for philosophy made me love the field to begin with. During my time as a graduate student, I was surrounded by first-rate philosophers who played essential roles in my academic career, among them Richard Kraut, Rachel Zuckert, Kyla Ebels-Duggan, and Paul Guyer. More recently, I relied on an extensive network of Kantians to help spark, develop, and refine the ideas put forward in this book. I have benefited greatly from study group meetings sponsored by the North American Kant Society and I thank the hosts who arranged these meetings, including Melissa Seymour Fahmy, Colin McQuillan, Huaping Lu-Adler, and, again, Rachel Zuckert. I am grateful to audiences that gave valuable feedback at several additional conferences and invited talks, including those held at the University of Oslo, the University of Vienna, George Mason University, the University of Chicago, and the Rocky Mountain Ethics Congress.

I also want to note my gratitude to the other members of the D.C./ Baltimore Kant Group, which has enabled me to be part of a supportive, warm, and intellectually fierce community. Mavis Biss, Joseph Trullinger, Mike Nance, Tim Jankowiak, and Oliver Thorndike have all been consistent and challenging interlocutors these past few years, and I am extraordinarily grateful to them for their input on earlier drafts of several of the chapters or ideas in this book. Our group was formed in 2014 by Huaping Lu-Adler, and I want to express how thankful I am to her for giving us such a special, intimate, and serious place to share our works in progress. In fact, without having had the opportunity to read some of Huaping's excellent work, and to learn about the kind of resource Kant's lectures on logic could be for those interested in Kant's practical philosophy, this book simply could not have taken shape. Within the realm of Kant studies, I finally want to note my debts, first, to Krista Thomason, who also has offered extremely helpful and incisive feedback concerning past drafts of my work, and, second, to the two reviewers commissioned by Oxford to review my manuscript. Their careful, thoughtful, and constructively critical replies to my earliest version of the text enabled me to produce a substantially revised and improved book, and while I am, of course, solely responsible for any mistakes or missteps that remain in the final version, their input was invaluable. I deeply appreciate the time and care both reviewers put into this project.

Finally, I want to thank the friends and family members who have supported me as this book project took shape. Alison Peterman has been a dear friend from our first days at Northwestern, and since then we have staked out a trail writing proseminar papers together, rallying each other through the job market, and taking much deserved breaks by eating her excellent pancakes and having cocktails in person and over Skype. Katherine

Wasdin, who is part of my cohort at GW, has explored D.C. with me, been my co-navigator of the tenure track, and both has exposed me to some of the coolest, strangest, movies I've ever seen and has accompanied me to more metal shows than I'm sure she'd like to remember. Luis Mier y Terán has helped make D.C. home with barbeques, trips, adventures, and an ever-increasing stream of cat videos and pictures. The Northeast's best bluegrass band—Calamity Row, which includes Josh McDonald, Jordan Cutler, and Annie Miller—has given me fun nights out throughout the school years and summers, and has helped make D.C. the best place I have ever lived. My family and in-laws have provided steady encouragement these past years, and I want to thank Rod and Jo Winther, Melinda Winther, Sara and Mike Kopp, Dave Riley, Genevieve Riley, Liz Papish, and my mother Mary Ann Papish. She and my adored, late father Richard Papish never once doubted my choice of philosophy as a profession, and I am extremely fortunate to have known, from the time I was a child, that I should do what I love for work and do it well. My father was so pleased when I declared a major in philosophy that he went to Labyrinth Books in New York City and picked out for me Gregory Vlastos's *Socrates: Ironist and Moral Philosopher*. If I was going to do philosophy, he said, I would want to start at the beginning. I have tried my best to produce work as serious as he thought me capable of.

Finally, my deepest thanks go to Chris Winther, my husband and best friend. Chris is the funniest, most fun, and best person I have ever known. I spent many late nights and weekends at the office working on this book, and even on the most sleep-deprived, writer-blocked, and frustrating days, it never really bothered me since I knew I would come home to someone who would have me laughing within minutes without even trying. The partnership and home we share, complete with the two most darling cats that have ever existed, Schuylkill and Catharine, are the most valuable things in my life.

ABBREVIATIONS AND TRANSLATIONS

References to Kant's writings are cited in the body of the text and according to the volume and page numbers in *Kants gesammelte Schriften*, herausgegeben von der Deutschen Akademie der Wissenschaften (Berlin: Walter de Gruyter, 1900). The only exception is the *Critique of Pure Reason*, where my citations follow the standard A/B pagination. References to Kant's *Reflexionen* also include the number assigned to them by Erich Adickes.

My quotations of Kant rely on English translations from the Cambridge Edition of the Works of Immanuel Kant, edited by Paul Guyer and Allen W. Wood where available, and I have had to supply my own translations for only a few *Reflexionen*. The following list contains both the translations used and abbreviations for Kant's works.

Anth	*Anthropologie in pragmatischer Hinsicht. Anthropology from a Pragmatic Point of View*, translated by Robert B. Louden. In *Anthropology, History, and Education*, edited by Günther Zöller and Robert B. Louden (Cambridge: Cambridge University Press, 2007).
EAD	*Das Ende Aller Dinge. The End of All Things*, translated by Allen W. Wood. In *Religion and Rational Theology*, edited by Allen W. Wood and George di Giovanni (Cambridge: Cambridge University Press, 1996).
GMS	*Grundlegung zur Metaphysik der Sitten. Groundwork of the Metaphysics of Morals*, translated by Mary J. Gregor. In *Practical Philosophy*, edited by Mary J. Gregor (Cambridge: Cambridge University Press, 1996).
IaG	*Idee zu einer allgemeinen Geschichte in weltbürgerlicher Absicht. Idea for a Universal History with a Cosmopolitan*

Aim, translated by Allen W. Wood. In *Anthropology, History, and Education*, edited by Günther Zöller and Robert B. Louden (Cambridge: Cambridge University Press, 2007).

KpV   *Kritik der praktischen Vernunft. Critique of Practical Reason*, translated by Mary J. Gregor. In *Practical Philosophy*, edited by Mary J. Gregor (Cambridge: Cambridge University Press, 1996).

KrV   *Kritik der reinen Vernunft. Critique of Pure Reason*, edited and translated by Paul Guyer and Allen W. Wood (Cambridge: Cambridge University Press, 1998).

KU   *Kritik der Urteilskraft. Critique of the Power of Judgment*, edited and translated by Paul Guyer and translated by Eric Matthews (Cambridge: Cambridge University Press, 2000).

Log   *Immanuel Kants Logik: ein Handbuch zu Vorlesungen. Immanuel Kant's Logic: A Manual for Lectures*, edited by Gottlob Benjamin Jäsche, translated by J. Michael Young. In *Lectures on Logic*, edited by J. Michael Young (Cambridge: Cambridge University Press, 1992).

MAM   *Mutmaßlicher Anfang der Menschengeschichte. Conjectural Beginning of Human History*, translated by Allen W. Wood. In *Anthropology, History, and Education*, edited by Günther Zöller and Robert B. Louden (Cambridge: Cambridge University Press, 2007).

MAN   *Metaphysische Anfangsgründe der Naturwissenschaft. Metaphysical Foundations of Natural Science*, edited and translated by Michael Friedman (Cambridge: Cambridge University Press, 2004).

MpVT   *Über das Mißlingen aller philosophischen Versuche in der Theodicee. On the Miscarriage of All Philosophical Trials in Theodicy*, translated by George di Giovanni. In *Religion and Rational Theology*, edited by Allen W. Wood and George di Giovanni (Cambridge: Cambridge University Press, 1996).

MS   *Die Metaphysik der Sitten. The Metaphysics of Morals*, translated by Mary J. Gregor. In *Practical Philosophy*, edited by Mary J. Gregor (Cambridge: Cambridge University Press, 1996).

NG	*Versuch den Begriff der negativen Größen in die Weltweisheit einzuführen. Attempt to Introduce the Concept of Negative Magnitudes into Philosophy*, translated by David Walford. In *Theoretical Philosophy: 1755–70*, edited by David Wolford in collaboration with Ralf Meerbote (Cambridge: Cambridge University Press, 1992).
Päd	*Pädagogik. Lectures on Pedagogy*, translated by Robert B. Louden. In *Anthropology, History, and Education*, edited by Günther Zöller and Robert B. Louden (Cambridge: Cambridge University Press, 2007).
Prol	*Prolegomena zu einer jeden künftigen Metaphysik, die als Wissenschaft wird auftreten können. Prolegomena to Any Future Metaphysics That Will Be Able to Come Forward as Science*, translated by Gary Hatfield (Cambridge: Cambridge University Press, 1997).
Refl	*Reflexionen.*
RGV	*Die Religion innerhalb der Grenzen der bloßen Vernunft. Religion within the Boundaries of Mere Reason*, translated by George di Giovanni. In *Religion and Rational Theology*, edited by Allen W. Wood and George di Giovanni (Cambridge: Cambridge University Press, 1996).
SF	*Der Streit der Fakultäten. The Conflict of the Faculties*, translated by Mary J. Gregor and Robert Anchor. In *Religion and Rational Theology*, edited by Allen W. Wood and George di Giovanni (Cambridge: Cambridge University Press, 1996).
TP	*Über den Gemeinspruch: Das mag in der Theorie richtig sein, taugt aber nicht für die Praxis. On the Common Saying: That May Be Correct in Theory, but It Is of No Use in Practice*, translated by Mary J. Gregor. In *Practical Philosophy*, edited by Mary J. Gregor (Cambridge: Cambridge University Press, 1996).
VASF	*Vorarbeit zum Streit der Fakultäten. Draft for the Conflict of the Faculties*, translated by Frederick Rauscher. In *Lectures and Drafts on Kant's Political Philosophy*, edited by Frederick Rauscher (Cambridge: Cambridge University Press, 2016).

V-Anth/Busolt	*Vorlesungen Wintersemester 1788/1789 Busolt. Anthropology Busolt (1788–1789)*, translated by Allen W. Wood. In *Lectures on Anthropology*, edited by Allen W. Wood and Robert B. Louden (Cambridge: Cambridge University Press, 2012).
V-Anth/Collins	*Vorlesungen Wintersemester 1772/1773 Collins. Anthropology Collins (1772–1773)*, translated by Allen W. Wood. In *Lectures on Anthropology*, edited by Allen W. Wood and Robert B. Louden (Cambridge: Cambridge University Press, 2012).
V-Anth/Fried	*Vorlesungen Wintersemester 1775/1776 Friedländer. Anthropology Friedländer (1775–1776)*, translated by G. Felicitas Munzel. In *Lectures on Anthropology*, edited by Allen W. Wood and Robert B. Louden (Cambridge: Cambridge University Press, 2012).
V-Anth/Mensch	*Vorlesungen Wintersemester 1781/1782 Menschenkunde, Petersburg. Menschenkunde (1781–1782?)*, translated by Robert B. Louden. In *Lectures on Anthropology*, edited by Allen W. Wood and Robert B. Louden (Cambridge: Cambridge University Press, 2012).
V-Anth/Mron	*Vorlesungen Wintersemester 1784/1785 Mrongovius. Anthropology Mrongovius (1784–1785)*, translated by Robert R. Clewis. In *Lectures on Anthropology*, edited by Allen W. Wood and Robert B. Louden (Cambridge: Cambridge University Press, 2012).
V-Anth/Parrow	*Vorlesungen Wintersemester 1772/1773 Parrow. Anthropology Parrow (1772–1773)*, translated by Allen W. Wood. In *Lectures on Anthropology*, edited by Allen W. Wood and Robert B. Louden (Cambridge: Cambridge University Press, 2012).
V-Anth/Pillau	*Vorlesungen Wintersemester 1777/1778 Pillau. Anthropology Pillau (1777–1778)*, translated by Allen W. Wood. In *Lectures on Anthropology*, edited by Allen W. Wood and Robert B. Louden (Cambridge: Cambridge University Press, 2012).
V-Lo/Blomberg	*Logik Blomberg. The Blomberg Logic*, translated by J. Michael Young. In *Lectures on Logic*, edited by J. Michael Young (Cambridge: Cambridge University Press, 1992).

V-Lo/Dohna	*Logik Dohna-Wundlacken. The Dohna-Wundlacken Logic*, translated by J. Michael Young. In *Lectures on Logic*, edited by J. Michael Young (Cambridge: Cambridge University Press, 1992).
V-Lo/Wiener	*Wiener Logik. The Vienna Logic*, translated by J. Michael Young. In *Lectures on Logic*, edited by J. Michael Young (Cambridge: Cambridge University Press, 1992).
V-Met-L2/Pölitz	*Metaphysik L_2 (Pölitz). Metaphysik L_2*, translated by Karl Ameriks and Steve Naragon. In *Lectures on Metaphysics*, edited by Karl Ameriks and Steve Naragon (Cambridge: Cambridge University Press, 1997).
V-Mo/Collins	*Moralphilosophie Collins. Moral Philosophy: Collins' Lecture Notes*, translated by Peter Heath. In *Lectures on Ethics*, edited by Peter Heath and J. B. Schneewind (Cambridge: Cambridge University Press, 1997).
V-MS/Vigil	*Metaphysik der Sitten Vigilantius. Kant on the Metaphysics of Morals: Vigilantius's Lecture Notes*, translated by Peter Heath. In *Lectures on Ethics*, edited by Peter Heath and J. B. Schneewind (Cambridge: Cambridge University Press, 1997).
V-Phil-Th/Pölitz	*Philosophische Religionslehre nach Pölitz. Lectures of the Philosophical Doctrine of Religion*, translated by Allen W. Wood. In *Religion and Rational Theology*, edited by Allen W. Wood and George di Giovanni (Cambridge: Cambridge University Press, 1996).
WA	*Beantwortung der Frage: Was ist Aufklärung? An Answer to the Question: What Is Enlightenment?*, translated by Mary J. Gregor. In *Practical Philosophy*, edited by Mary J. Gregor (Cambridge: Cambridge University Press, 1996).
ZeF	*Zum Ewigen Frieden. Toward Perpetual Peace*, translated by Mary J. Gregor. In *Practical Philosophy*, edited by Mary J. Gregor (Cambridge: Cambridge University Press, 1996).

Introduction

Immanuel Kant's account of evil remains one of the less explored and more controversial elements of his broader moral theory. The reasons are manifold.

Kant's moral writings largely discuss the metaphysical underpinnings of morality, such as the possibility of moral motivation, how freedom and rationality relate to the ability to bind oneself to moral principles, and the need to specify the terms of the moral law independent of historical context, generalizations about human nature, or the specific desires or goals of any given individual. This allows Kant to purify his moral theory of any cultural, anthropological, or personal elements, and to develop an account of the moral law that would hold for any rational agent whatsoever, but it also forces much of Kant's moral theory to gravitate toward both the wholesome and the ideal. Thus, while Kant focuses on articulating the conditions of a Kingdom of Ends, wherein all rational wills are aligned in the pursuit of moral goodness, he does not offer a sufficiently extensive or fully clear account of the shortcomings that human beings are vulnerable to or the apparent variety of evil in everyday life. Though we know much about the hallmarks of morally worthy action, Kant spends comparatively little time explaining wrongdoing or evil actions or characters.[1]

These difficulties are aggravated by the context in which Kant finally, albeit briefly, addressed the problem of human evil and the reception

---

1. Throughout this chapter and this book, I use the notions of evil and immorality interchangeably, as I think Kant himself is inclined to. This is in contrast to the work of certain contemporary Kantians, such as Ernesto Garcia, who argue for a distinction between evil and immorality. See "A Kantian Theory of Evil."

he has received. Part One of *Religion within the Boundaries of Mere Reason* contains Kant's most thorough account of evil and a striking claim—namely, that the evil in human beings is universal. Kant's contemporaries fiercely objected to this idea, finding implicit in it an unacceptable commitment to the doctrine of original sin. Goethe, for example, wrote to Johann Gottfried von Herder that Kant "slobbered on his philosopher's cloak" with these claims about the universality of evil.[2] Schiller likewise deemed Kant's claim about the universal evil in human nature "scandalous."[3] Such concerns shaped the views of even the most sympathetic of early-twentieth-century commentators. For example, Ernst Cassirer argued that Kant's thesis regarding universal evil was an attempt to strike a balance between commitments that pulled Kant in different directions. In Cassirer's view, Kant sought to retain a rationalist moral theory while finding the truth in biblical dogma, and he needed to write ambiguously enough to deflect the attention of political authorities at a time when Frederick the Great's intellectually permissive reign had just ended. For Cassirer, these tensions rendered Kant's account of evil an unsatisfying, opaque, and inadequately developed product of compromise.[4]

Cassirer's and other similarly gloomy assessments have persisted, causing contemporary scholarship on Kant's theory of evil to lag behind scholarship on Kant's moral theory more generally. Within the commentary we do have, responses range from chilly and skeptical to warm and sympathetic. On the former end, Kant's *Religion* often gets treated as a work that cannot offer insights that stand up to those found in his more canonical ethical writings, such as the *Groundwork of the Metaphysics of Morals*. The wariness many feel toward the *Religion* is evident not only in still-lingering worries regarding the specter of original sin; it also underwrites objections Kant often faces for his views about the motivations behind evil. Kant has come under intense criticism from Kantians and non-Kantians alike for at least appearing to claim that all action contrary to the law is driven by a commitment to hedonistic pleasure or what Kant calls "self-love." The worry is that in arguing that all evil arises from self-love or a concern for one's own happiness or pleasure, Kant commits himself to a crude, simplistic, and implausible account of human behavior and motivation. Among the many cases one can put forward as possible counterexamples

---

2. *Goethes Briefe, Bd. 2, Briefe der Jahre 1786–1805*, 166. Cited in Robert Thomas Clark, *Herder: His Life and Thought*, 319–320.
3. Cited in Emil Fackenheim, "Kant and Radical Evil," 340.
4. See *Kant's Life and Thought*, 361–397.

to the idea that evil involves self-love are: terrorists and religious fanatics[5]; vengeful individuals who do terrible things even though these actions thwart their own happiness; those who appear to do evil at the behest of an authority figure—such as the participants of the Stanley Milgram shock experiments[6]—but not out of self-love; and Adolf Eichmann, particularly as he is immortalized in our public consciousness and through the writings of Hannah Arendt.[7] This final example has served as something of a rallying cry for those rejecting Kant's theory of evil, for as Bernstein has pointed out, it seems absurd to think of Eichmann as a sensualist or a hedonistically self-indulgent man.[8] And for many commentators and philosophers, this failure is fatal. In their eyes, it damages both Kant's standing as a moral theorist and Kant's ability to be considered relevant to contemporary accounts of evil in ethical theory.[9]

On the warmer or more sympathetic end, the scene looks different. The past five years in particular have seen revived interest in Kant's theory of evil and instilled a new-found optimism that his account is more viable than previously thought. I share that enthusiasm, though as we will see, some of the warmth felt toward Kant's theory of evil has been somewhat hastily or preemptively offered. It seems one reason why Kant's notion of evil has found new admirers is because Kant is inclined toward what many see as a highly attractive view about the cognitive dimensions of evil. Several aspects of Kant's moral philosophy appear to commit him to the position that evil is facilitated by or perhaps even requires self-deception. And for those who stand convinced that moral failure is accompanied by

5. On terrorists and religious fanatics as possible counterexamples to Kant's theory of evil, see Richard Bernstein, *Radical Evil: A Philosophical Interrogation*, 42. See also Robert Louden, "Evil Everywhere: The Ordinariness of Radical Evil," 101.

6. I discuss these experiments and commentary on them in Chapter 2.

7. See *Eichmann in Jerusalem: A Report on the Banality of Evil*. See especially 21–55, 82–111, and 135–150. This final selection discusses Eichmann's infamous depiction of himself as a Kantian, a description that Arendt herself does not wholeheartedly endorse.

8. See again Bernstein, *Radical Evil: A Philosophical Interrogation*, 42. I revisit the case of Eichmann at the end of Chapter 1 and again in Chapter 4.

9. Indeed, contemporary philosophers of religion and moral philosophers doing research on evil seem to have picked up on this disregard for Kant's views, as his theory of evil receives little mention in their work and, when mentioned, even less favorable support. For example, Peter Brian Barry is quick to criticize Kant's theory of evil in *Evil and Moral Psychology* (see 23–26), as are John Kekes in *The Roots of Evil* (see especially page 5) and Claudia Card in *The Atrocity Paradigm* (see 75–87). In Colin McGinn's *Evil, Ethics, and Fiction*, Kant is only nominally noted, and barely a passing glance is made at Kant by Adam Morton is his interesting book *On Evil* (see especially page 3). Thus, Kant's almost non-existent influence on contemporary scholarship on evil stands in stark contrast with the influence he has had on contemporary meta- and normative ethics.

internal dissonance, confusion, and a sense of self-betrayal, any indication that Kant seems sympathetic to this view will count strongly in his favor.

This explains the recent urge to take seriously Kant's theory of evil and helps us appreciate what this theory stands to offer us. But unfortunately, the literature has up until now lacked any sustained inquiry into the connection between evil and self-deception. It is more assumed than argued that doctrines such as the fact of reason, or Kant's broader commitment to moral rationalism, lead to the conclusion that evil is tightly or necessarily linked to self-deception. It is not acknowledged that despite scattered remarks alluding to such a connection between immorality and self-deception, Kant never really advocates it; indeed, as we'll see in Chapter 3, Kant only very rarely even uses the term "self-deception." It is also assumed that we Kantians all know what one another means when we refer to the notion of self-deception in the first place. Finally, though these deficiencies in the scholarship are serious enough, at least two more exist. Since there is not an adequate body of literature to facilitate debate, disagreements with those Kantians who are less convinced that evil demands self-obfuscation have remained unresolved and, worse, largely unaired.[10] And though Kantians most broadly have taken seriously the need to show the viability of Kantian ethics from an ahistorical or contemporary point of view, they have not yet begun to determine whether, if Kant does put self-deception alongside evil, he has defensible philosophical reasons for doing so. To at least some extent, Kant scholars interested in the relation between self-deception and evil, or self-deception and practical irrationality more generally, should take into account what those working in contemporary ethics and the philosophy of action have to say regarding this connection.

The following book is a response to these deficiencies, as well as to those cool and warm strains in Kant scholarship. It continues the trend of the last several years by interpreting Kant's theory of evil in a largely sympathetic light, as I try to show that there are good grounds for the new sense of promise that surrounds the *Religion*. I offer a chapter-by-chapter synopsis shortly, but one reason why I think this optimism is deserved is that we can, to a surprisingly successful degree, defend Kant against those who would charge that his theory of evil relies on a simplistic account of human motivation. Beyond this, one of the central and animating ideas of this book is that the possibility of a connection between evil and self-deception

10. As I note in Chapter 4, Paul Formosa, Matthew Rukgaber, David Sussman, and Allen W. Wood are among those Kantians who have expressed at least some skepticism about whether evil requires self-deception.

can not only be developed but also provide a new lens through which we can approach Kant's theory of evil. By trying to figure out what self-deception is and the different ways in which it seems to relate to evil, we secure a new way of both explaining what is so attractive about Kant's theory of evil and illuminating controversies surrounding it, including Kant's claims about an evil universally spread throughout human nature. We also, crucially, obtain a new way to conceptualize moral reform. For if cognitive failures are implicated in evil, then we should expect that an agent who performs a moral revolution and endeavors to make moral progress needs, likewise, to make certain strides in self-cognition. Given that Kant's account of moral reform can often seem to involve mysterious, or as he would say "inscrutable" (RGV 6:21), elements, any interpretive framework that can perhaps demystify some aspects of moral reform is highly desirable.

To explain further this book's goals and how we will get to these final points about self-cognition and moral reform, a chapter-by-chapter overview is needed. To begin, and as already noted, Kant argues that there are only two incentives of practical reason, namely, self-love and respect for the moral law. And because of this dualism, he is vulnerable to the charge that his theory of motivation lacks nuance and that people can surely want something other than the gratification of desire or pleasure. The first two chapters respond to this criticism, with the first chapter focusing on how this criticism plays out in the context of Kant's nonmoral psychology and the second chapter shifting to the context of Kant's theory of evil. In Chapter 1, I argue that we can develop a more sophisticated version of Kant's nonmoral psychology, one that is markedly different from Andrews Reath's influential attempt to rehabilitate Kant on this score. Whereas Reath tries to secure a more complex Kant by stripping out much of the hedonism that seems to run throughout Kant's account of nonmoral motivation, I proceed by attending closely to the role and demands of the *self* that seeks pleasures or that self-loves in Kantianism. I believe that in doing so, we'll lend much-craved texture to Kant's views and do so while remaining quite faithful to Kant's stated claims. At the end of this chapter, I also note how this focus on the self anticipates important questions regarding personal moral reform. If, as I'll argue, egoistic concerns are at the core of nonmoral motivation, then it might seem as though a person's sense of self—complete with the social, historical, and empirical markers of one's identity—must be struck down or diminished in order to ensure the proper place of the moral law. Indeed, several influential critics have expressed just this prediction and concern about Kant's ethics.[11] I take this

11. Hegel, Schopenhauer, Iris Murdoch, and Bernard Williams are among these critics.

worry seriously, and throughout the course of the book, I offer an account of why this suspicion is ultimately unfounded.

While Chapter 1 tries to defend Kant's nonmoral psychology and explain exactly what self-love is, Chapter 2 turns to what we can refer to as Kant's immoral psychology, or the question of what it means to say, as Kant does in the *Religion*, that evil consists of the "subordination" of the moral law to self-love (RGV 6:36). Here, my main goal is to determine what kinds of formal arrangements between the incentives of practical reason—self-love and respect for the law—are possible in an evil will. I show that just as we were able to find nuance within Kant's nonmoral psychology in Chapter 1, so can we find nuance within this notion of subordination and mitigate the worry that Kant sees evil as simply the putting aside of moral respect for the sake of self-love or, as some commentators put it, the "prioritization" of self-love.[12] Such prioritization is one way the incentives of practical reason can be wrongfully arranged, but it is not, I argue, the only way. As we'll see, there is good reason to think that, for Kant, evil can result from *overdetermination* or from the attempt to incorporate the incentives of *both* respect and self-love alongside one another in the same fundamental maxim. I defend this idea of evil in terms of overdetermination throughout the chapter, taking special care to explain its philosophical value and the textual points that speak directly or indirectly in its favor.

Once this discussion of evil is concluded, we can then begin to shift to a central concern of this book, namely, how evil relates to self-deception. But as the concept of evil required closer inspection, so does the concept of self-deception. Thus the next task, and the task of Chapter 3, is to explain what exactly self-deception is from a Kantian point of view. Beginning with his writings in moral philosophy, I argue that though Kant seems to explain self-deception by drawing on the concept of an internal or inner lie, this would not provide a fruitful way to understand self-deception. Moreover, I argue that Kant himself was aware that this type of explanatory strategy was problematic. I then show that if we broaden our textual resources and turn to materials generally not investigated by those working on practical philosophy—in particular, Kant's lectures on logic—then we can develop a much more promising account of what self-deception is. As I'll demonstrate, self-deception is a rationally sophisticated and rationally minded form of irrationality, one that involves a process Kant refers to as *rationalization* (*Vernünfteln*). I also explain that since the border between impermissible self-deceit and justified doxastic voluntarism depends on the laudability

12. Examples of such commentators are given in note 31 of Chapter 2.

of our motives and goals, self-deceptive rationalization must ultimately be understood more as a normative concept than a descriptive one.

With this account of self-deception by our side, I then explore in Chapters 4 and 5 whether we can substantiate the intuition that self-deception is crucially related to evil. This is the point at which Kant's views concerning a "radical evil" become pertinent, and I proceed by teasing apart three different ways in which we can think of evil as rooted. I argue at the outset of Chapter 4 that the root of evil can be fleshed out in terms of, first, the *necessary conditions* of evil; second, that which explains the *entrenchment* or the obstinate quality of evil; and, third, the *universality* of evil throughout human nature. I then examine carefully whether self-deception is implicated in each of these senses of rootedness. Thus in Chapter 4, I consider whether Kant can say that self-deception is a necessary condition of evil and whether self-deception explains how evil can become entrenched or firmly anchored in a human will. To summarize, I argue that while there are some philosophical and textual difficulties that initially threaten to undermine our ability to establish that evil is rooted in self-deception in these two ways, these difficulties can largely be addressed. By the end of Chapter 4, we can conclude that the vice of self-deception is linked necessarily to an evil disposition, and that self-deception does, in fact, help explain how evil can become entrenched in a human being.

I then dedicate Chapter 5 to a discussion of whether self-deception can explain and validate Kant's notoriously controversial remarks regarding the universality of evil throughout the human species. Much preliminary work must be done to set us up for this inquiry, and so a bit more than half of this chapter sorts through unavoidable yet challenging questions, such as: whether Kant intends his claims about a universal evil to be *a priori* or empirically grounded; whether the social (or unsocial) aspects of human life are relevant to Kant's proof; if Kant can justifiably describe the evil that runs throughout human nature as both a propensity or willingness and a chosen disposition; how the universality of evil can exist alongside the possibility of individual moral reform; and what to make of the claim that evil attaches to our "species" character. After sorting out these issues, a path by which Kant can get to the conclusion that an evil is universally present in human nature begins to emerge. As we'll see, it also becomes clear that while self-deception as it was described in Chapters 3 and 4 cannot be implicated in this proof, a nearby kind of practical-epistemic failing, namely, dissemblance or dissimulation (*Verstellen*), can be. I then conclude that while Kant's account remains at least somewhat vulnerable to certain criticisms, he has a reasonable argument for the conclusion that an evil attaches to the human species, and that this evil consists in universal and willful acts of dissemblance or dissimulation.

The end of Chapter 5 marks the completion of my main inquiry into evil and self-deception, and the beginning of Chapter 6 marks the start of my account of moral reform and its relation to self-cognition. Now, since the concept of self-deception was given a stand-alone treatment in Chapter 3, I do the same for the concept of self-cognition in Chapter 6. In this chapter, I argue that self-cognition is not simply what results from the mitigation of self-deception. More specifically, I argue that self-cognition is a distinctive task, one with pitfalls and obstacles that outstrip self-deception and that plague even the most well-intentioned agent. I also demonstrate that while Kant can at points seem deeply pessimistic about the possibility of self-cognition, a more modest and at least somewhat hopeful view about its prospects can be secured. There are several components to my argument, but the most novel is likely my claim that self-knowledge or self-cognition must take the form of a provisional, experimental exercise in self-interpretation. To develop my view, I again rely both on core texts and claims within Kant's practical philosophy—including, most notably, his evocative reference to Johann Georg Hamann's statement that "only a descent into the hell of self-cognition can pave the way to godliness" (MS 6:441 and SF 7:55)—and Kant's writings on epistemology and anthropology.

In Chapter 7, I return to the text of the *Religion* and examine Kant's two-stage model of moral reform. Kant explicitly argues at RGV 6:47–48 that an initial stage of conversion must be followed by continual moral progress in the empirical realm, but scholars have not yet properly explained why two stages are needed or how, exactly, they differ from one another. I take up this question, arguing that we can best understand the first stage if we frame conversion as a kind of commitment, and that we can best understand the second stage if we conceive of moral progress more as a cognitive, as opposed to volitional, type of effort. Thus, to understand the second stage of moral reform in particular, we need to appreciate how, in a manner that mirrors how evil involves self-deceit, moral goodness requires a certain set of cognitive and self-cognitive achievements. In the final section of this chapter, I step briefly outside the *Religion* and consider whether the *Metaphysics of Morals* presents a compatible notion of moral reform. I argue that it does, and that in forging a parallel between these two texts, we can elucidate further aspects of moral progress and lend increased support to my attempt to develop a cognitive account of moral progress.

Lastly, in Chapter 8, I explore an additional aspect of Kant's theory of moral reform. More specifically, my topic in this chapter is Kant's concept of an ethical community. Because it is initially unclear how this community figures into Kant's account of moral progress, I consider at length an analogy made in the *Religion* between the ethical state of nature—which is left behind once we enter the ethical community—and the state of nature in a juridico-civil context (RGV 6:95–96). This analogy ultimately allows me to argue that the central task of the ethical community is to help its members adjudicate disagreements about the social aims appropriate to good life conduct. I also explain why the ethical community should be centered on a "historical" or "ecclesiastical faith," arguing that a faith-based community can promote moral knowledge, self-understanding, and interpersonal communication. A church's traditions, conventions, and texts help a person comprehend what virtue demands, articulate priorities in the pursuit of good works, and, crucially, provide a shared touchstone or common vocabulary among persons. As such, an ethical community provides, in the *Religion*, a discursive space, one which recognizes that while we must embrace the heterogeneity of moral beliefs and practices, we also cannot be sanguine or casual about moral disagreements or failures to understand each other's views regarding what socioethical problems are most salient.

Finally, some words of caution before we begin. It is not my intention in this book to delve into the historical reception of Kant's *Religion* or to offer an exhaustive commentary on this text. Numerous books and articles that are already available cover quite well the relevant historical issues, and section-by-section commentaries have also been published very recently.[13] My interest is in the core features of Kant's mature theory of evil and, most centrally, the cognitive aspects of evil and moral reform. As such, I must set aside those topics in the *Religion* that are not directly relevant to my inquiry. This includes, for example, Kant's account of grace. Given, first, how Kant himself describes this as a "parergon," or an issue that borders, but does not fall within, his main inquiry into evil (RGV 6:52), and, second, that the possibility of grace does not inform an account of the cognitive dimensions of evil or its overcoming, any treatment of grace lies too far outside the scope of this book.[14] Lastly, since my focus is not on the *Religion* per se, I will rely, as needed, on other texts from Kant's corpus, including writings that are somewhat unconventional in the context of an

---

13. See, for example, Lawrence Pasternack, *Routledge Philosophy Guidebook to Kant on Religion within the Boundaries of Mere Reason*; James DiCenso, *Kant's Religion within the Boundaries of Mere Reason: A Commentary*; Stephen Palmquist, *Comprehensive Commentary on Kant's Religion within the Boundaries of Mere Reason*; and Eddis Miller, *Kant's Religion within the Boundaries of Mere Reason: A Reader's Guide*.

14. There are, moreover, numerous helpful treatments of grace available, perhaps most especially Jacqueline Mariña's "Kant on Grace: A Reply to His Critics."

investigation in practical philosophy; the most notable examples are the aforementioned selections from Kant's logic lectures, which are highly important to the work I do in Chapter 3. The reader can thus expect to find in these pages only what is necessary for an inquiry into Kant on evil, self-deception, and moral reform.

CHAPTER 1
The Self of Self-Love

A cornerstone of Kant's views is the claim that there are two, and only two, incentives structuring human action: the incentive of respect for the moral law and the incentive of self-love. Because of its importance to both Kant's theory of evil and his broader nonmoral psychology and practical philosophy, I will start this chapter and this book by offering an account of the incentive of self-love.

To make progress, we can situate ourselves in the context of one of the most well-known articles and debates regarding the incentive of self-love and Kant's motivational dualism. The article is Andrews Reath's "Hedonism, Heteronomy, and Kant's Principle of Happiness," which explores whether Kant has a purely hedonistic understanding of self-love and thus thinks pleasure alone guides nonmoral action. This interpretation of Kant dominated the literature prior to Reath's article, and one would have only had to rely on Theorem II of the Analytic of the *Critique of Practical Reason* as evidence. In Theorem II, Kant repeatedly makes points such as the following:

> All material practical principles as such are, without exception, of one and the same kind and come under the general principle of self-love or one's own happiness. (KpV 5:22)

And:

> [A]ll material principles, which place the determining ground of choice in the pleasure or displeasure to be felt in the reality of some object, are wholly *of the*

same kind insofar as they belong without exception to the principle of self-love or one's own happiness. (KpV 5:22)

Such comments might appear to cut off Reath's inquiry before it even gets underway, as Kant seems to state unambiguously that nonmoral action, or action governed by "material" practical principles, is "without exception" driven by a self-love that aims only to secure pleasure. Yet even in light of these passages, Reath argued that Kant allows human beings to have nonmoral motives that are not hedonistic and nonmoral ends that are not valued or sought because of their potential to please. Reath's Kant would argue, for example, that though you were originally drawn to baseball simply because it pleased or gratified you—and this, Reath claims, is really what Kant is maintaining in the above passages—over time the quality and focus of your attachment can shift.[1] Gradually, we become motivated to watch baseball not because we seek pleasure but because we are taken in by the complexities of the game or identify with certain players or a team's city; hedonism informs not nonmoral action as such but only its starting points. Reath's interpretation therefore promised a reading of Kant that seemed better able to account for the diversity of human choice and that was unconstrained by what many saw as a crudely dualist view of motivation, as it was thought implausible and even embarrassing that Kant would maintain that any human being not motivated by respect is instead motivated by pleasure or the expectation of pleasure.

In light of these advantages, Reath's interpretation is frequently endorsed by commentators interested in Kant's account of self-love, and I will consider some of these endorsements in the next chapter. However, I now want to focus on some difficulties with Reath's proposals. First, even if Reath's Kant can establish that an agent's pursuit of nonmoral ends can be guided by non-hedonistic concerns, this point does not allow Reath to conclude that an agent who, say, appreciates baseball is responding correctly to a nonmoral good or value. Whatever virtues she ends up finding in the game, they do not transform a Kantian account of normativity. Such appreciation does not produce a distinctive kind of reason for action, and the development of such non-hedonistic interests does not instill them with any additional weight against the demands of morality. Thus we must note how little Reath's argument would appease Kant's critics, many of whom find an insufficient pluralism not only within Kant's theory of motivation but also within his theory of value. To see this, we need only consider Michael

1. Throughout this introduction, I reference Reath's own example about baseball. See "Hedonism, Heteronomy, and Kant's Principle of Happiness," 48.

Stocker's well-known criticisms of Kant. Stocker argues that Kantianism forces agents to suffer from a break between their motives—those direct concerns and personal attachments that guide them to act—and their values, or the justifications they can give for those actions.[2] Clearly, advocating pluralism about motives in an agent's nonmoral psychology while leaving untouched monism about what is unconditionally good does not make for a stronger link between motives and values. Insofar as Reath's argument does not sufficiently address Kantian axiology, Reath does no more than offer to some of Kant's critics an olive branch none of them care to accept.[3]

Second, we must note that Reath, in broadening the possibilities for nonmoral motives, must in the end abandon a central feature of Kant's theory of nonmoral motivation, namely, its ability to provide a substantive psychological thesis or framework for understanding nonmoral agency. On Reath's reading, hedonistic motives become overshadowed by an extensive proliferation of other desires. But with so many possible objects and concerns shaping nonmoral life, the only way to retain a reference to the concept of hedonism would be to strip it of any connection to pleasure. We could, on Reath's proposal, perhaps say that attention to the subtleties of pitching provides an agent a kind of "satisfaction," but it would be inappropriate to say that she sought pleasure or a feeling of agreeability.[4] But since most any end an agent sets—even an end that promises to bring pain or discomfort—can issue this neutered form of satisfaction, Reath's Kant ends up with no way to limit what could count as a nonmoral motive. This is problematic not only because, in an attempt to distance Kant from a reductivist approach to motivation,[5] Reath has ended

2. See Stocker, "The Schizophrenia of Modern Ethical Theories," 459. As is well known, utilitarianism is also criticized by Stocker on the same grounds.

3. Reath makes some suggestions regarding how his reading of Kant's nonmoral psychology intersects with a theory of value, but they are, as he notes, only sketched ("Hedonism, Heteronomy, and Kant's Principle of Happiness," 67). More importantly, the few comments Reath offers, while interesting, are not plausible as a Kantian theory of value. He speaks of nonmoral choice as being shaped by what an agent takes to be a valuable state of affairs ("Hedonism, Heteronomy, and Kant's Principle of Happiness," 65), but the claim that a state of affairs has a value that a person both observes and directly responds to implies a pluralistic value realism difficult to align with Kant's broader account of humanity as the only self-subsisting value.

4. In making this point, I am relying on Andrew Johnson's criticisms of Reath in "Kant's Empirical Hedonism." See especially Johnson's point that Reath equivocates between two senses of "satisfaction" on page 59. Also see Iain Morrisson, "On Kantian Maxims: A Reconciliation of the Incorporation Thesis and Weakness of the Will," 89n11, for like-minded skepticism regarding the textual evidence for Reath's interpretation.

5. This is Reath's stated goal at "Hedonism, Heteronomy, and Kant's Principle of Happiness," 43–44.

up with more an empty nonmoral psychology than a plausibly heterogeneous one. It is further problematic since there are real interpretive costs
to the proposal that Reath has made. As a handful of commentators have
pointed out,[6] Reath's interpretation runs directly contrary to Kant's stated
claims. To return to Theorem II of the Analytic of the second *Critique*—
which, it is important to note, is Kant's most sustained treatment of nonmoral practical psychology—we are repeatedly told, for example, that
when the lower faculty desire is engaged, the expected feeling of pleasure
"alone . . . constitute[s] the determining ground of the will" (KpV 5:23).[7]
In other words, Kant explicitly endorses hedonism as a substantive view
about the nature of our nonmoral motives, not a formal claim that we have,

6. See Barbara Herman, *Moral Literacy*, 179–180, and Samuel Kerstein, *Kant's Search for the Supreme Principle of Morality*, 26–29. See also note 4 above.

7. Reath himself seems to acknowledge, albeit implicitly, the difficulty of accounting for remarks like this one in Theorem II. He notes several passages from this section of the second *Critique* as he reviews why we tend to read Kant as a hedonist about nonmoral action, but after he proposes his alternative, Reath never revisits specific Theorem II passages or explains how they don't significantly undermine his own pro-posal. This omission is unfortunate, particularly in light of questionable arguments made by Reath in his paper. Reath argues, for instance, that Kant's incorporation thesis should lead us to conclude that material pleasure is not the basis on which nonmoral choice is determined ("Hedonism, Heteronomy, and Kant's Principle of Happiness," 53–54). But as others have already pointed out, Reath's appeal to the incorporation thesis is peculiar, since this thesis rules out only that pleasure, or the expectation of pleasure, can directly determine the will to act (Johnson, "Kant's Empirical Hedonism," 58). The incorporation thesis explains only Kant's position on determinism and the conditions of free choice; it has no impact on his nonmoral psychology. Reath also claims that Kant does not need, in texts like the second *Critique*, a reductivist hedonism in order to reach his ultimate goal of distinguishing moral principles from nonmoral ones ("Hedonism, Heteronomy, and Kant's Principle of Happiness," 53). But this is too quick since Kant's hedonism does at least help him at crucial junctures. For example, in Kant's explication of the higher faculty of desire, he argues that reason can deter-mine the will "immediately" and "not by means of an intervening feeling of pleasure or displeasure" (KpV 5:25). This feature is supposed to enable a contrast with the lower faculty of desire, but it becomes much harder for it to do so once Reath's suggestions are brought into the picture. For in Reath's view, the "intervening feeling of pleasure" ceases to be present not only in cases of action from duty but also in at least some (and perhaps many) cases of nonmoral action and choice. Finally, Reath puts much weight on a passage at MS 6:212, where Kant discusses how our inclinations presup-pose pleasure. Reath argues that we should understand Kant as making a chronological or genetic point, one according to which pleasure is not the motive or goal of action but instead a shared historical feature of all inclinations. But as Herman, Kerstein, and Johnson all point out, Kant's clear intent at MS 6:212 is to argue that the *anticipation* of pleasure precedes the determination of the lower faculty of desire (see Herman, *Moral Literacy*, 180; Kerstein, *Kant's Search for the Supreme Principle of Morality*, 29; and Johnson, "Kant's Empirical Hedonism," 52–53). Thus, this passage, in fact, turns out to support a hedonistic interpretation of nonmoral action. Given just this sampling of problems with Reath's argument, it is clear that a new approach to Kant's hedonism and his theory of self-love is required.

and hope to satisfy, an almost limitless assortment of nonmoral ends and desires.[8]

Thus, although Reath seems right that Kant's hedonism and his account of self-love beg for reconsideration, his proposals are problematic. And yet in noting Reath's shortcomings, we do get a sense of how a reexamination of Kant's hedonism regarding self-love and nonmoral motivation ought to proceed. We should not hope to satisfy all of Kant's critics or address a criticism such as Stocker's, since, as noted, his criticism covers not only Kant's theory of motivation but also fundamental Kantian commitments about rational agency being the sole unconditional value. If we aim to appease those whose opposition to Kant extends to matters beyond his nonmoral psychology, then this will distract us from narrower, more attainable goals. It is also worthwhile to abandon hopes that hedonistic motives can be so drastically filtered out of nonmoral choice, since, as shown above, any such project will not satisfy those interested in Kant's stated views. To uncover a more plausible Kant, we need to lend nuance to hedonistic self-love without abandoning his commitment to the substantive claim that concern for one's own pleasure is what motivates nonmoral actions.

In this chapter, I propose that we develop the requisite nuance by attending closely to the *self* that seeks pleasures or that self-loves in Kantianism.[9] I believe this focus has been missing in Kant scholarship, and that we are not going to make sufficient progress if, as Reath did, we think only about how to rework the concepts of pleasure or gratification. We will not understand the role or significance of pleasure or gratification in nonmoral life unless we know more about who is trying to be pleased or gratified, what can count as pleasure or sensual gratification to such an agent, and why pleasure or gratification matters to us. Thus, I'll try to establish both that we can see an emphasis on the self in Kant's nonmoral psychology and how attention to the self can enrich an understanding of Kantian self-love.

Over the course of this chapter, I will also work out some of the implications of my account. By attending to the interests and wants of the self, we will be able to develop a richer understanding of the different varieties of hedonism and the peculiar shapes that imprudent, nonmoral, and immoral action might take in Kant's philosophy.

---

8. I make this same point about Reath in "Expansionist Interpretations of Radical Evil."

9. Others, such as Herman, develop the requisite nuance simply by exploring further the concept of hedonism itself. My approach can exist easily alongside Herman's. See Herman, *Moral Literacy*, 176–202.

To bring into focus the self of self-love, two initial points are in order. First, we need a temporary metaphysical disclaimer. Throughout the start of this chapter, I referenced the self implicit within self-love without commenting on its ontological status, and I continue to do so within this section. I do not, for example, discuss at the outset whether a person's sense of self corresponds to a fiction, a construct, or something else entirely. I set these issues aside because at this point I want simply to show how a human subject cannot have a will governed by the incentive of self-love unless she operates with certain presuppositions and commitments concerning her selfhood. I will, however, engage to a certain extent these metaphysical questions in due course, both in footnotes and in subsequent sections of this chapter. Second, while my goal is to discuss a person's sense of self insofar as it relates to practical philosophy and the incentive of self-love, I will not restrict myself to Kant's moral writings or to those parts of the second *Critique* where Kant outlines his nonmoral psychology.

Instead, I will begin by outlining the introductory topic of *Anthropology from a Pragmatic Point of View*, which is a discussion of egoism and one's sense of self. We quickly learn that egoism divides itself into three different kinds: logical egoism, where one thinks it "unnecessary to test his judgment by the reason of others" (Anth 7:130); aesthetic egoism, where a person is content with her own taste, even if failure to listen to others deprives her of better enjoyments in the future; and moral egoism, where someone "concentrates the highest motives of his will merely on profit and his own happiness, but not on the concept of duty" (Anth 7:130).

Now, even without elaboration, Kant's discussion is, for our purposes, encouraging. Since Kant speaks repeatedly and consistently of this three-fold egoism and egoism more generally in both the *Anthropology* and in the lecture notes on anthropology recorded by his students,[10] and since he

---

10. See V-Anth/Collins 25:10–15, V-Anth/Parrow, 25:244–246, V-Anth/Fried, 25:473–477, V-Anth/Pillau, 25:735–736, V-Anth/Mensch, 25:859–867, V-Anth/Mron, 25:1215–1217, and V-Anth/Busolt 25:1438–1439. Despite the clear consistency with which Kant oriented his lectures around the threefold egoism, some small exceptions and other observations should be noted. First, the threefold division of egoism into aesthetic, logical, and moral egoism does vary on rare occasion. Thus, for example, the Busolt lectures replace logical egoism with "physical egoism," a condition typified by hypochondria and present in people who pay attention to themselves by making themselves into objects of study (V-Anth/Busolt 25:1438). Second, and predictably, Kant's remarks about egoism reflect the development of the Critical philosophy. Thus, the earlier lectures notes, such as the Collins and Parrow transcripts, have Kant speaking affirmatively about the I as a soul and as a simple that "expresses my substantiality" (V-Anth/Collins 25:10), whereas such pre-Critical language is absent in the lecture

always puts this topic first in these discussions,[11] it is clear that in Kant's eyes, a person's sense of self actively and extensively informs subjective mental life. Furthermore, since moral egoism is just one aspect of a broader egoism—an egoism that infects everything from a person's general manner of thinking to her aesthetic pursuits—it is also clear that there will likely be much to say about the self besides that it is that for the sake of which pleasure or gratification is sought. This is particularly evident in the idea of an aesthetic egoist who "deprives himself of progress toward improvement" in order to keep his sense of self-importance intact (Anth 7:129). In this case, the satisfaction of egoistic desires threatens to leave more material pleasures unsecured, thus suggesting that the demands of the self do not always align neatly with demands for pleasure. If this is right, then along with the ubiquity of egoism in the anthropological writings, these points thus would seem to redeem, at least provisionally, my claim that it can prove fruitful to approach Kant's account of self-love by first developing a more adequate understanding of the self on its own.

Notwithstanding the initial promise of Kant's threefold egoism, there are, admittedly, some conceptual points missing in this account. For example, Kant does not really clarify what sort of element egoism is in our nonmoral psychology. He never explains whether egoism is a nonmoral *principle* of choice, that is, a subjective policy that an agent uses to guide her deliberations, thoughts, and actions; whether egoism is a *motive*[12] or ground according to which some object or action appeals to us or inclines

transcripts that approach or occur after the publication of the first *Critique*. Thus, these claims about the I as a substance, which are, of course, ruled out by Kant's treatment of the paralogisms of pure reason, are absent from the 1777–1778 Pillau transcripts and the 1784–1785 Mrongovius transcripts. A trickier case is the *Menschenkunde*, which has an *Akademie* date of 1781–1782 but still has Kant referring to the soul in his comments on egoism. Now, the dating of the *Menschenkunde* is controversial (see Brandt and Stark's *Einleitung* to the anthropology lectures, 25:CXI–CXIV), but even if we endorse the *Akademie* date of 1781–1782, we do not find anything that is necessarily out of keeping with this historical trajectory. While Kant does discuss the soul in the section on the I at 25:859–867 of the *Menschenkunde*, he speaks mainly of the soul by contrasting how it is understood by various parties, such as the speculative understanding or popular thought. Even when he does speak in his own voice and in more positive terms about the soul, he does not describe the soul as a simple or a substantiality. Instead, he identifies soul with *Gemüth* and also with the "sum of feelings [*Empfindungen*]" (V-Anth/Mensch 25:861).

11. Predictably, egoism and the I are also the first topics of the section on empirical psychology in Alexander Baumgarten's *Metaphysics*, from which Kant draws much inspiration for his own empirical psychology and practical anthropology. See Baumgarten, *Metaphysics: A Critical Translation with Kant's Elucidations, Selected Notes, and Related Materials*.

12. *Bestimmmungsgrund* or *Bewegungsgrund*.

us to its pursuit; or whether egoism is better described as something else entirely. This is frustrating because Kant is obviously aware of this distinction, as he made it clear enough in Theorem II of the second *Critique* that hedonism is both a motive and a principle of choice. Moreover, we have to acknowledge that there are some immediate technical obstacles that complicate matters further. We are accustomed to thinking about principles and motives in the context of practical philosophy, but since Kant's threefold egoism implies the relevance of the ego outside of typical practical domains, any terminological structure we impose on egoism must be sufficiently general; we cannot use terms that would only make sense in a discussion of how the faculty of desire is structured or in contexts of practical choice and action. Despite these obstacles, I think it is easiest and safe—at least with some eventual qualifiers[13]—to conceptualize egoism as both a motive or ground of attraction and a possible decision-procedure or principle. As the case of logical egoism makes clear, an agent's preoccupation with herself clearly inclines or disposes her to think of herself or to reason in specific ways. Insofar as an agent can also endorse this tendency, it seems clear that egoism can likewise be a policy or worldview wherein the interests of the self are taken to have prime importance.

To understand further the egoistic currents within our mental lives, I will now say more about why a sense of self necessarily stands behind, and is presupposed by, hedonistic self-love. As students of Kant's anthropology lectures have noted, Kant must give a certain priority to the self insofar as hedonism clearly requires a sense of personal identity. Drawing on Heraclitus's well-known river fragment, the notes from the 1772–1773 Collins transcripts contain Kant's comments about how our bodies are in constant flux, "like a stream flowing with other water, yet the I is unalterable, and this I is indivisible" (V-Anth/Collins 25:13). Even though we need to be cautious with remarks such as these, which stem from Kant's pre-Critical period and will not align neatly with Kant's mature views about how we cannot claim knowledge of the I as a substance or a simple,[14] we can still take away from this comment the fact that our bodily awareness is ordinarily underwritten by my supposition that I enjoy a self-same identity. Insofar as I take myself to be a distinct, self-identical I, I acquire the means to see self-persistence despite the changes that occur with respect to

13. I add these qualifiers to my claim that egoism can count as a principle of choice on pages 25–26 of this chapter.
14. We find these remarks about a "simple" or substantial I throughout early lectures on anthropology, including the Parrow, Collins, and Friedländer transcripts. These comments about the substantiality of the I are missing from the 1777–1778 Pillau transcripts and all later transcripts. For more on this point, see note 10 of this chapter.

my body and despite how drastically my specific inclinations might change over time. Without a sense of one's own ego, hedonistic urges could never translate into a commitment to *one's own* pleasure. The very idea of oneself as an enduring, self-same person is active in someone committed to making herself alone the recipient of as much pleasure as possible. Thus, hedonism can become a practical principle for an agent only insofar as she operates with an active sense of self.

To highlight further the role of the self in Kant's hedonism, we can also observe how different the character of hedonistic motives would be if they were not attached to an agent that conceives of herself as a self. We generally do not experience hedonistic desires as unfamiliar forces of attraction that shoot through our physical person. Such desires would be more like affects (*Affekten*), which Kant treats in the *Anthropology* as singular rash urges that a person experiences like water breaking through a dam (Anth 7:252).[15] But with affects described as rare occurrences, they are in no way representative of the more routine phenomenology of desire that we find in Kant. Typically, hedonistic desires are infected with and conditioned by a sense of self.

This is clear when we consider, for example, how Kant understands both inclinations (*Neigungen*) and pleasure (*Lust*). Inclinations are those desires for enjoyments that a subject has previously experienced or that are informed by a habitual disposition (RGV 6:26n; see also V-Anth/Mron 25:1334 and V-Anth/Mron 1339–1340), and it is such historically informed inclinations or *Neigungen* that Kant repeatedly references when he discusses the nonmoral or immoral ends that stand apart from or against the commands of the moral law.[16] As Kant's chief focus, inclinations would seem to both make up a very significant portion of the desires we ordinarily experience and include the most classic examples of hedonistic desires. For example, desires for food and sex are ones that we have long experienced; their content and their appeal reference and are reinforced by past personal interactions with them. We can thus say that present inclinations are shaped by expectations and how a person remembers them, and that the quality of these desires would be deeply different if they were

---

15. Kant claims that affects cause us to "come out of composure" (V-Anth/Fried 25:589) and that they involve a "surprise through sensation" (Anth 7:252; cited in Patrick Frierson, *Kant's Empirical Psychology*, 216). Furthermore, Kant claims that affects belong to the faculty of feeling and not to the faculty of desire, which indicates that affects do not engage our capacity for action in the way that other subjective states (such as inclinations) do (V-Anth/Pillau 25:837 and V-Anth/Mron 25:1341; see also MS 6:407).

16. See, for example, GMS 4:398–399.

not experienced as belonging to a historically persistent I. Furthermore, pleasure or *Lust*, as Kant conceives it, is what I feel when I experience the furthering of my life or when I gain access to the force of vitality or the vital powers (*Lebenskräfte*) within myself as a specific human subject.[17] I will examine Kant's remarks about vitality in further detail shortly, but for now it should suffice to note that pleasure, for Kant, is a way of acquiring access to one's own broader welfare. Although we can never come face to face with the healthy arrangement of our constitution or the principles of life that animate us, we can secure indirect access to these states or capacities through the feelings of pleasure and displeasure.[18] The role of pleasure is to inform us of our well-functioning, whereas pain or displeasure speaks to the presence of some sort of hindrance to life.[19] Thus, activities that appeal to me based on the pleasure they promise are desired insofar as they will promote the vital force within my embodied and historically situated being. So again, an account of pleasure refers us back to the life, needs, and identity of the subject experiencing that pleasure.

We can now take a moment to summarize the results of this section. We have thus far seen that egoism either precedes or is implicit in hedonism in at least the following ways: one can have egoistic motives and engage in egoistic thinking outside of practical life. A person can act, as the aesthetic egoist does, on the basis of egoism without trying to maximize her experience of sensual pleasure. Hedonism, as a principle of choice or the commitment to promoting one's own pleasures, is possible only for someone who conceives of herself as a self with a concrete, temporally persistent, personal identity. Finally, my hedonistic desires are experienced as they are—as inclinations and as pleasures—only because I presuppose my continued material and mental existence over time. Without this drive or tendency to affirm the ego, Kant's phenomenology of sensual desire would be radically different.

These points provide textual evidence for the importance of considering egoism—both egoistic motives and egoism as a possible personal commitment or principle of choice—alongside hedonism if we want to

17. For a very helpful overview of Kant's account of life and vitality, see Rudolf Makkreel, *Imagination and Interpretation in Kant: The Hermeneutical Import of the Critique of Judgment*, 91–103. I am much indebted to these pages in Makkreel's book.
18. See Refl 823/15:367, V-Met-L2/Pölitz 28:586, and V-Anth/Fried 25:499.
19. Granted, given the way the body is arranged, access to the underlying principles of my life or vitality will be imperfect. Hence, a paper-cut hurts terribly, even though it poses no real hindrance to life, and we sometimes do not notice our lungs deteriorating even though this will eventually prove to be an obstacle to health (V-Anth/Fried 25:559, V-Anth/Pillau 25:786, and V-Anth Mron 25:1318–1319).

illuminate our nonmoral psychology. It is also worth noting that an additional argument can be canvassed on Kant's behalf to make the practical relevance of egoism even more clear. Let's step back and note that in Theorem II, Kant's overall goal is to show that pleasure is the sole determining ground of nonmoral action and that all nonmoral principles of choice are one and the same, that they are all at bottom a principle of self-love or one's own happiness. Now, I take it that those, like Reath, who object to this account of motivation and choice on grounds of its apparent crudeness have a deeper reason to be suspicious. What Kant never really seems to address is: Why is pleasure so important to me? Why should this be the only kind of nonmoral motive I can access in my ordinary life? We would be equally suspicious if Kant were to tell us, for example, that all nonmoral motives bottom out in a desire for beauty or that all principles of nonmoral choice are designed to promote the feeling of communal belonging. The reason for such suspicion is that in any of these explanations, there is a potential gap between us and the motive or principle assigned to us. In all these cases, we would ask why X is that thing I necessarily care about. But by carving out a foundational role for egoism in nonmoral life, we begin to close this gap. A preoccupation with or concern for oneself is necessarily presupposed in any possible answer that Kant might give to the questions of how *I* want to structure *my* life, what motivates *me* to act, and what kinds of objects are attractive to me.

In what follows, I continue to highlight the importance of egoism in Kant's theory of nonmoral motivation and choice. Specifically, I explain more exactly how the preoccupations of the self figure into how one pursues hedonistic satisfaction in nonmoral life. To show this, I will need to differentiate between two different models of nonmoral choice in Kant.[20] Each model revises in helpful, textually adequate, but non-Reathian ways the idea that Kantian hedonism in nonmoral action and motivation consists simply in the pursuit of maximal sensual gratification.

I spend the majority of my time in the next section outlining the first model, since it's in that context that some more general objections and questions regarding my attempt to focus on the self of self-love will arise.

---

20. The possibility that there may be two models of nonmoral choice is noted in my "Expansionist Interpretations of Radical Evil," though the claim is not really developed and not connected to Kant's account of the self.

Model One. My overarching goal in this section is, as noted above, to develop a more nuanced, textually defensible hedonism and to continue to remedy the underappreciation of egoism within Kant's nonmoral psychology. The first step toward a more thorough reassessment of Kantian hedonism requires that we briefly consider points about pleasure or self-love that have not been given proper attention in the literature. In particular, we must explain how the degree to which a person finds her state agreeable does not move in exact lockstep with the amount of pleasure she experiences in that state. This is made evident by Kant's remarks about how pain factors into hedonistic pursuits and the role of judgment in choices governed by hedonistic concerns.

Perhaps intuitively, Kant notes that encounters with pain raise (*heben*) the pleasure one experiences (V-Anth/Mron 25:1317). I will find my current state more agreeable when the pleasure I enjoy has been preceded by a limited amount of pain or a feeling of the hindrance of life (V-Anth/Fried 25:501–502), and it comes as no surprise that I will experience a cake as tasting better when I have been forced to wait in hunger for it. The alteration of pain and pleasure makes an agent especially aware of the aforementioned principle of life or vitality, which, as noted, cannot be felt directly but is accessed only through its being hindered or promoted. Thus, we might not only welcome but actively seek pain,[21] since one feels quite alive when, for example, suffering through an all-night card game rife with both wins and losses (V-Anth/Mron 25:1318). We can also observe that from as far back as the essay on negative magnitudes, Kant is clear that pain and pleasure are "real opposites," or distinct forces in the way that negative and positive magnetic charges, hatred and love, or vice and virtue are (NG 2:180). As such, the enjoyments of pain removal and the enjoyments of pleasure enhancement are experienced as distinct. Since the removal of pain is intrinsically comforting aside from the positive pleasure or enjoyment that, according to Kant, accompanies pain's removal, we can see that hedonism can take shape either as the pursuit of positive pleasure or as the removal of negative pains; neither hedonistic desires nor a commitment to hedonism as a principle of choice must resemble some singularly minded form of sensualism.

21. For a likeminded account of the importance of pain in Kant's theory of pleasure, see Susan Meld Shell, "Kant's 'True Economy of Human Nature': Rousseau, Count Verri, and the Problem of Happiness," especially 215–217. Thanks to an anonymous reviewer for bringing this piece to my attention.

These remarks alert us to the way that pain factors into feelings of pleasure. But they also anticipate Kant's well-known point that happiness is an ideal of the imagination and contribute further to our attempt to uncover the workings of the self in self-love (GMS 4:418). Hedonism cannot be a straightforward principle of choice or action for the simple reason that the material pleasures we enjoy lack the determinacy that would be required for a judgment of happiness to issue directly from the gratifying experiences we register. Pleasures, we know, have multiple sources, as sensibility is not the only faculty that can take the expectation of pleasure as its determining ground (KpV 5:23). Understanding and reason will also represent objects as gratifying, and a person might find pleasure in, for example, entertaining mentally an empirical concept such as an efficient kingship or in endorsing a maxim of reason, such as the directive to simplify as much as possible our inventory of the laws governing nature. But because these types of pleasing objects make no direct sensory appeal, an agent can judge them as contributing to happiness only because she takes them to satisfy her own idiosyncratic viewpoint about what is pleasing; she is not passively logging felt impressions. Moreover—and related to both this point about indeterminacy and my above remarks regarding pain—whether a pain is experienced as a simple hindrance to the feeling of life or as an invitation to exercise some other power of ours that would compensate for any unpleasantness is an open matter (KpV 5:24). Human beings are not so shortsighted as to forget that obstacles are at least partly of our own making, and even a devoted hedonist might have enough imagination and creativity to find something richer than simple aversion in the face of every unsatisfied need or want. The satisfaction of hedonistic desires is not a wholly natural state but a largely interpretive and manufactured experience.

We have thus proposed three amendments to the crude form of hedonism Kant initially appears to offer. First, a person will aim to promote the feelings of pleasure, but she will also welcome the presence of pain into her life to the extent that doing so facilitates her overall goal of increasing access to the feeling of vitality. Second, a person will not operate with the belief that pleasures must be presented to her immediately by nature. Instead, she will continually revise her thoughts about where gratification can be sought and what constitutes gratification, inventing and anticipating new pleasures from sources that are not yet available and that may even provide only pain or aversion in their current form. Third, because these interpretive efforts demand the use of creative powers that can themselves reveal the vitality of the human being (V-Anth/Fried 25:604), the very construction of the specific ideals of pleasure and happiness allows for a further increase in the feeling of well-being.

Given these amendments, we can see that hedonism, when it is conceived as a principle a person applies to her nonmoral choices, is not best thought of as an attempt to promote maximal gratification of desire. Rather, the maximizing principle at work in hedonism is one that pertains to an agent's striving to determine that her life is going well according to the terms she has laid out. Her aim is to reveal and enliven her sense of self by authoring the subjective standards by which her life should be assessed, and then by gaining hold of the experiences needed to do well according to those standards. Acquiring access to the right materials to construct such a self-affirmation is an agent's goal, and this goal differs both conceptually and experientially from a straightforward tallying of the quantity of material pleasures. The satisfaction of hedonistic desires matters to me chiefly because it forms a part of my goal of judging myself subjectively flourishing and unhindered from a very general and longer-term point of view. In light of this, we can securely conclude that egoistic motives and egoism as a principle of choice stand behind and are implicit within, respectively, hedonistic motives and principles.

Now, in making these points, I am trying to strike a balance between two interpretive demands. On the one hand, we wish to add complexity to Kant's apparent endorsement of hedonism. We secured this by highlighting remarks about both pain and judgment as they relate to the feeling of vitality and the egoistic presuppositions implicit in hedonism. On the other hand, we want to avoid Reath's failure to take seriously Kant's stated claims and his commitment to hedonism as a narrow and substantive psychological hypothesis. On this front, the amendments I've proposed to hedonism do not dislodge its place in Kant's theory of nonmoral motivation the way Reath's interpretation does. There are several reasons why.

To begin, note that Kant is very clear throughout Theorem II that an agent who adopts hedonism as a principle of choice plays the long game. The decision of which objects to pursue is not driven by instinct alone, and a great deal of reason and understanding is "used" in the pursuit of one's own happiness (KpV 5:25). Now, my argument that an agent might incorporate pain into her nonmoral pursuits is no stranger than the fact that a person might use foresight to postpone a fleeting pleasure for the sake of a more lasting one. Both decisions are designed to promote the feeling of vitality, and though I have highlighted Kant's remarks about pain in the anthropological writings, I have not argued that human beings have anything like an original or natural predisposition to seek pain. I have only pointed out that the pursuit of pain is carefully incorporated into the pursuit of self-love and the attempt to reveal the feeling of life. As such, my argument leaves intact Kant's claim that pleasure is the determining ground of all nonmoral action.

Furthermore, though I have pointed out that the pleasures of pain removal and the pleasures of pleasure promotion are irreducible to one another, this point does not constitute a departure from Kant's emphasis on pleasure in general in Theorem II. The observation that there is a qualitative difference in the satisfying sensations that accompany an increase in pleasure versus those that accompany a decrease in pain is an observation well within the confines of a hedonistic view.

Finally, despite the distinct strand of egoism we have uncovered in Kant's theory of nonmoral motivation and choice, the tie between egoism and hedonism will still be quite tight. To begin to explain why, we must attend to the ways in which our egoistic sentiments are illusory. Though we are often tempted to conclude that we exist as ready-made distinct selves, or as metaphysically basic substances, and though this belief in a substantive self runs implicitly through the motive or principle of self-love, there is, in Kant's view, no truth to this conviction. By emphasizing that the human subject consists of faculties, by carefully outlining how the "I" of every "I think" can exist only as a "completely bare representation" (KrV A443/B471), and by pointing out the failures of paralogistic inferences, Kant makes it clear that any reference a subject makes to herself as a determinate and unique substance is unfounded. Even in cases where Kant claims a person is warranted in drawing certain conclusions about oneself—for example, how I must think my existence as both a noumenon and as a ground of causality in the phenomenal world in order to escape the antinomy of practical reason—we are justified only in presupposing that we enjoy specific powers, not that we exist as unique selves whose metaphysical primacy could justify any peculiar attention or devotion.

Now because the self, which a person takes to ground concerns of the utmost practical importance, has no substantial basis, any attempt to cater to the ego will be unsatisfying unless it takes place by proxy. To explain what I mean, note that in the first *Critique* and in the *Groundwork* (GMS 4:451), Kant reiterates that the human subject cannot know herself as a thing-in-itself and that she can only intuit the way the self is affected through the capacity of inner sense. Similarly, it seems that the pull of egoism in practical life makes itself evident through feeling. Much of a sense of self is based on fiction, yet sensual pleasure, while it may be an indeterminate phenomenon, is quite clearly real and material. Because we cannot really focus on or attend to the idea of a self except through sensual feelings, the person who attempts to live out her egoistic preoccupations directly will find her efforts deeply unsatisfying; her attempt to bring herself into focus without the aid of sensual feeling would be like trying to grab hold of air. We can see the idea that we become aware of our selves through feeling play out in everyday life, such as when I instruct someone to "pinch me" so that I can conclude my existence is not illusory. And since attending to the feelings of pleasure and vitality is the sharpest way to act on our egoistic sentiments, this is why I noted earlier that I would have to qualify my claim that egoism can be a principle of choice. Although egoism can clearly become a policy, it cannot be acted on directly. Hedonism remains the principle of choice that governs agents at the ground level of action.

To reach this same conclusion from a different direction, we can consider in further detail how Kant thinks pleasure allows access to one's vital powers. In the third *Critique* and the anthropology lectures, Kant makes two important points about the peculiar way pleasures and bodily feelings relate to vitality. First, he argues that the sensual, physical qualities we ordinarily associate with hedonism cannot be experienced apart from mental life, and second, that the reason why sensual pleasure is so important is that a person cannot get evidence of the quality of her inner subjective life unless she has a body. In other words, one's sense of her physical existence presupposes mental existence, and yet her access to her mental existence is thin or threadbare unless she can rely on her bodily experience to put flesh on its bones. A person's body has on its own no animating principle, for as Kant says, the "first source of life" lies not in the "human machine" but "in the mind" (V-Anth/Fried 25:604). Those enjoyments that would seem to provide raw, unmitigated bodily pleasure can only be experienced if they cater to a person's sustained need to prove herself generally vital and alive, and yet this sense of mental vitality takes on no color or qualitative richness unless it can enliven itself with sensuality. As Kant says,

> [L]ife without the feeling of the corporeal organ is merely consciousness of one's existence, but not a feeling of well- or ill-being, i.e., the promotion or inhibition of the powers of life; because the mind for itself is entirely life (the principle of life itself), and hindrances and promotions must be sought outside it, though in the human being himself, hence in combination with his body. (KU 5:277–278)

Thus, a focus on sensual desire is both indispensable in an account of nonmoral agency and somewhat misleading if not understood from a more holistic point of view. I seek pleasure as a way of making contributions to my life as a specific human *being*, not, primarily, a specific human *body*. Nevertheless, because a sensitive, nuanced assessment of how my life is going is possible only through my sensuality, we can understand why, despite the more complex egoistic hedonism we have uncovered, Kant often sounds like a crude Benthamite when he describes how an agent will decide which nonmoral ends to pursue. Reason, sense, and understanding all suggest a range of objects that will affect the force of vitality within us, and to make comparisons between these objects, we can appeal only to the degree or "magnitude" of the "feeling of agreeableness" that they promise (KpV 5:23). Thus, Kant's reliance on hedonism is firmly in place, though behind this hedonistic orientation is a prudent, pain-tolerant, and egoistically minded agent.

To conclude this discussion, I will revisit a promise I made in the beginning of this chapter. My goal in this discussion has been not only to rethink our interpretation of self-love but also to spell out at least some implications of this revision. In other words, we hoped to lend nuance to Kant at both the theoretical level and the applied level, that is, in Kantian diagnoses of certain instances of nonmoral, imprudent, or immoral action. I will briefly note some instances where such new diagnoses seem possible.

First, recall the aesthetic egoist, who puts his self-esteem ahead of acquiring future delights. Because of his disregard for his own material pleasure, this individual might have otherwise seemed to present an example of unmotivated behavior. Yet focusing on Kantian egoism helps us grasp the motivations behind such an individual. Along similar lines, Kantian egoism can help us see how other cases that initially appear to feature unintelligible behavior are, in fact, willful and intentional. For example, consider Kant's discussion of passions (*Leidenschaften*) in the *Anthropology*. Passions are what we have when desires concerning other people, like dominance and lust, become "manias" that preoccupy us no matter what their cost to our overall sensual gratification (Anth 7:266). Now, there are many difficult points in Kant's discussion of the passions, and my goal here is not to sift through these debates.[22] I want only to point out that if we neglected Kant's remarks about egoism and viewed nonmoral action only through the lens of a sensualist hedonism, cases of dominance and lust might seem to indicate a complete failure of agency. We might find ourselves at a loss as to why an agent would act this way, and we might even question whether we can hold her responsible for her actions when she

22. Perhaps the most pressing question concerns whether an agent has the ability to resist passionate urges. Kant's commitment to transcendental freedom would seem to require this ability, but Kant also maintains that the passions exclude our mastery over them. I discuss this question in other work in progress, but see also Frierson, *Kant's Empirical Psychology*, 248–257; Frierson, *Freedom and Anthropology in Kant's Moral Philosophy*, 59–66; and Morrisson, "On Kantian Maxims: A Reconciliation of the Incorporation Thesis and Weakness of the Will," 85–87.

seems so divorced from her own nonmoral reasons for action and concern for her own pleasure or happiness. But by stressing the egoistic element of hedonism, we can see that the passionate person's actions are not unwillful or divorced from her subjective motivational set. The propensities to dominance and lust are clearly born of egoistic motives, and by putting egoism at the heart of Kant's theory of nonmoral motivation, these manias are rendered far less mysterious or threatening to practices of holding people responsible.[23]

Second, this focus on egoism casts a new light on Kant's claim in the *Religion* that a person's happiness cannot be established without comparative measures. Kant claims that "only in comparison with others does one judge oneself happy or unhappy" (RGV 6:27), and while the Rousseauian influence on this remark is clear enough,[24] Kant fails to add his own defense of this claim, particularly with regard to how it squares with the emphasis on hedonic pleasure in his nonmoral psychology. From the standpoint of Kant's nonmoral psychology, it may be readily granted that an agent needs the ability to make a certain sort of *intra*personal comparison. After all, hedonism—especially hedonism as a principle of choice—makes little sense if a person lacks the ability to compare her own hedonic states; it would be impossible to set an increase in pleasure as her end unless she could compare her current state with that state she anticipates entering, and it would be similarly impossible to judge actions as successes or failures absent an ability to compare past and present levels of satisfaction. From these points alone, however, nothing yet follows about why hedonic judgments require *inter*personal comparisons. But once we recognize the illusory presuppositions behind egoistic concern, it begins to make more sense that nonmoral action will be deeply informed by cares about one's interpersonal standing. If I cannot access or affirm my self-importance directly, I can at least feel good about myself by reveling in the miseries of others. Interpersonal comparisons can—like the experience of pleasure

---

23. My understanding of the passions is especially informed by David Sussman's work, particularly *The Idea of Humanity: Anthropology and Anthroponomy in Kant's Ethics*, 198–203. I revisit the passions in Chapter 4.

24. Wood, in his editorial notes to the Cambridge translation of Kant's *Religion*, flags this comment as showing Kant's reliance on Rousseau's distinction between a "love for oneself" that is concerned with whether one's "true needs" are satisfied and a self-love that thrives on—and, predictably, is routinely frustrated by—a desire to see oneself as better off than others (*Religion and Rational Theology*, 458). This is an important observation, and I wish to add to it only that Kant somewhat improves upon Rousseau by showing why self-love takes on this complex character. As will become clear from what follows in this section, there are deep reasons why a Kantian account of self-love must reference our desire for interpersonal advantage.

more generally—provide self-affirmation, since the more other people are badly off, the more probable is a judgment about my own well-being.

Notice also that in offering this explanation, we can approach from a new angle the emphasis several commentators have put on the importance of unsocial sociability in Kant.[25] Now, the idea that human beings tend to balance within themselves dispositions toward both social harmony and interpersonal antagonism is one that I will further comment on in subsequent chapters, particularly Chapters 5 and 8. At this stage, I want only to note how the emphasis I have placed on egoism in interpersonal comparisons would and would not coincide with an emphasis on unsocial sociability.

On the one hand, egoism and unsocial sociability would seem intimately related. Each of us will desire to have other people around, since egoistic gratification functions only by proxy. That is, I'll be able to see myself as flourishing only if I am surrounded by people—people whose ill-being I can leverage to render more probable a judgment about my own well-being. As such, egoism and unsocial sociability appear nicely aligned and perhaps to be two sides of the same coin.

Yet on the other hand, calling attention to egoism can bring out features of Kant's view that a focus on unsocial sociability cannot. Even if one is tempted to view egoism and unsocial sociability as two sides of the same coin, it must be granted that the former has reach that the latter appears to lack. Unsocial sociability, considered in isolation, seems to be a drive that we as finite human beings may not necessarily have. Egoism, however, appears to be inextricably linked to the human condition. As beings that have both mental and physical powers, but whose physical sides remain the points of access to holistic senses of self, we necessarily rely on our bodies, our capacity for sensual pleasure, and the people around us in ways that will likely diminish the care we give to others. The role of interpersonal comparisons in judgments of happiness reveals not merely an unsocial sociability that overlays human life; rather, these interpersonal judgments point to a deep fact about how any human being strives to shore up a sense of self and yet, in light of its evasive quality and a person's inability to gather lasting evidence of her importance and even her existence, must resort to other measures to prop herself up.

Model Two. Despite the attention paid to the first model of nonmoral choice, we should not think it Kant's only model for how feelings of vitality and judgments of subjective flourishing are accessed and made. We also

25. Of the commentators that focus on unsocial sociability, Wood and Sharon Anderson-Gold tend to be the most frequently cited.

should not assume that a person's attention to her self invariably displays the megalomaniacal quality present in agents driven by dominance or people who worry more about their place on the social ladder than they do about the quantity of pleasure in their lives. I will now argue that we can develop a second model of nonmoral choice, one that features both a different procedure for furthering the feeling of vitality and a different account of how the concerns of the self inform nonmoral practical reason.

To begin, it will be helpful to note that we should expect there to be two ways that the feeling of vitality can be promoted. In the previous section, I discussed the various things an agent might do in order to further the feeling of life she experiences. By seeking to remove those pains that she is wholly averse to, pursuing the right degree and kinds of pains needed for increased pleasure, and generally gathering the materials needed to make a judgment of maximal subjective flourishing, an agent tries to actively manipulate the world's offerings to her so that they better suit her interests. But, of course, this isn't the only direction that our efforts can take. If the goal is to achieve a fit between our needs and the world, then the feeling of vitality is furthered not only by making the world adjust to us but also by making ourselves conform better to it. In other words, the feeling of vitality can be promoted either through an actively pursued hedonism or through a disposition toward passivity. Central to a hedonistic orientation is an agent's desire to feel unimpeded or unhindered, and this means that those motivated by self-love might simply pursue the path of least resistance or do what is easiest.

Although Kant never lays out explicitly this second option, it directly follows from the core insight that the feeling of vitality registers a relational dynamic, one that is strengthened or diminished given the accord or discord that exists between the agent and her environment. This second option is also unquestionably operative in both published writings and lecture notes spanning an extensive time period. For example, he is careful to note that even though we often purposively stimulate our vital powers through sensual gratification, there exists also "enjoyment of the well-being resulting from the equilibrium of the various vital forces" (KU 5:274). This point is echoed by Kant's claims that "the human being who does not feel his body at all is properly healthy," that an equanimity or lack of "touchiness" constitutes the "self-awareness of a healthy soul," and that feelings of health pertain when there is a balance or *Gleichgewicht* of the vital forces or life powers (V-Anth/Mron 25:1219, V-Anth/Fried 25:561, and Refl 1539/ 15:963, respectively). Kant moreover discusses how we often seek pleasure by minimizing tension between ourselves and whatever situations we find ourselves in. In both the *Anthropology* and the lectures on anthropology,

Kant remarks that we do not always seek pleasure tempered by the appropriate interactions with pain. On the contrary, we often want to experience no alterations whatsoever, and want simply to subsist in a state where we are neither hungry nor being gratified by food, or to avoid both the highs and lows of card games and instead feel mere contentment or the absence of pains and pleasures altogether.[26] There is also, as Kant notes, a common desire to be absent to ourselves and not notice our own existence, which comes across fairly clearly when he remarks that we know we've really enjoyed some activity when we use expressions concerning how fast the time flew by (V-Anth/Mron 25:1316). Since we experience ourselves through the intuition of time, my not noticing how much time has elapsed means that I have let my sense of self slip out of view and that I am not trying to find evidence of my self in experience. In other words, Kant appears to suggest that, at least sometimes, self-love is facilitated not by catering directly to our egos but instead by minimizing the extent to which we have to attend to ourselves or articulate an active list of demands that we want to make on the world.

Finally, in Part Four of Kant's *Religion*, we find a lengthy testament to how available and attractive this inclination toward passivity is. The context in which we find these remarks is rather removed from our current framework, since Kant's aim in this final part of the *Religion* is not to delineate the different dimensions of self-love. His subject matter is instead a certain set of ethical risks that human beings can encounter even when, as he puts it, they are "under the dominion of the good principle" (RGV 6:151). In cases where persons are not acting from self-love and are instead self-ruled in accord with the moral law, there is still evidence of a tendency to conform passively to those options made most available to us by our external surroundings. We see this in Kant's constant reminders—which I revisit in Chapter 8—that we are routinely inclined to adopt a passive or servile attitude regarding faith, one in which traditions and practices are interpreted not as an occasion for active, deliberate moral reflection, but as inviting us into the comparatively less challenging performance of outwardly visible services and rituals. If it remains tempting for even a morally reformed human being to fall into an uncritical stance toward religion—one focused on obedience to the external trappings of a historical faith—then we have only further grounds for concluding that passivity can also be the face of self-love.

26. Granted, Kant notes, complete contentment can never be our goal. Pains, for example, are crucial to life, since they prompt us to activity and are something whose absence indicates our near death (Anth 7:35).

Thinking about how we can reveal the feeling of vitality through an attitude of passivity puts us in an excellent position to appreciate further nuances within Kant's hedonism and explore additional examples that may otherwise seem incompatible with it. For example, it allows us to see as hedonistically driven an agent who takes her cues from situational factors. I mention this both to give an illustration of this second model of nonmoral choice and so that we can connect this discussion to recent and increasing interest in whether Kant can adequately accommodate certain empirical findings relevant to both ethics and practical psychology.[27] If Kant thinks I can feel alive and pleased by reducing a sense of opposition between me and the world, and by accommodating whatever outside forces are encouraging me to do, then there are a number of cases of nonmoral action that immediately look more intelligible and open to a Kantian interpretation. Thus, we can take, for instance, the widely cited "dimes" experiment, in which Alice Isen and Paula Levin concluded that a person's willingness to help a nearby woman pick up dropped papers depended disproportionately on whether he had just been fortunate enough to find a dime.[28] It is reasonable to interpret someone who lets a dime's absence or presence direct him as someone who is trying to maintain an easy feeling of being unbothered or unhindered. This holds even for someone who, after finding a dime, puts aside his own wants and offers aid to a passerby. The person who offers help may appear to suffer a reduction in hedonic satisfaction, but Kant's second model of nonmoral choice can show us that by simply taking direction from an external cue, one has also secured a feeling of being unopposed or unobstructed by the surrounding world.

To continue to illustrate this second model of nonmoral choice, and to conclude this section, we can note that even if an agent who acts from self-love does not necessarily exhibit the obviously self-centered tendencies highlighted by the first model of nonmoral choice, we can still say that

27. John Doris is largely responsible for introducing these questions about whether ethical theory is sufficiently sensitive to empirical research. His overall point in *Lack of Character* is that if we look at personality and social psychology research, we must conclude that we neither have, nor have the capacity to develop, character traits of the kind envisioned by Aristotle and other philosophers similarly reliant on a character-centered moral psychology. Recently, certain Kantians—including Frierson and Pauline Kleingeld—have begun to consider how Kant fares against charges of empirical inadequacy. See Frierson, "Kantian Moral Pessimism," and Kleingeld, "Kant against Situationism." I revisit this issue and Doris's research in Chapter 2. I also explain how my approach to Doris's research is different from, for example, Frierson's.

28. In this experiment, a woman dropped papers in front of a phone booth. At those booths, some people had just found a dime planted there, while others had not. Of those who had found a dime, 87.5 percent helped the woman gather her papers, compared to 4 percent of those who had not found the dime. See Doris, *Lack of Character*, 30.

passivity is nonetheless self-interested insofar as it takes a fundamentally protectionist stance regarding the self. This observation lets us appreciate the hedonistic and self-centered undertones of certain depictions of Eichmann, an example routinely referenced by those attempting to criticize hedonism in Kant's nonmoral and immoral psychology. Bernstein, for example, rightly points out that Eichmann, at least as he is understood through the writings of Arendt,[29] does not appear to be a man driven by sensualist concerns[30]; in other words, Eichmann does not seem well explicated by the first model of nonmoral choice. But what Bernstein overlooks is the possibility of a second model of nonmoral choice, one where hedonism takes shape through a passive and uncritical willingness to be amenable—to obey orders and to identify with positive law. Eichmann achieves a consistency that a person vulnerable to situational factors does not, but both have in common how they can feel subjectively unhindered by adapting easily to socially recognized norms or behavioral prompts.[31] This kind of example shows us all the more vividly how Kant would conceive the possibilities of and explanations behind nonmoral or immoral actions, while remaining committed to motivational dualism and hedonism about nonmoral psychology.

CONCLUSION

The goal of this chapter has been to develop a more adequate account of self-love, both because of its general importance to Kant's practical psychology and our interest in how action driven by self-love can manifest itself. But before we move on to further considerations regarding the incentive of self-love in Chapter 2, it is natural to ask what, in light of Kant's two models of nonmoral choice and their shared emphasis on the egoistic preoccupations underwriting self-love, can be proposed within Kant's framework to help curb this egoistic streak.

One possible answer begins with how Kant routinely emphasizes that an essential power of the moral law is its ability to render us humiliated, to infringe upon a human being's "opinion of his personal worth," and to force

---

29. Unfortunately, whether Arendt's Eichmann is indeed the historical Eichmann, and whether Bernstein's understanding of how Arendt presented Eichmann is accurate, are not questions I can consider in this context. A nice summary of debates relevant to both issues is offered by Roger Berkowitz in "Misreading 'Eichmann in Jerusalem.'"

30. Bernstein, *Radical Evil: A Philosophical Interrogation*, 42.

31. I make a similar point about Eichmann in my "Expansionist Interpretations of Radical Evil."

a human being to realize that in the "absence of agreement with the moral law" his personal value is "reduced to nothing" (KpV 5:78). Comments like this can give the impression that Kant's remedy for egoism is to strip away all that is unique or personally distinct in our self-conceptions. In other words, it may seem that what endorsement of the moral law leaves us with—and what a person's sense of self is to include—are only those features that any rational agent whatsoever could build an identity on, such as a recognition of oneself as free, as capable of autonomous self-legislation, and as enjoying properties in virtue of which any person can demand respect.

But as will become clear in the course of this book, this cannot be the core of Kant's response to either the egoism discussed in this chapter or the other practical failings I discuss shortly, namely, evil and self-deception. To begin to explain why, we can note that if this were Kant's main reply, it would soon run headlong into some of the most unattractive depictions of Kantian agency in the literature. I have in mind a cluster of objections broadly shared by Williams, Murdoch, Schopenhauer, and, most distantly, Hegel. Notwithstanding some general sympathies with Kant's attempt to improve ethics by turning attention to a person's inner life or character, these critics argue that Kant leaves human beings saddled with a decimated, thin, and indistinctive conception of agency like that described above and forcefully reject his view on this basis.[32] However, like many contemporary Kantians, I find that Kant's conception of human selfhood and agency, in fact, turns out to be at odds with this conjecture. To appreciate why, we need only follow through to the final chapters of this book. There, I consider Kant's theory of moral reform and show where it features a self who relies on empirical conditions to gain moral insight, whose ethical progress is impossible in social isolation, and who is dependent on historically situated and culturally robust institutions. Toward the end of Chapter 6, for example, I explain why Kant believes that self-knowledge—which is essential to the task of moral transformation—requires social relationships and interactions with others. In Chapter 7, I explain how, for Kant, concrete experiences in the mode of sense help us learn more about what it means to be devoted to the moral law and how to cultivate virtue. And in Chapter 8, I discuss how social collectives—including churches and

---

32. For some of their most germane and forcefully articulated criticisms, see Schopenhauer, On the Basis of Morality, 61–62; Murdoch, The Sovereignty of Good, 30–31; and Williams, Shame and Necessity, 100–101. For an excellent overview of some of Hegel's criticisms of Kantian morality, see Karl Ameriks, Kant and The Fate of Autonomy: Problems in the Appropriation of the Critical Philosophy, 309–331.

an inclusively minded ethical community—are needed to resolve threats to moral progress so grave that they can render us "instruments of evil" (RGV 6:97).[33] These final chapters are thus valuable on multiple fronts. For one, they are where I develop a reading of Kant's theory of moral reform, one that has no analogue in the existing literature and thereby warrants consideration in its own right. And because of this, the final arguments of this book also give fresh insight into how Kant displaces both the egoistic streak of self-love featured in this chapter and the interpretation of Kantian selfhood and agency popularized by some of his fiercest critics in the history of philosophy.

33. I explain what I take "instruments of evil" to mean in Chapter 8. See pages 221–222 in particular.

CHAPTER 2

Evil and the Subordination of the Moral Law

Kant's account of evil remains one of the more challenging elements of his moral theory, and there are at least three reasons why his account has proven so controversial and difficult to interpret. First, the *Religion* is really the only text from Kant that offers a sustained, mature commentary on the nature of human evil.[1,2] Since we find exceedingly little on evil

---

1. This is not to say that if we put the *Religion* aside, then Kant's works offer no consideration of any element of moral wrongdoing. One element of immorality that receives sustained attention is the question of how to conceive of an agent's relationship to freedom when the moral law is violated. As Gerold Prauss notes, Kant struggled throughout his ethical writings to find a way to articulate how freedom relates to non-moral or immoral action, particularly when freedom of the will is conceived as practical reason. See *Kant über Freiheit als Autonomie*, 92.

2. The pre-Critical and strictly Leibnizian "New Elucidation" and "Optimism" essays are not helpful for fleshing out a mature Kantian theory regarding the nature of evil. Even the account of evil in the transcripts of Kant's lectures on philosophical religion, which are dated sometime between 1783 and 1786, is of limited use. Part of the difficulty stems from the fact that the text used for these lectures was, predictably, Baumgarten's *Metaphysics*. Thus, where Kant's own thoughts on evil start, and where Baumgarten's thoughts end, is unclear. Perhaps because of this, and because of the influence of Rousseau on Kant, much of the discussion seems to be an amalgamation of Rousseauian ideas about unsocial sociability and Baumgarten-inspired ideas about how human limitations or imperfections are implicated in evil (see Baumgarten, *Metaphysics*, 146). Thus, even though much of Kant's early, pre-Critical Leibnizian commitments regarding evil—such as Kant's early sympathy for a theodicy—are shed by the time of the lectures, I nonetheless agree with Gordon Michalson that the lectures on philosophical religion are not an example of Kant's mature thinking about evil. See Michalson, *Fallen Freedom*, 26.

in Kant's other main moral writings,[3] commentators are left with few re-sources to help them sort through problematic dimensions of the view presented in the *Religion*. This lack of complementary resources is per-haps not surprising with respect to Kant's pre-1790 writings, but special comment should be made about the *Metaphysics of Morals*, published sev-eral years after the *Religion*. This 1797 text is exactly where we would expect to find some echo of Kant's discussion of evil, yet instead we are met with silence when we turn to it for guidance. The *Metaphysics of Morals* contains few uses of the term *Böse* and absolutely no systematic discussion of evil, let alone a *Hang zum Bösen* (propensity to evil) or an evil that is radical and rooted in human nature. This state of affairs has led one recent commen-tator to claim that it is as if Kant looked in the abyss of evil in the *Religion* and then, unable to grasp what he saw therein, jerked back.[4]

Second, beyond the difficulty of situating the *Religion* in Kant's broader corpus on practical philosophy, the *Religion* itself seems as though it can be read under significantly different interpretive lenses. From an existential point of view, the *Religion* shifts between the bleakest pessimism, insisting on a universal and "inextirpable" evil (RGV 6:51), and later affirmative talk of a victory (*Sieg*) of good over evil. Additionally, the text appears to be: both a transcendental inquiry into the conditions of the possibility of evil[5] and an anthropological treatment of evil that shows Kant's interest in being a philosopher of history[6]; committed to both an individualistic[7] and communitarian theory of evil and moral reform[8]; and intermittently resistant to and in need of biblical themes, Christological assumptions, and a belief that goodness requires divine assistance.[9]

Third, and as discussed in the Introduction to this book, the peculiar stance Kant develops vis-à-vis Christian theology helps explain the histor-ical reception of the *Religion* and the skeptical or disinterested attitudes

---

3. Kant explicitly discusses good and evil in the second *Critique*, but only very briefly and in a manner that is difficult to map onto the discussion of evil in the *Religion*. The discussion in the second *Critique* (5:58–67) offers more or less a formal definition of evil by deeming it that which is an object of aversion, with regard to either what is agreeable or what is contrary to the law of reason.

4. Hans Peter Lichtenberger, "Über die Unerforschlichkeit des Bösen nach Kant," 130–131.

5. See, for example, Pablo Muchnik, "An Alternative Proof of the Universal Propensity to Evil," 130.

6. See Anderson-Gold, *Unnecessary Evil*, especially 53–62.

7. Michalson, *Fallen Freedom*, 50–51.

8. For a communitarian approach to Kantian moral reform, see Kate Moran, *Community and Progress in Kant's Moral Philosophy*.

9. Examples of these theological tensions are given throughout Michalson, *Fallen Freedom*.

toward the text that persisted until relatively recently. Noteworthy contemporaries—most famously, Goethe and Schiller—objected in particular to Kant's claim about a universal propensity to evil, or an evil that is rooted in human nature, finding implicit in it an unacceptable commitment to the Christian doctrine of original sin. And though, as we'll see, recent commentators are much more willing to treat Kant's claims sympathetically than were Schiller or Goethe, it remains the case that scholarship on the *Religion* has not benefited from the same sustained engagement that texts such as the *Groundwork* have. Commentators interested in Kant's theory of evil have some catching up to do.

Despite these significant obstacles, the present chapter and the subsequent ones contribute to current efforts to revitalize interest in Kant's theory of evil, thus trying to stare into that abyss long enough to make out the answers to the following essential questions regarding evil.

The first question concerns what characterizes an evil will, and to explain how I'll proceed, a contrast with the prior chapter will help. In Chapter 1, we established that we could find new depth in the concept of self-love by considering the presence of the self in nonmoral life. In doing so, we saw that an agent who incorporates self-love into her fundamental maxim may not pursue the actions and ends that we would immediately associate with hedonistically motivated behavior. As such, the goal of Chapter 1 was to reconsider Kant's account of the *content* of self-love. The current chapter picks up on this inquiry by arguing that the theory of evil Kant builds on this concept of self-love is likewise more complex than it initially appears to be. More specifically, I proceed by considering what kinds of *formal* arrangements between the incentives of practical reason—self-love and respect for the law—are possible in an evil will. Along the way, I will also try to determine whether Kant can prove sufficiently sensitive to influential objections regarding his moral psychology and to contemporary, empirically minded research relevant to evil.

The second question is far broader, and it concerns the pervasive and yet insufficiently understood or defended suggestion that an especially close relationship must exist between evil and self-deception. This question will frame Chapters 3 through 5, and as we explore it, we will have occasion to comment on additional issues including, for example, what self-deception is, different ways one can argue for a connection between self-deception and evil, whether Schiller and Goethe's dismissal of a proof for a universal evil is justified, and the other tensions I've noted in this chapter's introductory remarks concerning Kant's theory of evil. I will give a detailed overview of these issues later, and for now return us to the question of how to understand evil itself.

INCORPORATION, SUBORDINATION, AND EXPANSIONIST ACCOUNTS OF EVIL

The proper place to start in *Religion within the Boundaries of Mere Reason* is with what Henry Allison has dubbed Kant's "incorporation thesis" and Kant's further claim that evil consists in the subordination (*Unterordnung*) of the moral principle to self-love. The incorporation thesis is well known: it states simply that no human being can be determined to act except by those incentives that she willingly incorporates (*aufnimmt*) into her maxims (RGV 6:24).[10] This claim is introduced in the context of Kant's defense of moral rigorism, but even before we delve into that discussion, we can see why the incorporation thesis is important to both Kantian ethics more generally and Kant's theory of evil. The incorporation thesis makes explicit Kant's commitment to transcendental freedom, as it emphasizes the bedrock Kantian claim that human action can only be conceptualized under the idea of a free independence from antecedent conditions in space and time. Thus, the thesis both immediately puts out of contention one possible account of evil—namely, that evil would consist in being overcome by inclination—and points us in the general direction that a Kantian account of evil must proceed along—namely, that evil must be grounded in how human beings use their freedom.[11]

The next point to discuss is Kant's claim that what determines whether a man is of good and evil character is "which of the two"—the "two" being the incentives of self-love and respect for the law—he subordinates to or "makes the condition of the other" (RGV 6:36).[12] I will gradually develop some more novel ways of understanding this claim about subordination, but first we need to recall and further appreciate what rests in the background. Kant's arguments about subordination rely on his idea that human beings are constitutively vulnerable to the incentives of both self-love and respect for the moral law. The most it seems we can do is shove aside one in favor of the other, and the reason we may suppress but not eliminate either respect for the law or self-love can be found in Kant's account of exactly

---

10. See Allison, *Kant's Theory of Freedom*, 40.

11. Incidentally, these arguments also do much to combat those critics who find in Kant a "deep suspicion of our bodies" (Michalson, *Fallen Freedom*, 69) or, to use Kant's own words momentarily against him, critics who think evil indicates that we should "wish to be free" of our vulnerability to inclination (GMS 4:428).

12. Later in this book, I will show that Kant adds more nuance to his account of good character. At this early point in the *Religion*, Kant is focused on showing how character is related to the incentive incorporated into one's maxim. Further into the *Religion*, Kant adds that goodness requires not only adopting the right principle but also making moral progress over time. I discuss this point at length in Chapter 7.

what it means to describe them as incentives or *Triebfedern*, as incentives are experienced by human beings as forces that pull against one another. Kant emphasizes this in a crucial footnote (RGV 6:22n) that recalls once again the 1763 essay on negative magnitudes[13] noted briefly in Chapter 1. Kant's chief goal at 6:22n, which I revisit in a few pages, is to argue that a human being only removes herself from the force of one of these two incentives by putting herself under the sway of its opposite. Thus, it may help to note, this account also informs Kant's rejection of diabolical evil. This rejection has in the past proven controversial, and my current goal is not to challenge Kant on this point or to sift through this controversy but instead to note how it references Kant's account of the incentives.[14] If the most a person can do is turn away from one incentive and toward another, then there is nothing worse one can do than embrace self-love and turn away from the moral law. No agent can eliminate her receptivity to respect, and so diabolical evil is an impossibility.

With these introductory points now clear, I want to begin to shift the discussion to my own interpretation of Kant's theory of evil in the *Religion*, focusing specifically on what Kant means when he discusses the subordination of respect to self-love and how these incentives are formally arranged in a person of evil character. Part of what motivates the interpretation I will soon advance are concerns about how some interpreters have tried to rebuff a specific line of criticism regarding Kant's theory of evil.

The points offered thus far seem to indicate that Kant's dualism regarding human motivation also constrains his theory of evil. Evil, it would seem, results from an agent having made self-love her priority, and goodness, it would seem, consists in respect for the law being put first. But given this, criticisms in line with those we discussed in Chapter 1 would appear to get traction, only now Kant's theory of evil, as opposed to his more general practical psychology, becomes the explicit target. Insofar as the disposition or volitional structure of a given evil agent seems identical to that of any other—each being committed to self-love, each subordinating the moral law to one's own pleasure, and each being incapable of

---

13. Perhaps more than any other commentator, at least in the English literature, Melissa Zinkin has repeatedly emphasized the importance of Kant's *Attempt to Introduce the Concept of Negative Magnitudes into Philosophy* for a proper understanding of Kant's theory of the incentives and Kant's practical philosophy more generally. My debt to her papers is great.

14. Since I aim only to elucidate how Kant's rejection of diabolical evil is relevant to his theory of the incentives, I am putting to the side other important aspects of this rejection, such as how Kant leverages it to explain why we can be held morally accountable for evil. On this point, see Allison, *Kant's Theory of Freedom*, 150. I give a more detailed account of diabolical evil in Chapter 4.

diabolical motivation—Kantianism has appeared to some philosophers to be saddled with not only a crude theory of nonmoral motivation but also a correspondingly crude theory of what constitutes evil.

It is perhaps unsurprising that a number of commentators have tried to handle this worry in much the same way that Reath handled concerns about Kant's nonmoral psychology. Just as Reath tried to strip away the hedonism within self-love, many have tried to argue that we must similarly broaden the range of motivations that should count as evil. While these views differ in their details, we can think of all such views as offering "expansionist" accounts of Kantian evil. For example, Louden, in his recent work on Kant's theory of evil, explicitly relies on Reath's "Hedonism" article to argue that self-love should be understood simply as a commitment to "do what I desire" and that Kantian evil thus "has extremely wide scope."[15] At points, Wood also endorses this expansionist reading, arguing that evil is found in "*anything* people do when they violate their duties and fail to live up to the dignity of their rational nature."[16] Frierson has developed a sophisticated version of an expansionist view of evil as well, one motivated in large part by the argument that Kantianism needs to, and in fact is able to, accommodate empirical work on human character.[17,18]

Now, in Chapter 1 I argued that Reath was correct to think that our interpretation of Kant's theory of nonmoral motivation needed revision but incorrect to think that we could secure the needed amendments by cleansing the incentive of self-love of its hedonism. Here, I similarly want to concede that our understanding of Kant's theory of evil needs revision but resist the proposals offered by Louden, Wood, and Frierson. I consider Louden and Wood first, and then move on to Frierson's expansionist interpretation of evil.

While the urge to expand Kant's account of evil by deeply broadening Kant's conception of self-love is understandable, the work I have done in Chapter 1 makes clear the problems with any such approach. Both Wood and Louden think we can lend complexity to evil by augmenting what it can mean to be motivated by self-love. And though both commentators, of

15. "Evil Everywhere: The Ordinariness of Kantian Radical Evil," 102.
16. "Kant and the Intelligibility of Evil," 145. My italics.
17. See "Kantian Moral Pessimism" and "Character in Kant's Moral Psychology: Responding to the Situationist Challenge."
18. My "Expansionist Interpretations of Radical Evil" offers a brief review of how Frierson joins Wood and Louden in advocating expansionism. However, it neglects both to explain several important aspects of Frierson's view—including certain oversights in his description of Doris, which are discussed shortly—and to respond adequately to the expansionist trend.

course, agree that an action from respect for the law is not motivated by self-love, they put no other boundary on what can count as an action from self-love. In light of this, they end up where Reath did—with a theory of evil and self-love that lacks definitive shape and that does not deliver an adequate explanation of where their expansionism about evil ends.

Now, in making this criticism, I am not refuting the possibility of a limited form of expansionism about evil. Quite the contrary, I have already set the stage for a narrow, principled expansion by developing in Chapter 1 my account of two different models of nonmoral choice and by arguing that the desires contained in an evil maxim might not be those that bear the hallmarks of unbridled hedonism. The goal of the current chapter is to develop further a properly constrained expansionism by exploring additional, different resources for dealing with Kant's theory of evil.

To develop these resources, I'll next engage Frierson's attempt to expand the possible forms that Kantian evil can take. One reason why Frierson's expansionism differs from Wood's and Louden's is that Frierson's most recent inquiries into Kant's theory of evil are situated in a broader attempt to determine the relevance of certain findings in empirical psychology to Kantian ethics. More specifically, Frierson's account of Kantian evil is part of a wider discussion about whether Kantianism can respond to those such as Doris, who argue that much contemporary and historical ethical theory takes for granted certain empirically inadequate assumptions about human character. There are thus two points we need to be clear about moving forward: Doris's criticisms and Frierson's responses on Kant's behalf.

As for Doris's criticisms, they will be well known to those who have witnessed the extensive influence of his work on virtue ethics, but since philosophers situated squarely within the Kantian tradition might be more unfamiliar with them, a brief review is in order. Doris relies on experimental research to undermine the idea that human beings can develop stable moral characters, whether good or evil. Two of the experiments that motivate his claim are the Isen and Levin "dimes" experiment—which was already explored and given a Kantian interpretation in Chapter 1—and the infamous Milgram shock experiments. In the latter, which are featured centrally in Doris's book and will be my focus, test subjects were found surprisingly willing to administer increasingly painful shocks to another person at the behest of an authority figure.[19] Doris argues that since situational factors are highly predictive of the behavior of the Milgram subjects,

---

19. Two-thirds of the subjects proceeded to the highest shock level, though only in those situations where the authority figure is physically present. See Doris, *Lack of Character*, 45 and 46. As Doris notes, this proportion has been replicated.

there is strong evidence human beings generally lack stable and consistent character traits.

This conclusion, Frierson recognizes, threatens to undermine central components of not only Aristotle's ethics but also Kant's moral psychology, such as his rigorism about character[20] and his claim that human beings rely on a *Denkungsart* or a "fundamental maxim" to guide their everyday choices.[21] In order to save Kant from these worries, Frierson notes that in the *Anthropology*, Kant briefly but explicitly discusses the general difficulty in becoming a principled person, a difficulty that holds regardless of whether one positions herself with or contrary to the moral law. Kant, according to Frierson, maintains that many persons, instead of acquiring the stable character of either a monster or a saint, will find themselves "shifting hither and yon like a swarm of gnats."[22] This characterization, Frierson claims, speaks to the finding that, for example, the presence of an authority figure bears disproportionately on whether a person demonstrates a willingness to cause pain to another human being. Frierson then offers the expansionist thesis that evil consists in anything less than fully consistent adherence to the law. Once he does so, he can connect expansionism to these points about the difficulty of aligning oneself with either self-love or the moral law: evil, he argues, is present in both those who steadfastly give self-love priority over the moral law and those who resemble an unaffiliated "swarm of gnats." That is, his expansionism allows Kantians to argue that those who alternate in trivially different situations between inflicting and not inflicting high-level shocks are bad or evil.

Yet the difficulty with this application of an expansionist approach becomes evident if we return to Kant's claim in the *Religion* that failure to take the moral law as one's sole incentive must stem from a positive resistance to the moral law. There is, Kant insists, no room for a kind of forbearance or abstention from the incentive of respect for the moral law that takes the form of indifference, just as there cannot be a magnetic charge that is neither positive nor negative.[23] If a person fails to incorporate respect for the law alone into her maxims, Kant insists that this

20. I say more about Kant's rigorism later in this chapter.

21. See Frierson, "Character in Kant's Moral Psychology: Responding to the Situationist Challenge." On a *Denkungsart* as a "fundamental maxim," see Allison, *Kant's Theory of Freedom*, 40.

22. Anth 7:292. Cited in Frierson, "Kantian Moral Pessimism," 36. Also cited in Kleingeld, "Kant against Situationism."

23. Or, according to the shorthand Kant uses to summarize this claim, if we symbolize the moral incentive as "a," any failure to determine the power of choice to "a" must be due to "-a," or the incentive of self-love.

can be "possible only as the consequence of a real and opposite determination of the power of choice, i.e. of a *resistance* [*Widerstrebung*] in its [the power of choice's] part" (RGV 6:22n).[24] Moreover, Kant's insistence that we frame our theory of the incentives in a way that eliminates the possibility of indifference or lack of engagement with the incentives of human action is not unique to the *Religion*. To give just a brief example, in the second *Critique*, Kant maintains that the incentive of self-love is not only natural to human life but also "active" (*rege*) in us "even prior to the moral law" (KpV 5:73),[25] thus emphasizing the extent to which a human being cannot avoid at least trying to negotiate the competing pulls of respect for the moral law and self-love. Because both the moral law and self-love impress themselves upon us in an undeniable manner—that is, because the move away from one incentive can happen only by way of an endorsement of the opposed counterincentive—real devotion to self-love must be implicated in our resistance to the moral law. But if we entertain the expansionist approach offered by Frierson, and the proposal of a kind of blank space in human beings that precedes or marks disengagement from the incentives constitutive of human life, we would lose the ability to understand Kant's claims about how the motivational underpinnings of evil necessarily involve active opposition to respect for the moral law.

These difficulties with Frierson's expansionism, as well as Wood's and Louden's, may seem to put us in an impossible position. We have seen that neither form of expansionism is able to both lend nuance to Kant's theory of evil and abide by other Kantian commitments, such as the claims reviewed in Chapter 1 regarding how hedonism must meaningfully shape our account of self-love or my claims here concerning how the incentives of self-love and respect actively inform the practical life of any human being. However, we should not give up on expansionism entirely. Wood and Louden are right that something more needs to be said about the possible shapes of evil. Frierson is likewise correct that we should strive to make Kantian sense of examples like those of the participants in the Milgram shock experiments. And, in fact, I think that a closer look at just this example can motivate a different approach to Kant's theory of evil.

I want to take a moment to emphasize two points about this case that are generally overlooked by philosophers trying to respond to Doris. First, I want to stress that the subjects who continued to administer shocks in the experiments generally did so despite being in an agonized

---

24. See also KpV 5:75 for another reference to this idea of resistance.
25. This passage is also noted in Zinkin, "Respect for the Law and the Use of Dynamical Terms in Kant's Theory of Moral Motivation," 41.

state of conflict. Many subjects are recorded as crying, groaning, digging "their fingernails into their flesh," wringing their hands, saying, "Oh God, let's stop it,"[26] and generally exhibiting clear, anguished, and seemingly sincere moral disapproval of their own actions. Second, we should also clarify how, exactly, Doris interprets experiments such as Milgram's. The nuances of Doris's claim about lack of character are often missed or underappreciated, and it is easy to misinterpret him as arguing—to put the point bluntly—that there is no meaningful core within moral personality. But in arguing against character, Doris is arguing only against the idea that human beings generally possess rich, ethically informed dispositions or traits that reliably incline them to *act* in trait-relevant ways.[27] The subjects' failure to take the right or compassionate action is for Doris evidence that the subjects lack the character traits of compassionate persons, but this is fully compatible with the claim that there are other meaningful and legitimate aspects of moral identity and moral comportment. Indeed, the experiments seem to reveal that the participants do, in fact, have something like sincerely held moral allegiances; otherwise, such intense and consistent anguish would not be evident. We may even say that while the subjects *behave*—through cries, sighs of anguish, and so on—in a way that at least partially expresses sincere commitments, their *actions* do not express these commitments. Thus, when Doris says that subjects routinely lack (moral) character, he means only to say that they lack the traits, dispositions, or sets of reasons that reliably incline them to act in accord with their ethical commitments. A thesis regarding lack of character should not be read as a denial that there are significant and perhaps quite stable elements of moral personality and an agent's inner life that are different from and fall outside the scope of what Doris defines as character.

The question, then, that faces us is whether Kant's moral psychology and theory of evil are complex enough to do justice to this more nuanced reading of both Doris and the empirical evidence that Frierson and Doris rightly demand that any philosopher must attend to. I want to argue that Kant can, in fact, succeed on this front, and I will do so by reconsidering exactly how we should understand his argument that evil consists in the subordination of the moral law.

26. Milgram, quoted in Doris, *Lack of Character*, 43. As Milgram (and Doris) note, the subject who said, "Oh God, let's stop it" continued to the very highest shocks.

27. I am indebted to Doris for clarifying this during a discussion of his work at the 2013 Character Project Summer Seminar, which took place June 17–27 at Wake Forest University.

Recall that Kant's subordination thesis states that whether a man is of good and evil character depends on "which of the two"—the "two" being the incentives of self-love and respect for the law—he subordinates to or "makes the condition of the other" (RGV 6:36). I want to call attention to how commentators have glossed this concept of subordination. Allison has noted that subordination involves "letting the principle of self-love wear the trousers," and that a "morally evil agent does not repudiate the moral law as such but takes it as yielding a sufficient reason to act, or refrain from acting, only on the condition that it does not conflict with self-love."[28] For Seiriol Morgan, "the evil person subordinates duty to the gratification of his desires, acknowledging moral ends only insofar as they do not proscribe his pursuit of what he wants."[29] Similarly, Muchnik and Anderson-Gold claim that evil consists in putting aside "what we ought to do in favor of what pleases."[30] Numerous other examples can be given to document the interpretive trend of describing the subordination thesis simply in terms of "priority."[31]

Now, I do not want to dispute that some individuals do, in fact, give priority to self-love in just the way Allison and these other commentators argue. But we lose much of what is intriguing about the subordination thesis, and thus overlook a feature of it that can lend depth to an account of the possible shapes of evil, if we restrict ourselves to this claim about priority. In making his point about subordination, I do not think that Kant's goals are to remind us that the prioritization of self-love results in evil, or that an agent remains vulnerable to the incentive of respect even while she puts self-love first. To see why, we can focus our attention on a claim Kant makes immediately after he articulates the subordination thesis. He describes an evil agent as someone who attempts to incorporate the moral incentive *alongside* the incentive of self-love. That is, what characterizes an evil will is that an agent "indeed incorporates the moral law" into his maxims, "together with the law of self-love," and that what motivates

28. Allison, "On the Very Idea of a Propensity to Evil," 340.
29. Morgan, "The Missing Formal Proof of Humanity's Radical Evil in Kant's *Religion*," 66.
30. Muchnik and Anderson-Gold, "Introduction," 2.
31. See, for example, DiCenso, *Kant's* Religion within the Boundaries of Mere Reason: A Commentary, 62; Paul Guyer, *Kant*, 228; and Lichtenberger, "Über die Unerforschlichkeit des Bösen nach Kant," 130. Allison also used the term "prioritization" to characterize his reading of the subordination thesis at the 2015 Eastern Study Group of the North American Kant Society, which took place April 24–25 at Georgetown University.

this agent is an attempt to keep the incentives of self-love and respect for the law on "an equal footing" (RGV 6:36). In Kant's own words, the agent "*das moralische Gesetz zwar neben dem der Selbstliebe in dieselbe aufnimmt*," and tries to will that the one incentive can stand next to the other ("*eines neben dem andern . . . bestehen kann*"). Kant therefore tries to depict the motivations behind evil not in terms of a person who endorses self-love while remaining vulnerable to the moral law but in terms of someone who tries to *overdetermine* her will by incorporating *both* incentives into one and the same maxim.[32] Kant reaffirms this idea of a person striving to endorse both incentives when he states that respect for the law "should have been incorporated into the universal maxim of the power of choice as the *sole* [*alleinige*] incentive"[33]; the "sole" here clearly indicates that an agent who subordinates respect for the moral law can nonetheless be someone who— in a sense that needs further spelling out and qualifications—acknowledges and in some meaningful way accepts the burden of the moral law and its demands. We find the same emphasis, and even the same language as the *Religion*, in the second *Critique*. Much of the chapter on the incentives of pure practical reason in the second *Critique* centers on a discussion of re- spect as an *a priori* moral feeling and how the moral law can function as the determining ground of the will, but it is helpful to note that at the very beginning of this chapter, Kant emphasizes the hazards of letting a competing incentive, such as the incentive of advantage, "cooperate *along- side* [*neben*] the moral law" (KpV 5:72). The idea of trying to maintain parity between the incentives of self-love and respect is thus clearly not unique to the *Religion*, even if it is given more focus in the latter.[34]

32. It should be clear that in this section, I am using this term "overdetermination" to suit my own purposes of inquiring into the different motivational states permitted by Kant's theory of evil. I will not comment on and in no way rely on the use of this term in articles on moral worth from Richard Henson, Herman, and Marcia Baron. For their respective writings on moral worth, see "What Kant Might Have Said: Moral Worth and the Overdetermination of Dutiful Action"; "On the Value of the Motive of Acting from Duty"; and *Kantian Ethics Almost Without Apology*, 146–193.

33. My italics.

34. Thus, when Kant notices the way a human being seeks cooperation or coordi- nation between the two incentives, I take him to be making a point much stronger than the comparatively weaker claim that we are always vulnerable to both incentives. Allison offers this comparatively weaker claim, but to do so, he must rely on an ex- tremely thin or watered down reading of what it means to incorporate an incentive into one's maxim (see *Kant's Theory of Freedom*, 151). Instead of understanding incorpora- tion as he usually does—that is, in terms of where a person turns for practical guidance and what she concretely endorses as giving her a reason for action—Allison switches to a weak reading at this juncture in *Kant's Theory of Freedom*, arguing that any human must always incorporate both incentives into her or his maxim insofar all persons are constitutively vulnerable to both incentives. Very likely, Allison relies on this move be- cause he takes Kant's rigorism to rule out the possibility of an overdetermined will and

Now, while Kant has clearly pointed us toward the idea that evil can consist in overdetermination, we must, given other elements of Kantian thought, address some difficulties regarding this proposal.[35] We have to note, for example, that the idea of an overdetermined will seems problematic in light of Kant's theory of motivation. However, spelling out the difficulty is delicate because it can be cashed out in different ways depending on some broader interpretive issues, specifically whether one frames the idea of overdetermination in terms of reasons or incentives, and whether we think the moral law must motivate us by providing sufficient reasons for action or whether the law must be accompanied by a feeling—respect—that has sufficient force to determine the will to act.[36] I've emphasized the latter approach thus far, but I don't want to step deeply into this debate, both because the text of the *Religion* and Kant's writings more broadly support both interpretations[37] and, more importantly, because on either account, it would seem that an overdetermined will is impossible. If incorporating the law into one's maxim involves seeing the moral law as providing sufficient reason to act—sufficient regardless of whatever competing inclinations self-love presents—then the idea of a person who aims to take both the law and self-love as authoritative guides seems a contradiction. We get a similar problem if we think of overdetermination as an attempt to incorporate

thus must find another way to read these claims about how a person tries to hold the two incentives alongside one another. But as I will argue later in this chapter, we can reconcile Kant's rigorism with my thesis regarding the prospect of overdetermination.

35. It may also help to note that while the account of overdetermination I develop in this chapter is my own, some commentators have gestured toward the core insight at the basis of my account. For instance, instead of putting the subordination thesis in terms of self-love taking priority over the moral law, Ingolf Dalferth speaks of evil in terms of the moral law *not* taking priority over self-love ("Radical Evil and Human Freedom," 67). This negative formulation leaves good conceptual space for the idea that evil can be characterized as the attempt to incorporate both incentives into one's fundamental maxim. Thus, even though Dalferth doesn't consistently emphasize this negative formulation (see, for example, "Radical Evil and Human Freedom," 69), he, at least at points, offers support for my claim that the concept of overdetermination is highly relevant to Kant's theory of evil.

36. Commentators like Allison, who emphasize an intellectualist account of moral motivation, would align with the former view, whereas Richard McCarty and other "affectivists" would endorse the latter.

37. As McCarty points out in "Kant's Incorporation Requirement: Freedom and Character in the Empirical World," the language of the incorporation thesis at RGV 6:24 supports an affectivist account of moral motivation, since here Kant claims that we must incorporate into our maxim the *incentive* of either self-love or respect. However, McCarty does not note that at other points in the *Religion*, Kant discusses incorporating the law itself—not the incentive of respect—into one's supreme maxim. This is clear from the German, but less so in the Wood and di Giovanni translation. See, for example, the end of 6:24, 6:26, and 6:36. See also RGV 6:62, where Kant discusses the incentive of respect as a mere idea, as opposed to a feeling.

two competing forces into our will. If we think of respect for the law as a kind of power wrought against sensibility,[38] and if, as Kant himself does, we think of the incentive of self-love as something that positively resists the moral law, [39] then an overdetermined will would seem not to be a will at all; it would function as if it were a balance scale with equal weights on both sides, and no movement or action could take place.[40] So in either case, we must address the challenge: Is the idea of an overdetermined will defensible?

To answer this question, two points are needed. First, we should revisit the issue of how self-love and respect function as forces and our earlier observation that an agent only resists one incentive by leveraging its opposite. It is tempting to conclude from this account that the human will is constitutively incapable of bearing the force of both incentives at once, but this is not quite right. Envision a tug-of-war: one team resists the other only by pulling harder on its own side, and the rope is clearly capable of being acted on by both forces at once. Thus, we can argue that one incentive can be resisted only if we endorse its opposite, while also allowing that a person's will is capable of registering simultaneously each of the dueling forces. In other words, Kant's argument about the mutual resistance of self-love and respect does not show their complete exclusivity within a person's will. Second, even in light of this observation, I am willing to admit that given Kant's account of how self-love and the moral law can function as forces or reasons for action that mutually undercut or oppose one another, it is impossible to stably or fully overdetermine one's will. I've tried to allude to this concession a bit by referencing in these last few pages a person who "tries" or "aims" to overdetermine her will.[41] An account of the modality of an overdetermined will thus requires some fine-tuning, for even though it is impossible to incorporate completely into one's will both the moral law and self-love, Kant still regards the *attempt* to do so as a live and highly attractive possibility for human beings; the struggle to hold the two incentives alongside one another, and to not have to let go of either, is an important feature of the human condition. My goal, then, is not to dispute that there is a deep futility implicit within the task of trying to overdetermine one's will and live up to two competing incentives or reasons

38. On this point, see Zinkin, "Respect for the Law and the Use of Dynamical Terms in Kant's Theory of Moral Motivation," 46–48.
39. See RGV 6:22n.
40. I borrow this very helpful imagery from Zinkin, "Respect for the Law and the Use of Dynamical Terms in Kant's Theory of Moral Motivation," 45.
41. In what follows, when I refer to overdetermination in the context of human agency, it should be understood that I am referring to an *attempt* at overdetermination.

for action. My goal instead in the remainder of this chapter is to explain how these efforts toward overdetermination shed new light on a possible, limited expansion of Kantian evil and how this proposal regarding overdetermination gains support from Kant's broader corpus.

I want to be explicit about why I find Kant's remarks concerning how agents strive toward overdetermination so attractive and why I want to freeze our attention on them. In part, the attraction stems from how the concept of overdetermination coheres with what seemed to be the characteristic failure of human beings in Kant's first *Critique*, namely, that human beings want *more*.[42] This desire to strive for more than one can have, ought to have, or needs to have is implicit within the Dialectic. Reason, as we know, is characterized by a certain hunger or conative energy that can feel irresistible, even though it often works against human interests. In the first *Critique*, this insatiability has the peculiar result of undermining a person's ability to secure what is within her clear reach. Take, for example, Kant's discussion of a human being's desire to understand the world as a transcendental realist would, as someone convinced of the idea that the law of causality governs appearances so thoroughly that she thinks she can uncover the unconditioned in the series of conditions. Kant follows this discussion with his well-known comment that "if we would give in to the deception of transcendental realism, then neither nature nor freedom would be left" (KrV A543/B571). Freedom would disappear because of its fundamental incompatibility with transcendental realism, and nature would disappear because a human being can pursue this unconditioned only to the extent that she sacrifices nature as an intelligible network of appearances bound by the limits of space and time. In other words, in wanting more, human beings would be left with nothing. I think we see this same dynamic in examples of overdetermination. A human being wants to not sacrifice either of the two incentives that are constitutive of human life, and in holding on to both of them, she will often end up with either nothing or, more precisely, with a set of actions that secure neither of her interests. If the human being has done what Kant described—has "looked about for yet other incentives," and has tried to respect the law but "with an eye to other aims"—then we will likely be left with no achievable or coherent aims whatsoever (RGV 6:42).

This, I maintain, is how we should think of a case like the Milgram shock experiments. Those who kept administering the shocks despite such evident, intense anguish cannot be understood as individuals giving the

---

42. Allison made this observation at the May 2015 Eastern Study Group of the North American Kant Society at Georgetown University.

incentive of self-love "priority" over the moral law. Such a description would trivialize the experience of the test subjects and lead to an unreasonable explanation of their behavior. Frierson's explanation of these individuals in terms of a *tout court* failure to stand under principles is also less compelling than an explanation that focuses on overdetermination. It's not the case that the test subjects lack commitments or suffer from a kind of practical apathy; rather, the test subjects are engaged in a frantic effort at overdetermination, caring both about the right thing and a pleasing ease in social interactions (i.e., with the authority figure overseeing the administration of shocks). Moreover, I want to point out that my difference with Frierson is not merely a verbal one. Frierson and I both converge on the idea that there is something peculiarly faulty about a human being's commitments in many cases of evil. But if we want to understand properly the subjective motivational sets that can accompany evil and the kinds of self-understanding that can accompany an evil disposition, we very much need an emphasis on overdetermination.

There is a meaningful difference between trying to "serve two masters"[43] and being devoted to neither, and without an appreciation of this difference, we will not understand the extent to which human beings— even those failing miserably to be good, like the participants in the shock experiments—may not be insincere in their claims to be concerned about morality. However, precisely for this reason, we can predict that it will be especially unlikely that they will properly grasp their failings. The attempt to overdetermine one's will often leads individuals to settle on actions that can only be read as *compromises*, or attempts to negotiate a conflict, that leave the individual unable to secure any of the competing goods or values that she cares about. Unlike the straight prioritizers, on whom Allison and other commentators concentrate, who set aside their own consciousness of the moral law and thus at least set themselves up to get what they desire, someone with an overdetermined will remains in all likelihood deeply unsatisfied. Because the participants of the shock experiments, and other individuals struggling in vain to somehow do justice to both of the incentives they are trying to incorporate into the will, lose out on practical life in a distinctive way, any resistance to moral self-criticism is not altogether unreasonable. How can such individuals see themselves as selfish when they clearly don't come close to getting what they want? How can they assess their moral faults when they see themselves—again, not unreasonably— as already recognizing the good? How, when such individuals are already

---

43. Since the text of the *Religion* is interspersed with biblical references, it is fitting to note the famous verse found at Luke 16:13 on the folly of trying to serve two masters.

struggling to keep so many practical concerns in the balance, could they see the prospect of change as the occasion for anything other than loss and sacrifice? It seems that when a person has overdetermined her will and has already compromised so much on behalf of the moral law, the prospect of being part of a kingdom of ends cannot hold quite the appeal Kantians have hoped.

These points should show the explanatory advantages of overdetermination to Kantians of nearly any persuasion. But those who approach Kant from certain specific vantage points can likely find further reason to endorse it. Those Kantians interested in how the *Religion* blends biblical narratives with a discussion of evil can see a parallel to the Genesis depiction of Eve, whose characteristic failing is better understood as wanting "more"—in this case, an additional fruit—than as simply putting aside what is right in favor of what pleases. Kantians sympathetic to Aristotelian moral psychology will find in my depiction of the Milgram shock participants an echo of Aristotle's insight that the vicious "hate and shun life," finding themselves "full of regret" and simultaneously torn in "different directions."[44] Finally, there is something reminiscent of contemporary constitutivist readings of Kant in the idea that evil can consist in an attempt at overdetermination of the will. Philosophers like Christine Korsgaard have argued that since moral principles are constitutive of agency, individuals who fail to embrace moral principles will fail to count as agents or as moral persons.[45] This line of argument has attracted legions of both defenders and detractors, with the former arguing that those who are immoral nullify their chance for integrity or a coherent self-conception and the latter arguing that those who act immorally can be perfectly contented with the defective, alternative form of self-constitution that accompanies a rejection of the demands of the moral law.[46] My argument regarding overdetermination can act as a kind of compromise between these two sides. I am sympathetic to those who reject the constitutivist thesis that everyone will find the psychic toll of evil especially burdensome; those who simply prioritize self-love will have much more stability in their lives than those who struggle to endorse both incentives. Yet cases of overdetermination, where evil takes the form of an ill-conceived and ill-fated compromise to be as good as we are self-loving, fit well with the constitutivist view that wrongdoing is a recipe for personal disaster and disarray.

44. *Nicomachean Ethics*, 1166b13–26.
45. See, for example, *Self-Constitution*, 27–44.
46. See, for example, David Enoch. "Agency, Schmagency: Why Normativity Won't Come from What Is Constitutive of Action."

I have so far tried mainly to articulate the significance of the idea that evil can consist in the attempt to keep the two incentives of the human will next to one another in the act of incorporation. As such, I have still said little about where we can find further evidence in favor of overdetermination, noting mainly its initial appearance in the *Religion* and its overlap with the spirit of Kant's claims about the overreach of reason in the Dialectic of the first *Critique*. To loan additional support to the claim that overdetermination remains a neglected feature of Kant's discussion of subordination, I will now explain how it aligns with other aspects of the *Religion* and Kant's thought more broadly.

FURTHER DISCUSSION: EVIL AND OVERDETERMINATION

Kantian Purity and Interpretations of the Subordination Thesis. I want to begin by stressing that my focus on overdetermination should help clarify some of the murkiness that surrounds reconstructions of the subordination thesis. In general, it seems that commentators fall into one of two camps. Some commentators let the subordination thesis reduce down to Kantian touchstones that are already abundantly well established, such as the claim that a diabolical agent, or a human being whose will does not materially contain the incentive of respect, is impossible.[47] Other commentators manage to preserve the impression that there is something more complex on hand with Kant's subordination thesis, and that it can substantively inform and change our assessments of certain types of moral dispositions, but fail to clarify exactly how it does so.

In the latter camp, consider again Morgan's claim that the person subordinating the moral law is nonetheless someone who is "acknowledging moral ends only insofar as they do not proscribe his pursuit of what he wants."[48] Morgan leaves it unclear what this "moral acknowledgment" amounts to. Is it simply that the moral law remains present in an agent's consciousness but that the incentive of respect is in no way informing that person's actions and choices? In other words, is Morgan simply reminding us diabolical agency is impossible? Or would Morgan hope to advance the idea that a person, in fact, can act from duty at moments where the inclinations of self-love are quiet or satiated? If so, how could we reconcile this with

47. See, for example, Wood, *Kant's Ethical Thought*, 287. See also Allison and Guyer, who are discussed momentarily.
48. See page 47 and Morgan, "The Missing Formal Proof of Humanity's Radical Evil in Kant's *Religion*," 66.

Kant's commitment to the idea that lower-order maxims are expressions of a more basic or highest fundamental maxim? It is unclear how Morgan would sift through these options and what form of moral engagement he sees as possible within the confines of the subordination thesis.

In contrast to Morgan, both Allison and Guyer read the subordination thesis in a manner that removes this opacity but, unfortunately, also removes the possibility that the subordination thesis can help us see new dimensions of the moral psychology of evil. Guyer, for example, in discussing the "priority" we give to self-love, makes it clear that this prioritization indicates a "fundamental commitment" and "not merely an occasional exception to a commitment to morality."[49] In other words, Guyer is clear that there is no room for meaningful psychological variety within evil motivation, and that all the subordination thesis should do is to remind us that evil isn't always apparent. Yet this point won't push our understanding of Kantian evil in new directions, and neither will Allison's insistence that subordination is meant to show that an evil agent "does not repudiate the moral law as such."[50] Allison, as noted, likewise sees the subordination thesis as restating Kant's stipulation against the possibility of diabolical evil and regards any alleged profession of sincere concern for moral demands as a lie one tells oneself in order to evade responsibility for evil. In other words, we can say that both Allison and Guyer see any admixture of self-love as resulting in the nullification of the moving power of the moral incentive in a person's will.

However, if we highlight the possibility that subordination can take the form of overdetermination, we can avoid the difficulties Morgan faces and find an alternative to the singular assessment of evil given by Guyer and Allison. Unlike Morgan, we can be precise about what new light the subordination thesis can shed on evil dispositions, and unlike Allison and Guyer, we can let the subordination thesis point us toward a richer moral psychology of evil and variations in an account of how the incentives of self-love and respect can be formally arranged in a person's will. In other words, we can adhere to the constraints the subordination thesis puts on the possibility of diabolical evil without endorsing the idea that this is the sum of what Kant's discussion of subordination is meant to accomplish. We can also make more systematic the open-ended nature of many of Kant's remarks on lack of purity. Kant does not often spell out for us what we ought to take away from his characterizations of a will that has let an admixture of nonmoral motives into her maxim,[51] but my account

49. Guyer, *Kant*, 228.
50. Allison, "On the Very Idea of a Propensity to Evil," 340.
51. See, for example, KpV 5:72.

explains and redeems this open-endedness. On my view, a lack of purity exists both when the moral incentive has been stilled or immobilized by self-love, resulting in an agent who offers nothing more than disingenuous professions about her willingness to be moved by moral concerns, and when an agent's attentiveness to the law is evident in the compromises she makes from all corners of the faculty of choice.

Rigorism and Overdetermination. As additional support for the proposal developed in this chapter, we can note that a focus on overdetermination will help us isolate and clarify the argument used to generate moral rigorism in the *Religion*. Kant rather famously claims at RGV 6:24 that good and evil wholly exclude one another, and that there can be neither an indifferentism, according to which an agent is neither good nor evil, nor a syncretism, in which an agent is evil in some parts of her character and good in other parts.[52] Now, while my earlier remarks regarding how self-love and respect for the law necessarily function as incentives can explain why indifferentism is not an option in Kantian moral psychology, it may seem as though the arguments I have made regarding overdetermination are at odds with Kant's stipulation against syncretism of good and evil. However, there are three reasons why this is not the case. As we will see, my account of overdetermination not only preserves rigorism but also helps us appreciate its role in Kant's moral theory.

First, we should emphasize that good and evil are, for Kant, evaluative concepts.[53] Since concepts are that which allow us to bring unity to a manifold, good and evil, when they pertain to character, will function as designations that loan order to different possible arrangements of the incentives of practical reason. Insofar as they play this organizing role, it is clear that the concepts of good and evil need not merely reduce down to, or reiterate, the contents of an agent's fundamental maxim or a description of how the incentives are structured in one's power of choice. In other words, we cannot expect that our evaluative concepts will overlap in a straightforward or direct way with our descriptive assessments of human motivations. Even if we have a complex moral psychology, there may be reasons why the

52. Although moral rigorism has several applications, here I focus only on rigorism regarding character. In contrast, there is both Kant's rigorism regarding actions and, closely related to rigorism about specific acts, Kant's apparent rigorism about certain maxims, such as maxims that advocate deception. I do not comment on these issues, in part because they are not relevant to a discussion of evil and in part because there exists a robust literature on Kant's rigorism regarding maxims. See, for example, Korsgaard, "The Right to Lie: Kant on Dealing with Evil," and Tamar Shapiro, "Kantian Rigorism and Mitigating Circumstances."
53. That good and evil are concepts is most clear in KpV 5:65–67.

scheme we use to organize and morally evaluate these different possibilities should remain comparatively more simple. Thus, even if there exist both straight prioritizers and agents who strive to overdetermine the power of choice, Kant is within his theoretical rights to argue that the same evaluative concept should be used to categorize both types of character.

Indeed, if all types of immoralism involved a clear-cut and whole-hearted suspension of the moral incentive, and if there were no diversity within the manifold to begin with, then the application of moral concepts would be either unnecessary or obvious. In such a case, Kant's rigorism would more or less restate an account of how the incentives of the will are constrained to operate, and rigorism would, in light of this simplified moral psychology, be the only view with even minimal plausibility. But if trying to overdetermine one's will is a live option, then this possibility breathes new life into rigorism. The prospect of overdetermination requires taking a stand on how such a will should be interpreted in evaluative terms, and Kant's insistence that an agent trying to incorporate both incentives into her will is in no manner good shows both why moral rigorism is a necessary addition to Kant's views and how severe it really is.

Second, it is important to observe some of the different points Kant relies on to craft an argument in favor of moral rigorism. At RGV 6:24, we can note that to establish rigorism, Kant directs us to consider not only how the two incentives—self-love and respect—are arranged within a person's will but also the "freedom of the power of choice," that is, an agent's unmitigated responsibility for the quality of her will. While the first point may seem to indicate that character evaluations simply restate which of the incentives is active in a person, the second point shows that moral assessment can depend either on a person's motivational structure or how that person has used her capacity for freedom. In other words, our use of evaluative terms like good and evil at this point in the *Religion*—I say more about Kant's subsequent uses of these terms in Chapters 5 and 6—is dependent on whether an agent has engaged her capacity for moral autonomy, or whether her *Willkür* executes the demands legislated by *Wille*. Whether an agent has used the freedom of the power of choice as she both can and ought is a question that must get a yes or no answer, and Kant uses this insight to commit us to a rigoristic conclusion.[54] This again shows that moral rigorism is compatible with vast complexity concerning the incentive structure governing a human will.

54. Dalferth likewise touches on this claim that the use of freedom shapes Kant's argument for rigorism. See "Radical Evil and Human Nature," 62.

Finally, we can supplement this discussion by noting that outside the *Religion*, Kant's argument for moral rigorism seems to exist as part of a broader argument regarding how the presentation of morality must proceed. We see this, for example, in both the lectures on ethics and the *Groundwork*. Kant argues that one reason why moral theory and practice have not flourished as they should is because the moving power of depictions of the moral motive is diluted by the acknowledgment of other possible determining grounds of the will (V-Mo/Collins 27:303, GMS 4:389, RGV 6:48). Thus, it seems that Kant should be thought of as offering a moral argument for moral rigorism and for the treatment of good and evil as exclusive concepts: if we do not present examples of characters or actions in a clearly graspable form, then whatever instruction or power we would hope to find in these examples would be lost. Yet a moral argument for moral rigorism leaves intact the possibility of an overdetermined will and explains why Kant would insist that overdetermination is a case of evil.

The Three Stages of Evil. The possibility that evil can consist either in an attempt at overdetermination or the straightforward prioritization of the moral law over self-love can explain some of the difficulties that attach to an interpretation of the three stages (*Stufen*) of evil—frailty, impurity, and depravity; I soon define these terms more precisely—that Kant outlines in the *Religion*. Any discussion of Kant's theory of evil must make mention of these three stages, and yet several extremely difficult questions remain regarding them. To begin, though Kant discusses and uses the language of frailty, impurity, and depravity throughout his moral and practical writings, Kant does not attempt to reiterate this neat, organized threefold progression in any other writing. Moreover, even within the *Religion*, the significance that attaches to the three stages is unclear because Kant does not claim that there is necessarily or even often a development of evil in line with these stages. Finally, in maintaining that there are three stages of evil, Kant would appear to be implying that evil comes in degrees and that some forms of evil are somehow less immoral than others. But it is not clear how any such suggestion can cohere with Kant's dismissal of syncretism, since, were some evils to be less immoral, their dilution could only have stemmed from the adjoining of some additional feature of the will properly evaluated as good or indifferent.

In light of these difficulties, commentators propose different ways of understanding these stages.[55] Allison argues that the three stages can be differentiated from one another in terms of the degree of self-deception

---

55. For a selection beyond those I'll discuss here, see Michalson, *Fallen Freedom*, 45–46; Frierson, *Freedom and Anthropology in Kant's Moral Philosophy*, 110–113; Rukgaber, "Irrationality and Self-Deception within Kant's Grades of Evil"; Sven Bernecker, "Kant

present in an agent.[56] Baron, to give another example, has approached the three stages as part of a broader comment on whether Kant can allow for the possibility of moral weakness of will or a kind of practical irrationality in which an agent finds herself unable to follow through on her good intentions.[57] Muchnik, to name yet one more, has argued that the three stages align with a corruption of the three predispositions to animality, humanity, and personality that Kant discusses in the *Religion*.[58]

These proposals are promising and provocative, but I will not pursue or engage them here. The reason is that each proposal sees the three stages as part of a larger commentary on either the *Religion* as a whole or a significant issue in Kant's moral theory. But given how little Kant says about these stages of evil, any interpretation of them needs, I think, to be extremely modest and not to bear much weight either in a reconstruction of Kantian evil or on a broader question regarding Kant's practical philosophy. So instead, I will explore whether a less ambitious account of the three stages can be offered. And as I explain below, my own proposal is that Kant does not have in mind an especially clear account of how to differentiate the three stages of evil. Instead, then, of trying to pin down a static interpretation of these three stages, I want to try to let Kant's discussion remain fluid and use it as an opportunity to explore a broadening of the possible manifestations of evil. I will mine his ambiguous claims for their hints, suggestions, and nudges toward an account of subordination that may take us beyond the idea that evil consists simply in the prioritization of self-love over the moral law.

Take, for example, frailty (*Gebrechlichkeit*) and impurity (*Unlauterkeit*), the first and second stages. In the section in the *Religion* regarding the three stages, Kant describes the frail agent as someone who would echo Paul's remark, "What I would, that I do not!" in Romans 7:15; immediately, this suggests that the first stage of evil refers to what has traditionally been described as weakness of will. Kant then more fully explains the vantage point a frail person takes on her own actions:

> I incorporate the good (the law) into the maxim of the power of choice; but this good, which is an irresistible incentive objectively or ideally (*in thesi*), is

zur moralische Selbsterkenntis," 170n12; and Mark Timmons, "Evil and Imputation in Kant's Ethics," 122–132.

56. Allison, *Kant's Theory of Freedom*, 158–160. A similar view can be found in Wood, "The Evil in Human Nature," 51–52. I say much more about self-deception and how it relates to evil in subsequent chapters.

57. See Baron, "Freedom, Frailty, and Impurity."

58. Muchnik, *Kant's Theory of Evil*, 143–163.

subjectively (*in hypothesi*) the weaker (in comparison with inclination), whenever the maxim is to be followed. (RGV 6:29)

Kant also claims that the frail suffer from a weakness "in complying
with adopted maxims," and that impurity differs from frailty insofar as
the former consists in the wills of human beings who "adulterate moral
incentives with immoral ones" (RGV 6:29). Now, caution in differentiating
these stages is required here. As we will see in Chapter 7, where I discuss
Kant's account of moral reform, Kant is not always clear in how to differentiate frailty from impurity, nor does he put the concept of frailty to only
one use. But we can put these complications momentarily aside since we
have plenty of additional ones to deal with.

For example, just getting a firm handle on either frailty or impurity in
isolation of the other stages is difficult. The frail, on the one hand, seem
to be agents whose will is good; Kant could hardly be clearer about this
when he says that those with frail hearts indeed "incorporate the good
(the law) into the maxim of the power of choice." But, on the other hand,
elsewhere in the *Religion* he claims that frailty is a "pretext" or *Vorwand*, a
harsh term that Kant uses to criticize those people who misrepresent their
capacities in order to avoid the hard "moral labor" of introspection and
self-criticism (RGV 6:51 and RGV 6:77).[59] Impurity is just as perplexing.
Kant fairly consistently describes impurity in terms of the adulteration of
the moral motive, but what precipitates this impurity is far more difficult
to say. Within the very same passage in the *Religion*, Kant makes two claims
that seem irreconcilable. He claims that the supplementation of the incentive of self-love is needed to determine the power of choice, and yet he also
claims that the impure man's good maxim is, in fact, "powerful enough in
practice [*zum Ausübung kräftig genug*]" (RGV 6:30). Finally, even with depravity, or *Bösartigkeit*, it is hard to develop a fully unambiguous picture.
The description of the depraved we first find in the *Religion* is of someone
who "reverses" or *umkehrt* the rightful order that should hold between self-
love and respect (RGV 6:38). Kant then adds that the depraved man still
craves to find himself "justified [*gerechtfertigt*]" before the law (RGV 6:38),
and though one could insist on reading this sentiment as sheer artifice, it is
not obvious what Kant's intent is.

I believe it is fruitful to read these tensions as evidence of Kant's interest in adding nuance to his account of the different dispositional

59. Similarly, at RGV 6:169, Kant speaks sarcastically of someone who thinks himself too weak to obey moral commands but able to compensate for that weakness with
demonstrations of eagerness.

arrangements within evil agents. This interpretive strategy is highly ec-umenical, as it allows Kant to hold on to all the competing descriptions that he offers regarding these stages of evil. This strategy would account for possible ambiguity concerning the depraved, as Kant seems to enter-tain both the idea that the depraved prioritize self-love and that the de-praved may be partly moved by moral concerns. This strategy would also explain why frailty can be either a phony pretense offered by those who prioritize the moral law or a sincere expression of self-frustration in light of the sacrifices made to balance the two incentives; this self-undermining quality is even alluded to in the remainder of Romans 7:15, as Paul agonizes not only that he does not identify with his actions but also that he hates (*hasse*) them.[60] It is similar with impurity. We can agree with, for example, Rukgaber that the impure may, in fact, lack the motivation to comply with the law unless they can supplement the power of choice with the incorporated force of self-love.[61] We can also, however, see another possible manifestation of impurity, one wherein a person adulterates her own will with self-love even though respect for the law was, as Kant says, "powerful enough in practice." Granted, we will likely remain somewhat uncertain what Kant means by this, but we do not wholly lack interpre-tive options. In fact, one route for making more sense of this claim is even readily suggested by Baumgarten, whose *Metaphysics* served as a signifi-cant historical source for Kant's own account of how self-love and respect inform human choice.

Baumgarten's importance on this front is underscored both by how his text served as the basis for Kant's lectures on philosophical theology, which contain some of his pre-*Religion* considerations of evil, and by the fact that Baumgarten's overview of the faculty of desire is echoed in the substance of Kant's discussion of the incentives in the second *Critique*. In the chapter on the incentives of pure practical reason, we find Kant referring to the incentives of the mind (*elateres animi*) and thus echoing Baumgarten's own Latin terminology (KpV 5:72), and in his very brief discussion of evil in the second *Critique*, Kant offers a formal account of evil that directly mirrors Baumgarten's, defining evil as that which is an object of aversion.[62] Now, to begin to turn back to our discussion of impurity and the question of how adulteration of the moral motive can happen even when it is suffi-ciently powerful, it may help to note that in Baumgarten's text it is clear

60. This language of hatred is used in the Luther Bible.
61. Rukgaber, "Irrationality and Self-Deception within Kant's Grades of Evil," 252.
62. See Baumgarten, *Metaphysics*, section 670. See also KpV 5:58–67 and note 2 of this chapter.

that a theory of the incentives must account for more than the moving force needed in order for an aversion or a desire to be efficacious with respect to its object. More specifically, Baumgarten claims we must also pay attention to how we form anticipatory beliefs about our desires or our intentions to produce some object. Such anticipatory beliefs are familiar enough in everyday life. For example, if I need to pick up a paperweight in front of me, I'll form an implicit belief about how much force is needed to pick it up. I might undershoot and struggle to exert enough power to fulfill my intention or desire. But I might overshoot as well, in which case I pick up the paperweight successfully but am accompanied by a peculiar kind of dissonance, one that stems from the fact that I made an inadequate prediction about what level of force was, in fact, required for my will to be effective. It is possible that this same kind of dissonance underwrites impurity as it is described in the second stage of evil: the power of choice can perhaps be sufficiently powerful in practice, but an agent may nonetheless, perhaps because she uncritically anticipated a different, more exceptional or exotic phenomenology of goodness, incorporate another incentive into her supreme maxim. If this is right, it supports the claim that Kant invites us to consider impurity in terms of someone attempting to overdetermine her will.

Supplemental Texts. I noted earlier that the idea that evil can take shape as overdetermination has much promise, since it will enable us to build off the results of Chapter 1 and develop further a more narrow, constrained expansionist approach to evil, one that avoids the pitfalls associated with its more ambitious or broad forms. Given this, I will bring this chapter to a close by showing that we can further support my claims about overdetermination by putting the *Religion* in dialogue with other Kantian texts.

Note, for example, that at least one reason why a human being tries to overdetermine her will is that originally, the incentives of self-love and the moral law were not opposed to one another. In the *Religion*, this is evident in Kant's remark that in addition to being unable to reject the moral law outright, a human being remains "dependent on the incentives of his sensuous nature because of his equally innocent natural predisposition, and he incorporates them too [*auch*] into his maxim (according to the subjective principle of self-love)" (RGV 6:36). It is appropriate to take this claim about the innocence of self-love and animality seriously. Because he emphasizes here and earlier in the *Religion* how these two natural predispositions are dispositions toward the good (RGV 6:28), Kant is able to show us that in the prelapsarian conditions of human life, self-love and the moral law did not provide competing reasons for action or function as counterincentives. Though his remarks are too brief to make his thought fully transparent, the idea seems to be that the harmony between freedom and nature that Kantians usually see as a far-off prospect or ideal was at one point a fully actualized state of affairs. Furthermore, insofar as there is no logical contradiction between the demands of self-love and those of the moral law, such a state of affairs is not one that Kant can rule out on *a priori* grounds. We can confirm these points by way of Kant's claim in the *Conjectural Beginning of Human History* that the voice of God is present in human instinct, and that man did well before the fall if and when he did not break from instinct (MAM 8:111).[63] Given these observations, it should seem less strange to us that Kant would think someone may attempt to overdetermine her will. Striving for overdetermination is, in a way, the most natural thing a person could do.

We can also turn to Kant's logic to increase support for the claim that we should make room for a form of evil that does not involve the straightforward prioritization of the moral law.[64] That we would look here is somewhat less surprising when we note, first, that other commentators, such as Lewis White Beck, have already turned to Kant's logic to illuminate Kant's practical philosophy, and, second, that what we are trying to shed light on is the claim that in the subordination of the moral incentive, self-love is made the "condition" (*Bedingung*) of the moral law.[65] Since this is a term often featured in Kant's theoretical philosophy, we will want to incorporate these texts into our discussion.

Now, most generally, when Kant discusses the idea of a condition in a practical context, he is calling attention to that which allows a principle to gain a foothold in my will. So, for example, in the *Groundwork*, when Kant discusses hypothetical imperatives, rules of prudence become connected to my will under the condition that there is some inclination I intend to satisfy.[66] On the basis of this reference, we may think of self-love as an incentive taking hold in an individual and thereby displacing the possibility of action from respect for the law.

However, if we attend to additional points, other possible formal arrangements of the incentives will present themselves. We should consider Kant's account of a "condition" in his remarks on conditional or

63. See also V-Phil-Th/Pölitz, 28:1078.
64. I am indebted to Hyoung Sung Kim, who suggested I consider the connection between the subordination thesis and Kant's logic.
65. Beck, *A Commentary on Kant's* Critique of Practical Reason, 81.
66. See, for example, GMS 4:420n and Beck, *A Commentary on Kant's* Critique of Practical Reason, 81.

hypothetical judgments,[67] the most well-known discussions of which are in the first *Critique* and the *Prolegomena*. In such judgments, we have "the use of a given cognition as ground and another as consequent" (Prol 4:312), and to illustrate the form of such judgments, Kant gives as an example "if a body is illuminated by the sun for long enough, then it becomes warm" (Prol 4:312). It is also important to note that with respect to hypothetical or conditional judgments, Kant's logic requires a specific kind of relationship between the antecedent and the consequent. As others have pointed out, not any old set of cognitions or concepts can be paired together in a hypothetical or conditional judgment.[68] The sun and the warming of a body belong together in a hypothetical judgment because of an intimacy or community between the antecedent and the consequent. In contrast, Kant would not allow the form of a hypothetical or conditional judgment to extend to a juxtaposition of unrelated concepts, such as "if it rains outside, I will sew this fabric." The sun and the warmed body can serve as the components within a conditional judgment, whereas the sewing and the rain cannot, *even if* the former judgment about the sun warming the stone proves false and the latter judgment about sewing and raining proves true. This is because proper judicative form is distinct from and independent of the truth of a conditional judgment.[69]

Now, this observation should prompt us to consider whether the evil man, in making self-love the "condition" of the moral law, could bring the two incentives into a relationship that is more intertwined or intimate than that suggested by the language of prioritization. The account I have given regarding overdetermination succeeds on this front, as it prompts us to consider the possibility that self-love can act as the condition of the moral law insofar as a person determines her will to align with morality *through* or by way of the antecedent conditions imposed by self-love. In other words, an agent may determine her will in the pursuit of self-interest but only insofar as she also attempts to live up to the demands of morality. Such cases thus show the close proximity that a person establishes between the two incentives in the faculty of choice or in the subjective determination of the will.

Finally, within Kant's theoretical philosophy, there is an additional set of passages that help support my proposal regarding overdetermination.

---

67. Kant uses the term "conditional judgment" far more infrequently than he does "hypothetical judgment." Nonetheless, it is fairly clear they can be used synonymously. See, for example, Refl 3091/16:653.

68. See, for example, Kim, "Function as a Transcendental Term in Kant's Analytic," 10–11.

69. See again Refl 3091/16:653.

We know that Kant conceives of the incentives of respect and self-love as forces, and within both the Vienna Logic and the Dohna-Wundlacken lectures, Kant makes highly relevant comments regarding what happens when two forces collide with one another. I'll cite the more vivid of the two passages:

> When a body is affected by 2 powers, there arises a third movement, where it does not remain on the track either of the one or the other, i.e., the diagonal force. E.g., a ball that would have gone directly into the center of the target when it is pushed sideways by the wind, and it was pushed there neither by the power of the [gun]powder nor of the wind. (V-Lo/Wiener 24:824)

As Kant makes clear, and as is evident from experience, when an object is subject to two antagonistic forces, one force generally does not destroy the other without trace. Instead, the object affected bears the mark of both forces, settling into a position of compromise in which the object then begins a new trajectory along a diagonal. Now, Kant himself applies this model to the human being after offering these comments. He explains that when the two powers are the understanding and sensibility, a human being is at risk for error not because one power may simply trump the other but because this collision causes judgment to veer in a diagonal direction. As Kant says, all error is essentially "deviation," as errors involve "turnings of judgments to the diagonal—crosswise" (V-Lo/Dohna 24:721). He draws the same parallel between material forces and psychic ones in the first *Critique*, arguing that while a body controlled by one force "would always of itself stay in a straight line in one direction," a body that encounters a second force will move in a "curved line" (KrV A295/B351). Erroneous judgment can therefore be envisioned as a "diagonal between two forces"—namely, the understanding and sensibility—"that determine the judgment in two different directions, enclosing an angle, so to speak" (KrV A295/B351). In light of this, it is plausible that Kant's theory of the incentives of practical reason should reflect the same insight. That is, it seems Kant clears space for an overdetermined will characterized by a need to pursue the diagonal, that is, to find a third movement or path—namely, one of compromise—in action.

CONCLUSION

The goal of the present chapter has been to show how Kant's remarks about overdetermination, and the attempt to incorporate the incentives of both self-love and respect for the moral law into one's maxim, allow us to develop a limited expansion of how we understand evil. With this as my focus, I have not yet been able to consider some of those controversies regarding Kantian evil noted in the introductory section of this chapter. I now move on to these other issues, beginning with the aforementioned question of the relationship between evil and self-deception.

CHAPTER 3

Kantian Self-Deception

Kant repeatedly suggests the ubiquity of self-deceit in evil acts and agency throughout his corpus. He references in the *Groundwork* the rationalizing moves that the dear self makes in order to exempt itself from the categoricity of moral demands (GMS 4:405). When he insists, rather infamously, in the second *Critique* that the moral law exists as a fact of reason that forces itself to consciousness within every human being, the implication certainly seems to be that no human being can deny such consciousness except through an act of self-deception. In both the *Religion* and the *Metaphysics of Morals*, we find Kant maintaining that dishonesty begins inwardly and often "extends" or "spreads" externally (RGV 6:38 and MS 6:429), making the first lie the "inner lie" or the lie we tell to ourselves (MS 6:430–431). Finally, given the very nature of Kant's moral rationalism, it would seem that no rational agent can be honestly unaware of the claims of the moral law, as these are implicit in reason itself.

Although the connection between evil and self-deception in Kant's practical philosophy has not gone unnoticed by commentators, there is little consensus regarding how the relationship should be spelled out. It is helpful to note the views we find when we look toward the extreme ends. On the one end are commentators who acknowledge but contain the presence of self-deception in evil. We see this when Wood, in "Kant on the Intelligibility of Evil," maintains that "disguise or self-deception" is involved in "some" instantiations of evil but does not extend this point such that inner deceit will play a role in all such instances.[1,2] On the other end is a commentator such as Jeanine Grenberg, who maintains that self-deception, or the attempt to distance oneself from his or her own knowledge of the categoricity of moral demands, is implicated in both evil and other practical failures, such as a lack of virtue.[3] In order to quiet the voices of reason and conscience, and to will an immoral maxim that contradicts the universalizability demanded by the law, an agent must, she argues, suppress and deceive herself regarding the strictness of the moral law. Offering a somewhat different but still strong view regarding the relationship between evil and self-deception is Allison. Allison argues that "systematic self-deception" is implicated in Kant's account of evil, with self-deception's crucial role being that it helps us avoid introspection and evade responsibility.[4] Thus, Grenberg and Allison insist on the ubiquity of self-deception but differ in their assessments of how exactly it enables evil, while other commentators are unconvinced that any tight connection between evil and self-deception must exist.

I believe there are two reasons why these debates persist. First, and unsurprisingly, they persist both because of interpretive difficulties surrounding Kant's discussion of evil in texts such as the *Religion* and because of broader questions regarding how Kant thinks the faculties of desire and cognition relate to one another in the context of immorality. The second, and widely overlooked, reason why these debates persist is because it is not exactly clear what self-deception is within a Kantian framework; none of the commentators noted above try to work through this issue, but instead assume that the concept is self-explanatory. Thus in this chapter, my goal is to understand how, most generally, we ought to conceive of self-deception. Only following this can we then, in the next two chapters, explore how self-deception relates to evil.

Though the aim of this chapter is clear, it is appropriate to offer some caution as we settle into our first task of clarifying Kantian self-deception. While commentators are correct to see self-deception as a crucial topic

---

1. "Kant on the Intelligibility of Evil," 156. I should note that since Wood's remarks are made somewhat in passing, it is unclear how attached to this view he is. Indeed, in another work, Wood claims evil necessarily involves self-deception, though, given the context of the remark, he might only be referring to the type of evil that Kant describes as depravity (see "The Evil in Human Nature," 52). Thus I make sure, in Chapter 4, to note other commentators who are likewise unconvinced that self-deception and evil must be intertwined.

2. The most characteristic elements of Wood's approach to Kant on evil—particularly his claim that evil has a social origin—will be discussed in Chapters 5 and 8.

3. "What Is the Enemy of Virtue?," 162–166.

4. "Reflections on the Banality of (Radical) Evil," 148.

within Kant's practical and moral philosophy, Kant may not have been inclined to put the matter exactly this way. As others have pointed out, Kant likely thought of self-deception as falling within the domain of empirical psychology, anthropology, or perhaps even applied logic, thus making it the case that in his ethical writings and in related student lecture notes, we find exceedingly little explicit commentary on self-deception.[5] Increasing our challenge is the fact that only rarely and unsystematically does Kant use directly language that references self-deception. Take the *Religion*, a text that seems to affirm, not contradict, the importance of self-deception in Kant's practical philosophy. He speaks a few times of self-deception in explicit terms, but these references are quite sparse and with one exception in Part Four of the text (RGV 6:173, 6:174, 6:192, and 6:200), thus well after his main account of evil. Before this, there is really only one page where self-deception (*selbst zu betrügen*) is directly referenced, and here Kant's elaboration on the phenomenon is written in tantalizing but opaque language, characterizing it in terms of a "blue dust" we throw in our own eyes (RGV 6:38).[6] Now, it might seem that we would gain assistance elsewhere, since while Kant does not regularly use the language of self-deception, he does rely on the seemingly nearby concept of rationalization[7] at many points throughout his texts. But again, an obstacle emerges because what this is or how, precisely, it relates to self-deception is hard to know. I'll revisit these points and terms throughout this chapter and the next one, for now leaving us with the important takeaway that we have our work cut out for us and that any discussion of self-deception in Kant must be highly reconstructive.

LYING, SELF-DECEPTION, AND RATIONALIZATION

Kant appears to deal with the phenomenon of self-deception most explicitly when he considers the possibility of an "internal" or "inner" lie. This idea of internal lying can be found in several texts, but it is given the most attention in the *Metaphysics of Morals* and in a section that pertains to lying more generally and external lies (MS 6:429–431). Now, what would this seem to imply about Kant's strategy, or a Kantian strategy, for understanding self-deception? It will, of course, make it seem as though Kant treats self-deception as a subcategory of deception more generally, or as a

---

5. Bernecker, "Kant zur moralischen Selbsterkenntnis," 164.
6. Thanks to Martin Thibodeau for pushing me on this point.
7. Usually, he uses the verb *vernünfteln*, but variants of *räsonniren* appear on occasion (e.g., V-Anth/Busolt 25:1481, Päd 9:476, Log 9:28, and Anth 7:200).

kind of lying that differs from lies to others chiefly with regard to the fact that the one lied to is the same as the liar. But I will argue in this section the following: this would be an ill-conceived framework for understanding self-deception, and even though Kant, insofar as he speaks repeatedly of a lie to oneself, might initially appear to endorse this strategy, the substance of his discussion shows that he is aware of the ways that self-deception cannot be thought of as a form of deception more generally.[8]

I begin with how Kant himself points out that lies to others do not invite the paradox or "contradiction" that deception of oneself involves (MS 6:430). I believe that as a preliminary step in understanding this contradiction or paradox and what Kant does to shed light on it, it's helpful to appreciate the extent to which we have a comparatively easier task in conceptualizing a lie to another. Lies to others do not prompt inquiries into moral psychology with the same urgency that deception of oneself does. While we might not understand why an agent would want to convince others of particular falsehoods, our unclarity about her motivations would not stop us from understanding how such lies can be attempted. In self-deception, however, it seems we will have greater cause to limit from the start of our account what kinds of untruths we tell ourselves. The bare, logical possibility of someone telling herself an untruth unrelated to her own practical context is not Kant's concern, nor is it likely to illuminate the real work of self-deception in human life. Thus, to begin to understand both self-deception and why self-deception cannot be well illuminated by considering lies to others, it must be noted that we can bracket, or be silent about, one's motivations for other-deception in a way that we cannot for self-deception.

If we try to see self-deception as a self-directed version of the lying we typically do to others, we would fail not only to notice the special way motives are relevant to self-deception. We would also fail to

---

8. In making these points, it will become clear why and how my view is opposed to Joël Madore's. Madore maintains that, for Kant, the self-deceived agent must be deeply bifurcated, just as the liar remains distinct from the lied to in lying more generally. Thus, Madore argues that Kantian self-deception requires that "I become other to myself" (*Difficult Freedom and Radical Evil in Kant: Deceiving Reason*, 88), and that an agent displays a self-foreignness that results from really being "two persons": a "noumenal being" and a "natural being" (*Difficult Freedom and Radical Evil in Kant: Deceiving Reason*, 88 and 87). But this interpretation is highly problematic for numerous reasons. Not only does Madore rely on an unfortunate dualism to make sense of Kant's notion of self-deception. He also overlooks the many ways that Kant strives to differentiate self-deception from lies to others and, as a result, Madore thereby fails to unpack the interesting features of self-deception that I explore in this chapter, such as how self-deception requires a sensitivity to norms of evidence and belief formation.

understand the *epistemic* workings of self-deception as Kant describes them in the *Metaphysics of Morals*. Consider one example he gives of a person who deceives herself regarding a loved one, considering "only" the beloved's good qualities and willing herself "blind" to this person's "obvious faults" (MS 6:431). This is clearly an act of self-deception, but it is crucial to note that the agent engaging in this self-deception is partly observant of norms of belief formation. She does not wholly lack evidence for the positive she sees in her beloved, nor would we understand her well if we say that she simply manufactures evidence for her view. Instead, she is *selective* in how she reads or interprets the evidence available to her. In the example, the beloved does not altogether lack good qualities, and Kant does not accuse the person engaging in self-deception of constructing a high-flown fictional account of what good qualities the beloved has.

A similar point can be made by way of yet another example from the discussion of inner lying in the *Metaphysics of Morals*, an example in which an agent convinces himself that he believes in God even though he does not (MS 6:430). Clearly, this case is possible because experience does not supply objective warrant regarding the falsity of this proposition; disbelief is not the kind of thing that can be straightforwardly empirically evidenced. Thus, attentiveness to evidence and epistemic standards is essential to the very possibility of self-deception in a way that does not carry over to the lies we tell to other people. A person might not convince others with tall tales and brazenly false lies—such as the lie that the president is her brother, or that she has twice been to Antarctica—but she can still succeed in *telling* lies with flagrant disregard for norms of evidence and possible belief formation. By contrast, it is hard to think of cases of self-deception that could get off the ground without some respect for norms of evidence and possible belief formation.[9]

These points about how human beings remain guided by norms of evidence point us to yet another reason why we must emphasize the structural differences between deception of oneself and deception of others. For our discussion thus far has demonstrated how Kantian self-deception will not take hold in an agent in the form of her advancing two contradictory propositions. A set of contradictory propositions can be exactly what we find in cases of external lies, when, for instance, I tell a landlord that I do

9. In the contemporary, non-Kantian literature on self-deception, this point is made most forcefully by Dion Scott-Kakures. See, for example, "At Permanent Risk: Reasoning and Self-Knowledge in Self-Deception." I am greatly indebted to his insightful work on this topic.

not own a pet when I know full well that I do. But as we've seen from Kant's examples so far, such outright static contradictions are not what we should expect to see in cases of self-deception. To misinterpret willfully evidence, or to convince oneself of something that is at least minimally compatible with the empirical evidence before us, is not to both know some proposition P and attempt to convince oneself of ~P.

Looking more at texts beyond the *Metaphysics of Morals* and Kant's practical philosophy, we can find further materials by which we can reconstruct a Kantian account of self-deception. More specifically, Kant's lectures on logic are an underexplored resource. They are underexplored perhaps because they can be brought to bear on this phenomenon only in a roundabout way; nonetheless, we can find in them rich information concerning why the self-deceptive agent remains highly sensitive to epistemic norms, why self-deception is not well understood in terms of an agent believing both P and ~P, and what, in general, an agent must do in order to enter a self-deceived state.

In particular, at least one set of passages is highly relevant for our purposes. In both the early Blomberg Logic and the late Jäsche Logic, we find Kant commenting on whether a human being can withhold her assent to an unpleasant or unwelcome cognition that she nonetheless knows to be especially well evidenced (V-Lo/Blomberg 24:156–161, Log 9:73–75). Kant claims that

> [i]n most cases, such a procedure of giving our approval, or withdrawing it, or holding it back[,] does not rest at all on our free choice, but rather is necessitated through and by the laws of our understanding and our reason. (V-Lo/Blomberg 24:156)

I revisit the qualifying "[i]n most cases" remark in a moment so that I can first focus on the substance of Kant's point and how he develops it. He gives an example of a person who is using her own powers of arithmetic to tally what she owes to a creditor (V-Lo/Blomberg 24:157). Kant finds it utterly implausible to think that she can withhold assent from the final number of her calculations. Even if it pains her to see the outcome of the balance, she is nonetheless "too much and too evidently convinced of the correctness of the arithmetic in this matter, and the account of the debts contains far too much evidence" (V-Lo/Blomberg 24:157). He makes similar points elsewhere, arguing that "the will cannot struggle *against* convincing proofs of truths that are contrary to its wishes and inclinations" and that were it not for our inherent vulnerability to the truth, the debtor would be able to consider himself creditor, and, similarly, a person of ruined honor and position could immediately will his mind to remain "undisturbed or excited" (Log 9:73–74 and V-Lo/Blomberg 24:157, respectively).

Kant clearly denies that what we believe is under any form of straightforward control, but he follows these points with an important concession. The concession is more clearly stated in the Blomberg lectures, but since similar language frames the Jäsche discussion, there is no reason to think Kant abandoned the view. He argues that while it is absurd to think that the will has "any influence immediately" on what we hold to be true, it has nonetheless a "mediate" influence on the understanding (Log 9:74). More specifically, he argues that this mediate influence consists not merely in the will's Cartesian-esque ability to withhold or grant assent to a *given* proposition.[10] Rather, it consists also in the will's ability to mitigate the sense of being compelled to accept a certain proposition by exploring, and to some degree constructing, a cognitive basis for assenting to some alternative proposition. This alternative proposition does not contradict or in any outright manner deny the first, but it nonetheless softens or pleasingly distracts ourselves from the experience of having to assent to it. As Kant puts it, we cannot moderate our approval of the initial proposition "directly," but a person can, "according to one's free wish," manipulate assent "indirectly" and by "seeking out those grounds that could in any way bring about approval for this or that [other] cognition" (V-Lo/ Blomberg 25:158).

It is thus within the will's power to guide assent to this or that alternative cognition, but no human being can do so in a way that wholly contravenes her overarching commitment to norms of truth and evidence. Even though the grounds on which this alternative cognition is based are not ones that could survive public scrutiny or a "*consensus aliorum*," some grounds for belief must nonetheless be acquired (V-Lo/Blomberg 24:158). Moreover, though a person cannot deny or contradict the original cognition—particularly when it relies on the use of one's own rational powers, as it does when someone is required to calculate a debt by virtue of her own mathematical skills—she can focus her attention on some other minimally grounded cognition, perhaps such as how she has prospects for new income that will make the standing debt less of a concern. Thus, we do not lie to ourselves regarding the presence of our original cognition but deflect attention from it through a process of *rationalization*, a term Kant uses frequently and that—though Kant only rarely offers a neat definition of the phenomenon—generally seems to refer to a misappropriation of our

10. *The Philosophical Writings of Descartes*, Vol. II, 40–43.

cognitive powers to the detriment of reason's true or final ends.[11] As he is recorded as saying in the Busolt lectures, rationalization is an "empty use of reason which contains nothing in regard to the true ends" (V-Anth/Busolt 25:1481).

In general, then, rationalization is what occurs when we introduce a desirable cognition or hoped for justification into the reasoning process, thus disregarding reason's constitutive end of wisdom.[12] For further evidence of how Kant uses the term, consider, for example, his remarks in *Toward Perpetual Peace* about those who try to dispute the notion that it is a principle of moral politics that a people should unite themselves into a state governed by freedom and equality. Kant accuses them of engaging in rationalization, not because they try to deny straightforwardly the veracity of this principle but rather because they put forward countless examples of empirical failures to bring about such well-organized constitutions. In other words, these "political moralists" introduce a new and, to them, more desirable cognition that respects the truth of the original cognition concerning our internal, *a priori* moral principles of public right while refusing to stay focused on that truth (ZeF 8:378).

We are referred to this same sort of indirect cognitive activity when, in the *Doctrine of Right*, Kant inveighs against those who preoccupy themselves with historical features of how their sovereign came to power (MS 6:318). These people do not lie to themselves regarding who their ruler is, or tell themselves that the sovereign in question both is and is not their ruler. Instead, they try to shift the conversation by preoccupying themselves with how the sovereign secured his position, even though this genetic point does not contradict arguments about the sovereign's right to rule. To give yet another example, we can note Kant's discussion in the *What Is Enlightenment?* essay about public officers who challenge the authority of their superiors. Kant thinks they are guilty of rationalization, but he is quite clear that these officers do not directly assert that their superiors hold their position unlawfully. This would be a lie that directly contradicts what the officers know to be true, so instead the officers pose

---

11. Though the secondary literature does not often discuss Kant's concept of rationalization, some have noted it, even if briefly. See, for example, Meld Shell's *Kant and the Limits of Autonomy*, 199, and Guyer, *Kant on Freedom, Law, and Happiness*, 211. Though my approach shares little in common with it, the most extensive treatment of rationalization that I know of is Martin Sticker's "Legitimität und Grenzen moralischer Intuitionen bei Kant - Kant über gemeine Menschenvernunft und Vernünfteln."

12. On wisdom as the final end of reason, see, for example, V-Lo/Wiener 24:799, V-Lo/Dohna 28:698, Log: 9:24, and MpVT 8:256n. I say more about wisdom in note 20 of this chapter.

questions about the demands issued by these authorities in a way that only a private citizen should (WA 8:37). As with Kant's other examples, the rationalization in question involves a shift in attention to a more attractive and true yet comparatively less relevant alternative cognition.

Now, to be clear, Kant relies on the concept of *Vernünfteln* too many times in his writings to give an exhaustive inventory of every application of the concept. Given the frequent use of the term, we probably cannot expect that all examples bear out quite so clearly the features noted above. For example, at KU 5:286, Kant seems to use the term in a non-pejorative sense, as he discusses how even though art critics lack an objective principle of taste, they "can and should rationalize [*vernünfteln*]" about how our cognitive faculties might be set up for reciprocal subjective purposiveness. This non-pejorative use of *vernünfteln* likely explains why Guyer and Eric Matthews, in their translation of the third *Critique* for the Cambridge Edition of the Works of Immanuel Kant, appropriately translate the term as "reason" instead of "rationalize." Nonetheless, many references to rationalization—even those outside of the practical philosophy—clearly reinforce the interpretation offered here. For example, in the *Critique of Pure Reason*, Kant discusses rationalization in the context of the antinomies of pure reason (KrV A421/B449–A422/B450). The vacillation between two competing vantage points in metaphysics—the points of view of noumenal and phenomenal frameworks—calls to mind how rationalization is described in the above-noted political texts, as rationalization is in both cases not about refuting some initial cognition or perspective but shifting to another cognition that distracts from, rather than denies, the cognition within the original point of view.

To summarize, then, between this example and the other ones noted, a clear pattern has emerged. No matter how unpleasant, we do not and cannot directly contradict the truth of what we know,[13] such as that there's an *a priori* principle requiring that the state allow citizens maximal freedom and equality, that the sovereign has rightful power over us, or that public officers cannot and ought not, as public officers, undermine their superiors. Instead, we divert our attention by focusing on something that tempers the experience of having to assent to these cognitions. We do this by considering, for example, empirical facts that are irrelevant to the justification

---

13. Formosa partly tracks this insight when he claims that Kantianism has room to account for the activity of compartmentalization, but he otherwise neglects many crucial features of how self-deception works for Kant. To give one example, because Formosa overlooks how rationalization is essentially a form of distraction, he greatly overemphasizes the extent to which we can become "quite unaware" of our motives or intentions. See "Kant on the Limits of Human Evil," 200.

of *a priori* principles or the conditions of rightful power, or by imagining ourselves as mere private citizens when we are also public officers. As such, the kinds of propositions I put forward when I shift to these other perspectives are, from within some other point of view, not only legitimate but also reasonable and probably even quite sophisticated. Certain kinds of historians should, for example, diligently attend to the circumstances in which constitutions have been adopted or sovereigns came to rule, and private citizens should aggressively question whether the demands issued by officials—say, military officials—are smart, even if, for example, an army sergeant should publicly articulate no such claims.

RATIONALIZATION AS A NORMATIVE CONCEPT

We should by this point understand how rationalization works. But it is important to note that even as we try to describe how human beings go about rationalizing, such self-deceptive rationalization is best thought of chiefly as a normative concept, rather than a strictly empirical or descriptive one. As anyone familiar with Kant's postulates is aware, Kant maintains that a person's beliefs can and should be guided by the demands of practical life. In other words, Kant would not see self-deception as a culprit whenever an empirical state of affairs does not provide probable objective warrant for some belief a person holds. Rather, self-deception begins only where practically justified willful assent ends. A person's end, and her practical context, can be decisive in the question of whether she is, on the one hand, self-deceived, or, on the other hand, exhibiting the doxastic flexibility that is integral to our lives as practical agents and moral persons.

When, for example, the highest good is one's end, Kant is quite permissive about when we have sufficient warrant to believe in God. Even though, by Kant's own lights, belief in God is not probable or supported by "more than half of the [objective] grounds" (V-Lo/Blomberg 24:194; see also V-Lo/Blomberg 24:197, V-Lo/Wiener 24:882, V-Lo/Dohna 24:742, Log 9:82), belief in Him could be a case of self-deception only if experience showed the impossibility of God.

Moreover, though Kant does not mention this example in his main text on moral belief and holding-to-be-true (*Fürwahrhalten*), namely, the Canon of Pure Reason[14] in the first *Critique*, he at least flirts with another possible case in which concerns that stem from the faculty of desire can

14. The importance of this text for understanding Kantian belief is made clear in Andrew Chignell's "Belief in Kant." I am highly indebted to this article.

legitimately direct the faculty of cognition and what we ought to believe or assent to. The case I have in mind is that of "permissible moral illusion," which is brought up in the *Anthropology* (Anth 7:152). Despite having put forward in the *Religion* abundant evidence regarding the evil in humanity, and despite, in the *Anthropology*, discussing at length our certainty that there is a clear human tendency to dissemble or withhold one's true nature or inner thoughts,[15] Kant regards it as highly laudable to set aside these cognitions and instead embrace the good image that others put forward of themselves. He writes:

> In order to save virtue, or at least lead the human being to it, nature has widely implanted in him the tendency to willingly allow himself to be deceived. Good, honorable *decorum* is an external illusion that instills respect in others. . . . Even the illusion of good in others must have worth for us, for out of this play with pretences which acquires respect without perhaps earning it, something quite serious can finally develop.—It is only the illusion of good *in ourselves* that must be wiped out without exception, and the veil by which self-love conceals our moral defects must be torn away. For illusion does *deceive*, if one deludes oneself that one's moral debt is cancelled or even thrown away by that which is without any moral content. (Anth 7:152–153)[16]

Thus, even though it seems there are no more objective grounds for believing that others act respectably whereas I do not, belief in the good in others is permissible, whereas a favorable interpretation of myself involves succumbing to self-deception. In this case again, the normative dimension of the concepts of rationalization or self-deception is clear.

We can continue to outline the limits and shape of the doxastic flexibility that is allowed to exist side-by-side a Kantian prohibition on self-deception by adding to our account Kant's treatment of pragmatic belief (*Glaube*) in the *Critique of Pure Reason*. This discussion is helpful because it allows us to see that even in instances in which merely pragmatic exercises of reason are at stake, Kant allows for a limited manipulation of the cognitive power. As Chignell has helped illuminate, when one has a contingent end such as making a sale or curing a patient, the conditions under which we may justifiably assent to certain beliefs shift; a doctor, for example, is

---

15. I discuss these passages in Chapter 5. See pages 144–146 in particular.
16. Alix Cohen also comments on similar and nearby passages in a different context; however, I see nothing in her account that fails to cohere with my own. See "Kant on Anthropology and Alienology: The Opacity of Human Motivation and Its Anthropological Implications," 88.

allowed doxastic flexibility but only because of his practical stance, or because he is trying to bring about a change in his patient.[17] Assent to belief is licensed if: (1) some action, such as making a diagnosis, is required by the agent's end; (2) the belief assented to, such as that the patient has consumption, is required for that action to be taken; and (3) that which is held to be true is at least objectively probable.[18] In this type of case, the agent is aware that while the objective grounds for what he is holding to be true would ordinarily be insufficient, the assent is subjectively justified insofar as it is required in order for the doctor or the salesman to achieve the end in question. The idea driving Kant is that action will fail to be decisive unless it is supplemented by these firmly held beliefs, thus rendering these beliefs "hypothetically necessary" or necessary to achieve one's contingent end.[19]

Therefore, when Kant discusses rationalization as a violation of reason's legitimate ends, the ends under consideration include not only the true but also the good and the practically necessary.[20] What characterizes rationalization, then, is not the search, per se, for new and different grounds of cognition but the *improper* search for such grounds. And this seems to explain, at least in part, why rationalization is hard to avoid. To avoid rationalization, we are not to become strict evidentialists, nor are we to engage in cold-turkey abstention from the creativity and willfulness evident in self-deceptive rationalization in the way that a person in Alcoholics Anonymous swears off drink. Instead, it seems we must do something antithetical to what is recommended to those in recovery, which is keep the mental powers that enable self-deception active but curbed, and redirected back toward reason's proper ends. Presumably, to keep this cognitive agility without indulging in rationalization will be as difficult for us as it is for the

17. "Belief in Kant," 339.
18. Regarding these conditions that govern the permissibility of belief, two follow-up points should be made. First, Kant does not explain what alternatives should be considered when the third condition cannot be met. In other words, he does not say what, for example, the doctor should do if no diagnosis looks objectively probable and yet some course of action needs to be tried to stave off the imminent death of the patient. Second, while I revisit this final stipulation in the next section, it is important to repeat that a probable holding is one supported by "more than half of the [objective] grounds."
19. "Belief in Kant," 340.
20. Though Kant does not use the term "wisdom" or *Weisheit* systematically enough for me to be fully confident about this point, it seems that he describes the true end of reason as wisdom in the logic lectures because "wisdom" can account for how reason has both theoretical aims such as truth and practical aims concerning morality and prudence. Thus, Kant's references to wisdom recall the term's use in ancient Greek philosophy. See, for example, V-Lo/Dohna 28:698 and Log 9:24. See also the conclusion of Chapter 6.

alcoholic to have, and drink only with moderation from, a fully stocked bar.[21] We would thus be surprised if self-deceptive rationalization did not turn out to be a highly ubiquitous phenomenon.

REMAINING POINTS AND QUESTIONS

To summarize our findings so far, we have outlined the following features of Kantian self-deception: we have shown that any attempt to model it on the deception of others will turn out poorly for the following set of reasons. To begin to understand the possibility of self-deception, we need to hone our focus immediately on the reasons and motives attached to it, while this stipulation is not needed to make sense of how lies to others are possible. We have also seen that self-deception is undertaken by an agent who is overall sensitive to epistemic requirements and who, according to Kant's own description, is involved in a dynamic process of finding alternative grounds of belief that offer her distance from, or a reframing of, some unpleasant cognition. This means that self-deception is not merely a form of willful irrationality, but more a sophisticated and rationally mindful form of irrationality. In light of this, it also becomes clear that self-deception will not feature an agent believing in two contradictory claims. To complete this overview, I will also add that talk about self-deception in terms of illicit belief demands some caution. Note that in Chignell's account of belief, it is argued that Kantian *Glaube* does not fully resemble our contemporary and casual notion of belief. In ordinary language, if I say that I believe the museum is a mile away, or that it rained while I was at work, I am describing certain states of affairs. But as Chignell points out, when Kant describes the salesman, the doctor, or the moral agent assenting to God's existence, the assertoric attitude might better be described—as Kant himself sometimes describes it—as one of acceptance (*Annehmung*) or conviction.[22] This is especially clear from a phenomenological perspective.[23] Though a sense of imposition is present when I form the belief that it rained while I was inside, in cases of Kantian *Glaube*, the agent experiences no fact of the matter imposing itself on her. Something similar must, I think, hold for self-deception and thus be born in mind whenever we talk about some proposition we self-deceptively maintain or believe. Phenomenologically,

21. I make these points in part because Kant himself relies on the example of intoxicants to explain temptation more generally. See RGV 6:29n.
22. Chignell, "Belief in Kant," 341.
23. Ibid.

self-deception is something we do. The self-deceptive agent feels driven to her beliefs or point of view from within, not from without.

Finally, it is important to note that even in light of what we've established thus far, several extremely difficult interpretive issues remain for a Kantian account of self-deception. In general, it seems to me that much of the difficult interpretive work revolves around the way the border between self-deception and justified willful assent is likely to remain a contested one. Even though we have noted Kant's positions on how moral belief in God for the sake of the highest good is required, as well as how pragmatic belief can be justified, we still cannot account for or anticipate all complexities, particularly in regard to the ways that self-deception depends on a person's ends, motives, and other subjective dimensions of her agency. To bring this chapter to a close, I will offer a review of at least some of the different cases in which this border between self-deception and justified willful assent can become opaque.

Difficulties in Application: Non-Homogenous Grounds. We can briefly recall Kant's example regarding the doctor. Even though it would ordinarily be improper to hold it to be true that the patient has consumption, such belief is justified for the doctor because such belief is integral to his ability to heal and because the diagnosis is objectively probable or, as Kant claimed, supported by "more than half of the [objective] grounds." Although Kant does not call our attention to this in the Canon, it is clear in the logic lectures that the practice of assigning weights to objective grounds is fraught with ambiguity. It is difficult to assess when the objective grounds supporting a favorable judgment are more likely than not, particularly because—as Kant himself points out—such grounds are not homogenous (V-Lo/Wiener 24:880 and 24:882). The ground determining the probability of getting a five when one rolls a die is homogenous; the only factor is the six-sidedness. But to determine a patient's diagnosis, the doctor would need to assess a variety of qualitatively different factors, such as his personal testimony, what his family has observed in caring for him, whether his medical history inclines against or in favor of a given diagnosis, and his current symptoms. When we add to this that the doctor would also need to know how to weigh those factors, and that "the weights are not all stamped, so to speak" (Log 9:82), it becomes obvious that it will be exceptionally difficult for an agent to determine whether a holding-to-be-true is supported by the weight of evidence and thus ruled out as a possible instance of self-deception.

Beliefs outside the Context of Empirical Action as Described by Kant. As we may again recall, the doctor must settle on some diagnosis to bring about a cure in the patient. But Kant does not indicate what the patient's loved ones may hold to be true. Should their hope for a cure be considered similarly efficacious in some manner? Are we to envision them as bearing passive witness to the situation, and thus guided more by evidentialist norms, or can their beliefs be linked to the prospects of successful action in the way that the doctor's beliefs are? Part of the reason these questions remain is that Kant's remarks do not precisely indicate how generous or charitable to human beings he would be in shaping the boundary between self-deception and rightful or permitted doxastic voluntarism.

On the one hand, Kant's argument about the doctor in the Canon, and how he is in a unique position insofar as he "must do something" for the patient, may lead us to conclude that he would allow only the doctor, and not others mindful of the health of the patient, to try to redirect certain beliefs; the doctor seems to earn this doxastic flexibility by way of committing himself to a specific action undertaken on the patient's behalf (KrV A824/B852). On the other hand, Kant at some points seems more lenient and to suggest that doxastic flexibility is presumed permissible until we can detect either some violation of moral concerns or an egregious violation of epistemic standards. He appears to lean toward this position when, for example, he refuses to criticize fantasies of the imagination in the *Anthropology* (Anth 7:180). While it is unclear how to map the notion of fantasy onto a discussion of belief, we do know that fantasy occurs within the faculty of cognition—specifically within the power of the imagination—and that the point at which Kant thinks fantasy turns into self-deception is when a person "believes [*glaubt*] he sees and feels outside himself that which is only in his mind" (Anth 7:178). If we take this discussion as our guide, it would seem that Kant has a comparatively more permissive account regarding the manipulability of belief, allowing us to cognize what we will so long as we mind certain important epistemic and moral limits.

Beliefs outside the Context of Moral Action as Described by Kant: Loving Relationships. Earlier we discussed how an account of self-deception must not trespass on our ability to hold God's existence and human immortality as true, as these beliefs are indispensable to the realization of the highest good. But very clearly, action to promote the highest good is not the only end or action that stems from our moral vocation. Thus, even if briefly, we should note cases where belief would seem to facilitate ends and actions that are morally praiseworthy but not required by or essential to the willing of the highest good. Action in the context of loving relationships shaped by beneficence, gratitude, and other Kantian virtues can serve as our general backdrop, and as a more specific example we can consider a case noted by Chignell, where a parent is faced with evidence that his son is a drug user.[24] If the parent discounts evidence about the son's drug use and considers a possible but implausible alternative justification for the smells in the house, has a person crossed the line from justified assent to illicit self-deception?

It is helpful to explore briefly this issue, not because we intend to settle it but because reasoning through it will clarify what would need to be taken into account to generate a determinate answer. As far as I can tell, Kant's most germane comment is from a footnote in the Jäsche logic discussing why the highest good makes epistemic demands on us that do not carry over to other moral cases. Here, Kant argues that in the context of moral action in general—cases where we are fulfilling particular demands made on us by the moral law—no specific supplemental beliefs must be presupposed by the agent. For example, to discharge my obligations regarding truthfulness, I do not need to believe that others will take my words seriously and—this is more Kant's focus—I do not need to believe anything about God. As Kant says, "we do not need this [i.e. belief] for action in accordance with moral laws, for *these* are given through practical reason alone" (Log 9:67n). By contrast, however, "if we wish to extend ourselves through actions to possession of the end [i.e. the highest good] . . . then we must accept that this end is possible" and thus assent to those propositions that secure its "objective reality" (Log 9:67n).

Let's review Kant's reasoning here. The more familiar point is that the highest good is a necessary end even though the faculty of choice is bound to this end not by virtue of objective moral laws but by way of subjective grounds. Only beings like us—that is, creatures that take an interest in how otherwise disparate seeming actions and ends can be regarded and pursued as part of a broader and more harmonious whole—will be subject to the demand to secure this end.[25] The somewhat less familiar point is that

24. "Belief in Kant," 344. In framing the issue this way, I am distancing myself from the way Chignell himself handles the case. Chignell does not discuss this example at great length, but he does claim that we ought to rely on Kant's account of pragmatic belief at this juncture. Thus, on Chignell's reading, it would seem that the parent is justified in believing the son is not a drug user so long as it is probable or more likely than not that this is the correct judgment. This may be the view Kant himself would have endorsed, but I find this framing implausible. The case of the parent and the son does not fit the typical model of pragmatic belief, in which we have contingent or merely permissible ends. Thus, I have instead framed the case under consideration as one wherein we are trying to facilitate ends and actions that are morally praiseworthy, albeit not required by or essential to the willing of the highest good.

25. As Wood notes, in seeking the highest good, we can view ourselves as having a singular purpose and as finding something meaningful. See Wood, *Kant's Moral Religion*, 97–99. Wood makes this point so that he can respond to Beck's well-known worry that the highest good is superfluous in Kant's moral theory (Beck, *A Commentary on Kant's*

because of the peculiar way the will is taxed in the pursuit of the highest good, a cognitive supplement is needed. Any such supplement is highly atypical insofar as there is no other circumstance in which the higher faculty of desire requires such support, and though Kant is not entirely clear about why this is the case, it seems that the strain on the will has to do with the complex and distant character of the highest good, rather than the sacrifices required of someone trying to realize it. Because belief in God and in immortality mitigates this overwhelming quality, and because this quality is absent from other actions taken on behalf of duty, there is a justified supplement of moral belief only in the context of pursuit of the highest good.

If this is the whole and only story a Kantian can tell, then in a case where the balance of the evidence suggests that the son is an addict, it would be self-deception to favor the merely possible over the objectively probable for the sake of protecting the relationship more generally. But it seems if we push back on the above reconstruction, we will easily cause Kant one problem or another; any attempt to address a given objection will just give rise to different and new objections. To begin, we could ask whether outside the context of the highest good we might find a similar juxtaposition of moral necessity and cognitive strain. Kant's claim that we "extend ourselves" only in the pursuit of the highest good doesn't, I think, immediately ring true. A practically loving relationship seems to effect a similar extension in human beings, since such relationships survive and flourish only if we take a long-term focus and are willing to think that the very many smaller ways we tend to such relationships can together form a greater whole.

Now perhaps Kant would reply that we do not need to believe anything about our beloveds in order to have relationships with them, or perhaps he would reply that since no specific loving relationship is morally necessary, any relationship that would require such cognitive redirection should be abandoned. If so, then action in accord with the highest good would remain the only context in which favorable supplemental beliefs are justified as opposed to self-deceiving or illicit. But again, new objections seem within easy reach. To the first point, while I can certainly fulfill my perfect duties without any specific beliefs about those affected by my actions—for example, abstention from coercion requires absolutely no beliefs about the merit or personal character of those we treat justly—the actions needed

Critique of Practical Reason, 244). For a view similar to Wood's, see Friedo Ricken, "Die Überwindung des Bösen: Kant über die Aufgabe einer Religiongemeinschaft," 502–503.

to sustain personal relationships are not so obviously immune from the need to believe certain things about our beloveds. And to the second point, many philosophers, including Kantians, would be wary of any suggestion that enforces an overly voluntaristic view of personal relationships. Though we must be willing to revise our personal commitments, it is problematic if a mature moral agent thereby regards them as unnecessary or contingent.

Thus, for at least these reasons, it will likely remain unclear whether some of the turf that Kant initially seems to assign to self-deception can indeed stay there.

CONCLUSION

Despite areas where the border between justified assent and illegitimate self-deception becomes either blurry or contestable, the most important features of Kant's approach to self-deception are now in focus. With this, certain guidelines for interpreting his references to it throughout his practical philosophy are likewise established. As we encounter remarks about self-deception or rationalization throughout the practical writings, it is crucial to read them against a backdrop that features prominently his theory of mind and his long-standing commitment to the idea that human beings cannot deny or contradict well-evidenced cognitions. To revisit, then, an example noted at the beginning of this chapter, when Kant points out at the end of *Groundwork* I how innocent, common human reason is inclined to rationalize against the moral law and challenge its strictness and purity (GMS 4:405),[26] we now understand that reason is constitutively incapable of doing this directly. No agent forms a particular belief according to which laxness and impurity are permitted. Rather, the laxness and impurity Kant fears are generated only indirectly, that is, by means of the diversion of attention toward some pleasing alternative cognition that does not contradict what we know as true with regard to moral principles.

Or, to give another example, Kant's comments about self-conceit (*Eigendünkel*) must be interpreted in a similar manner. Self-conceit, which I revisit in the chapter that follows,[27] is generally described in the literature as a particularly corrupt form of self-aggrandizement, arrogance, or

26. Similar comments are made at GMS 4:407.
27. I should note that even in the next chapter, I focus only on the relationship between self-conceit and passions like ambition. I do not take up every issue relevant to an account of self-conceit. For an overview of the relevant issues, see Moran, "Delusions of Virtue: Kant on Self-Conceit" and Stephen Engstrom, "The *Triebfeder* of Pure Practical Reason."

sense of imperiousness,[28] and it is widely noted to involve some kind of self-deception or delusion.[29] Yet exactly how this self-deception functions is often misunderstood, and this is in no small part due to how Kant's most animated comments about self-conceit characterize more its upshot than its mechanics. In the Vigilantius lectures notes, Kant is reported as saying that in self-conceit, we ascribe to ourselves "without proof" a higher worth than we really possess (V-MS Vigil 27:611), and in light of such passages, Kant's readers often describe self-conceit as a false belief or a "fiction" that transpires when a person "ignores" rational standards.[30] In casual parlance, and if we are aiming to underscore how self-conceit is both morally and epistemically inadequate, such descriptions are sufficient. But if we are aiming to understand how self-deception gets traction, how it is possible for creatures constitutively inclined to truth, or the full set of reasons why self-deception is difficult to avoid, these descriptions come up short. As Kant himself notes in the *Metaphysics of Morals*, moral arrogance (*arrogantia*) or self-conceit stems not from the holding of a per se false belief,[31] that is, from a representation that lacks agreement with or correspondence to an object.[32] Self-conceit fuels itself on myopia rather than myth; it is a "conviction of the greatness of one's moral worth, but only from failure to compare it with the law" (MS 6:435).[33] We become self-conceited when we

28. Here, I am indebted to Moran's characterization of self-conceit in the literature. See "Delusions of Virtue: Kant on Self-Conceit," 422.

29. For example, see Moran, "Delusions of Virtue: Kant on Self-Conceit"; Engstrom, "The *Triebfeder* of Pure Practical Reason," 117; Robin Dillon, "Kant on Arrogance and Self-Respect," especially 203–210; Wood, *Kant's Ethical Thought*, 266; and Wood, "Self-Love, Self-Benevolence, and Self-Conceit," especially 148–153. I am indebted to Moran for bringing Engstrom and Dillon's papers to my attention.

30. Wood describes self-conceit as a false belief in "Self-Love, Self-Benevolence, and Self-Conceit," 153. The description of self-conceit in terms of fictions and the ignoring of rational standards is Moran's in "Delusions of Virtue: Kant on Self-Conceit," 442.

31. In the *Metaphysics of Morals*, Kant tends to treat the Latin *arrogantia* as interchangeable with self-conceit or *Eigendünkel*. However, the German term that is often translated as arrogance in the Cambridge edition—namely, *Hochmut*—is not the same thing as *arrogantia*. *Hochmut* is described as a "vice" at MS 6:465 and as a "passion" at Anth 7:272–273, and despite this terminological instability, it is clear enough that Kant is inclined to regard *Hochmut* as a further offshoot of self-conceit or *arrogantia*. See pages 108–109 and note 30 of Chapter 4 for additional discussion.

32. I put the point this way in order to reflect Kant's general commitment to a correspondence theory of truth. Though far outside the scope of this project, I do say a bit more about Kant's advocacy of a correspondence theory of truth in note 33 of Chapter 6.

33. Despite how the literature has widely overlooked the extent to which the self-deceiving agent is mindful of what is true, there are moments where several commentators come a bit closer to this position. For example, Wood at one point notes that in self-conceit an agent "selects" only certain touchstones by which she compares herself to others, and this locution is far more accurate than his later description in

observe—rightly—how our moral vocation exalts us above animal nature but *then* fail to attend appropriately to the deep imperfections we exhibit when seen alongside the moral law's unrelenting demands.

As this demonstrates, the "dear self" that Kant famously references at *Groundwork* 4:407 poses an obstacle to clear moral vision not only because, as noted in Chapter 2, we are inclined to incorporate self-love alongside the moral law or because, as noted in Chapter 1, one feels alive and vital only through the proxy of pleasure. In addition, human beings can harness the rational powers that instill them with dignity, and that are constitutive of one's "proper self," and redirect those powers to inappropriate ends (GMS 4:457). We must observe how the self-conceited agent can comfort herself with what is true, and thus nourish her vice with at least partly defensible cognitions, if we want to understand why human beings are so vulnerable to self-conceit in particular or self-deception in general. Moreover, and as we will see in the following chapter, we must continue to highlight these epistemic features of self-deceptive rationalization if we hope to spell out adequately the connections that exist between it and evil.

terms of false beliefs ("Self-Love, Self-Benevolence, and Self-Conceit," 151). Similarly, Moran at one point describes self-conceit in terms of "incomplete reverence for the law" ("Delusions of Virtue: Kant on Self-Conceit," 441). This is likewise more representative of Kant's views than her description of the self-conceited agent as one who "ignores" rational standards.

CHAPTER 4

Self-Deception, the Necessary Conditions of Evil, and the Entrenchment of Evil

With the prior chapter's inquiry into self-deception complete, we can now shift to a main concern of this book, namely, the relationship between self-deception and evil. As we may recall, commentators have thus far embraced a range of positions concerning how evil relates to self-deception, with some finding more an incidental connection and others advocating a much stronger link between these two failings. However, since these disputes remain and since across this spectrum none of these views has been developed in depth, a fresh, sustained inquiry into the connection between evil and self-deception is needed.

As a first step, it is helpful to remind ourselves why, from a very general point of view, the possibility of this connection has been attractive to many commentators. The appeal of self-deception stems in part from a concern to identify something different from and in addition to evil itself, or to find a phenomenon that can add an extra layer of explanatory power to an account of evil. As Morgan has put it, we need to do much more than characterize the nature of evil if we are to understand crucial issues regarding its place in human life, such as why evil is so attractive to us and why evil seems so difficult to avoid.[1] This demand underwrites many interpretations of Kant and evil, whether implicitly or explicitly. For instance, when Wood and Anderson-Gold highlight the importance of unsocial sociability in an

---

1. "The Missing Formal Proof of Humanity's Radical Evil in Kant's *Religion*," 89–91.

account of evil, they do so because they see the need to explain some of the deeper causes behind a human being's failure to let the moral law assume its proper role. In Morgan's own account, which I say more about in the next chapter, that deeper element is a human being's desire for freedom and maximal license.[2] Even the biblical statement that the root of evil (radix malorum) is desire, greed, or cupiditas embraces this same basic tactic, since cupiditas is supposed to explain something like the more fundamental motive or goal structuring all bad actions.[3]

Put simply then, commentators are thus trying to uncover what many would describe as the root of evil. And as we know, Kant is no stranger to this language of rootedness. We may recall from earlier in this book that the Religion is where we find Kant arguing that there is an evil "rooted" universally in human nature, an argument that drew scorn from Kant's contemporaries and continues to be regarded with skepticism. But I now wish to show that Kant's talk of a "root" (Wurzel) of evil is not restricted to this context. In fact, he draws on the notion of rootedness in three different ways. One concerns the above-noted question of an evil that is "rooted" (gewurzelt) in human nature, while the other two pertain to other important features of Kantian evil. I'll briefly discuss these, since on the basis of these distinct uses of the notion of rootedness, we'll be able to develop a helpful strategy for inquiring into how evil relates to self-deception.

First, the notion of a root directs our attention to the firm and intractable quality of a state of mind or states of affairs. Loosely speaking, something is rooted when it is not transient or fleeting, or when it has "taken [gefaßt] root" or been allowed to einwurzeln. Kant uses such an expression to explain, for example, how the prospects for moral reform are strengthened when the causes that lead to the dominion of the good principle are fulfilled (RGV 6:151). We see this same usage at work when Kant claims that the propensity to be insincere is "the hardest to extirpate if it is just allowed to take root" (RGV 6:190n), and when, in the Metaphysics of Morals, Kant briefly describes how desires can harness the power of reason to produce a form of evil that is rooted in an especially deep way (tief zu wurzeln) (MS 6:408).[4] On its own, there is little metaphysical baggage that must attach to this concept of rootedness. That which is rooted can be either contingent or necessary, and that which is rooted may or may not remain immune from change or corruption. In either case, a root explains

2. See note 47 of Chapter 5.
3. 1 Timothy 6:10.
4. I discuss this last passage in greater detail later in this chapter.

what allows something—such as the evil in a human being—to become entrenched or strongly fixed in place.

Second, to isolate the root of something is to focus on that which is an indispensable condition of that thing, or to call our attention to that which makes possible what appears at the surface. To consider the root system in a tree is to look beyond the leaves and the branches and toward that which is needed to nourish, anchor, provide sustenance, or generally serve as the sine qua non of what we see in front of us. This point is captured in part by Kant's distinction between a root, or that which is original to something and accounts necessarily for the possibility of that thing, and a graft, which contingently attaches to something and is thus not a condition of the possibility of that thing (RGV 6:27–28). Thus, while the surface view of evil focuses only on those "cruel" and "savage" human deeds that "parade before us" or particular human vices (RGV 6:33), such as envy or ingratitude (RGV 6:27), a Kantian considering the root of evil would ignore these appearances and instead look for that which serves as a necessary condition of the possibility of their existence.

Finally, and in its most explicit, sustained, and infamous context, Kant relies on the notion of a root to discuss how evil is rooted in and spread throughout human nature in general. In other words, this aforementioned notion of how evil is rooted refers to evil's universal scope. We see this, for example, in Kant's claim that the "supreme subjective ground" of evil is "somehow entwined in humanity itself and, as it were, rooted [gewurzelt] in it" (RGV 6:30) and in his repeated insistence that there is a "radical evil in human nature" (RGV 6:19; see also RGV 6:37–38).

In sum, then, we can consider rootedness as what allows evil to become entrenched, as the necessary condition of evil, and as a way of referring to the universal entwining of evil into human nature. Now, in laying out these three different senses in which Kant speaks of rootedness, we have determined how to be more precise regarding the different ways evil may prove dependent on something else, such as self-deception. Thus, my suggestion is as follows. In this chapter and the next, I explore each of the three senses of rootedness explained above and consider how self-deception figures into them. In other words, we will ask: if and how self-deception allows evil to entrench itself; whether self-deception functions as a necessary condition of evil; and whether self-deception can help explain how evil pertains universally to human nature. The first two questions will be treated in this chapter, while I wait until the next chapter to address the third.

Finally, before beginning our inquiry, we need to acknowledge three challenges associated with this task of finding something that roots evil. First, it is plausible that more than one candidate can fulfill one of the senses of rootedness outlined above. After all, there can be several reasons why an evil disposition is hard to dislodge, several necessary conditions of evil, and—though Kantians would be quite satisfied to find one adequate proof for the evil universally entwined in human nature!—several proofs could be given on this final score as well. Indeed, Kant's talk of a root may make us think that such overlapping explanations are acceptable and perhaps even desirable. While the literature has often tried to hone in on one distinct root of evil—such as unsocial sociability, or, in Morgan, a desire for maximal freedom—it is not clear that talk of some root of evil should push us in this direction. In nature, a root system is not qualitatively monolithic but instead characterized by conceptually distinct functions and subsidiary parts. These complex subparts and functions form a singular root system, and if we rely on this analogy, it may seem that we would ultimately hope to explain the network of factors that together structure evil. Luckily, however, though we need to appreciate this complication, we can more or less put it aside. The goal of my inquiry is to assess exactly how and why self-deception belongs in an account of the root of evil. I neither need nor intend to show that self-deception *alone* explains the root of evil. Thus, for example, there may be more than one reason why evil entrenches itself in a human being, as perhaps unsocial sociability should exist alongside self-deception in an account of the root causes of evil's entrenchment. In light of this, I will often, if not always, be able to bracket throughout this and the next chapter more extensive discussions of some of these alternative interpretations of evil's roots.

Second, and relatedly, just as there may be more than one root cause of entrenchment or necessary condition of evil, we also need to be aware that when commentators are discussing the importance of self-deception, there won't always be a singular task assigned to it. So, for example, in Grenberg's remarks about self-deception,[5] there is not an explicit endorsement of the idea that self-deception is *only* a necessary condition. Indeed, it would seem that she—quite reasonably—thinks self-deception both allows for the possibility of evil and makes evil harder to overcome by entrenching it in a human will. Thus at various points throughout this and the next chapter, we may see the same commentators and indeed the same basic views referenced in our different discussions of the rootedness of evil.

Third, the difficulties we face discussing the root of evil are compounded by the fact that *any* answer to the question of what this root consists of is bound to be unsatisfying in a very specific sense: no answer can promise

5. See page 68 of Chapter 3.

to shut down all new questions that would then emerge regarding the root itself. To explain how a root system functions is not to explain why trees or other plants exist, why soil is amenable to such structures, or why a host of other conditions make the roots themselves possible. Similarly, then, while we must hope to isolate a root of evil, our account of it may still have limited explanatory potential. And as we will see, it will prove especially important to be aware of this limit at the end of this chapter.

SELF-DECEPTION AND ROOTEDNESS AS THE NECESSARY CONDITION OF EVIL

While many have thought it clear that self-deception necessarily functions as a condition of evil, there are a few reasons to be cautious about endorsing this view too hastily. To begin, even those inclined to see this as obvious ought not take it for granted without first establishing what precise aspects of Kant's moral theory can, and cannot, lead him to this position. Second, it is important to reiterate that there is not a consensus in the literature that would allow us to assign immediately to Kant the claim that evil must always be underwritten by self-deception. While Grenberg, Allison, and others such as Pasternack, Timmons, Reath, Madore, and Muchnik are comfortable with this attribution—Pasternack is explicit that self-deception is a "necessary condition" of evil[6]—there are Kantians who articulate at least some resistance to the idea that evil always presupposes self-deception, including Formosa, Rukgaber, Sussman, and, as noted earlier, Wood in at least one article.[7,8]

6. "Can Self-Deception Explain *Akrasia* in Kant's Theory of Moral Agency?," 92.
7. See notes 1, 3, and 4 of Chapter 3 for the references to Wood, Grenberg, and Allison. See also Timmons, "Evil and Imputation in Kant's Ethics," 131–132; Reath, *Agency and Autonomy in Kant's Moral Theory*, 20; Madore, *Difficult Freedom and Radical Evil in Kant: Deceiving Reason*, 73 and 94; Muchnik, *Kant's Theory of Evil*, 75; Formosa, "Kant on the Limits of Human Evil," 199; Rukgaber, "Irrationality and Self-Deception within Kant's Three Grades of Evil," 235–243; and Sussman's review of Muchnik's *Kant's Theory of Evil* (see especially Sussman's comments about how frailty, Kant's first "stage" of evil, does not seem to require self-deception). I am indebted to Rukgaber for bringing Reath's comment to my attention.
8. In addition to those who either affirm that self-deception is a necessary condition of evil or express resistance to this idea, there is a group of commentators whose precise stance on self-deception is a bit difficult to make out. In "Duties to Oneself, Motivational Internalism, and Self-Deception in Kant's Ethics," Nelson Potter appears inclined to treat self-deception as a necessary condition of evil, though he never really develops the argument. Samuel Duncan maintains that self-deception "comes with evil," but the modality of this coupling is not discussed ("'There Is None Righteous': Kant on the *Hang zum Bösen* and the Universal Evil of Humanity," 156).

Third, and on general philosophical grounds, we have to proceed slowly once we appreciate what a strong position it is to tie self-deception to *every* instance of evil, as someone who argues this will likely remain in a permanently defensive position, open to a litany of compelling counterexamples. The wider contemporary literature on self-deception provides a host of potential counterexamples, and while these examples need to be amended in order to reflect certain fixed Kantian commitments and thus prove useful, they can nonetheless provide helpful touchstones for our discussion.

Consider an example from Mark Sanford, in which a person who knows full well the incredibly low odds of winning a "sleazy" stuffed animal at a carnival decides to waste a good deal of money attempting this feat.[9] Under Sanford's description, the person is not unaware of the poor odds or how lame the prize is, but is nonetheless so attracted to the prospect of winning that she decides to make this irrational use of her time and her money. Sanford thinks it is clear that no self-deception is necessary in this case, and he also notes that we can imagine that it is only after the fact, if someone else forces her to address her disregard for rational norms, that the agent claims to have been self-deceived all along concerning, for example, what her chances of success were or how desirable the prize was. Now, if this example is at least somewhat compelling—and it seems to me that it is—it should prompt us to think carefully about why, for Kant, self-deception is, in fact, a necessary condition for every instance of evil. If it is plausible that the norms our carnival participant violates in a clear, non-self-deceived frame of mind are norms that she herself regards as binding on her, and perhaps even norms that are woven into the fabric of rationality in a way sufficiently similar to how Kantians regard moral laws, we must address the challenge that Kant or those working within his framework can similarly admit that a human being can violate the law of autonomy with a parallel lack of confusion and cognitive dissonance.

Let us briefly entertain another example from Richard Holton. The case he uses is that of a meat eater who, while fully versed in and sensitive to the reasons in favor of vegetarianism, continues to eat meat. Such an example interests Holton because it shows there can be an action against one's better or best judgment that is nonetheless *not* an example of acting contrary to

DiCenso, in his commentary on the *Religion*, makes several references to self-deception but does not attest to whether he sees it as necessary for evil (see, e.g., *Kant's* Religion within the Boundaries of Mere Reason: A Commentary, 65). Finally, Mathew Caswell claims that "evil's hallmark" is self-deception, but it is unclear what we should take this to mean ("The Value of Humanity and Kant's Conception of Evil," 645).

9. Sanford, "Self-Deception as Rationalization," 167.

one's intentions; the meat eater may not endorse her own actions, but that doesn't mean she didn't intend to act as she did. Moreover, Holton adds that there is no reason to ascribe self-deception to this meat eater.[10] The meat eater fails to act rationally by her own lights, but she does not necessarily rely on self-deception in order to act against her own best judgment. We need not assume that such a person must attempt to provide, either before or after she sits down for a steak dinner, some moral justification for her actions. Similarly, Holton claims, with smoking, since no one, he thinks, can argue that smokers necessarily tell themselves that their activity is justified.

Since these examples help us see that different forms of practical irrationality—such as the failure to act as one intends, the failure to act in accord with one's best judgment, and the failure to be sincere with oneself about what one believes or how one acts—do not invariably coincide with one another, they can likewise prove helpful cases for distinguishing between different aspects of moral failure and practical unreason in a Kantian context. No Kantian can deny that evil is irrational. Nor can a Kantian deny that every agent is implicitly committed to moral standards simply by virtue of her status as a rational agent. We would also not deny that evil is grasped by the agent herself as displaying a fundamental rational failure. The only question is on what basis commentators would be able to conclude that this type of practical defect necessarily occasions self-deceptive activity wherein an agent tries to hide from herself, or manipulates evidence regarding, either what her actions or intentions are or what the moral law demands. In other words, is there a good reason why many of Kant's readers see self-deception and action against one's best moral judgment as coextensive, even while other philosophers and commentators come to the conclusion that each can be kept distinct? Ideally, we would answer this question by tracing back to a place in Kant's works where it is discussed, but, unfortunately, no explicit discussion or sustained engagement with it can be found in Kant's writings.

In light of these challenges both from contemporary philosophers and from within Kant scholarship, I will proceed as follows in the remainder of this section. Since the majority of commentators see self-deception as a necessary condition of evil for Kant, I will presume that this is the case and consider what arguments can, and can't, be used to generate strong support for this claim. If an argument in its favor can be developed, then we will have done the important work of not only affirming that self-deception

---

10. Holton, "Intention and Weakness of Will," 255.

is a necessary condition of evil but also, in explaining precisely why this is so and ruling out rival explanations, filling in a crucial gap in the literature. I also, along the way, address those readers of Kant who, like Sussman and Formosa, dispute the claim that self-deception invariably underwrites evil, as well as the above-noted challenges and counterexamples that Kant faces from a more general philosophical perspective. I take it as a given that there are meaningful reasons why some commentators—again, both Kantians and philosophers more broadly—have resisted the conclusion that self-deception is a necessary condition of evil, and a test of my argument favoring this conclusion is its ability to make sense of and address reservations about it.

Our next task, then, is to consider what arguments can be given to substantiate the claim that self-deception is a necessary condition of evil. A few options quickly suggest themselves, since there are a host of commitments from within Kant's moral philosophy that may appear to demand that self-deception is a necessary condition of evil. They include Kant's stipulation against diabolical evil in the *Religion* (RGV 6:35 and RGV 6:37), the claim that the moral law forces itself onto human consciousness as a fact of reason (KpV 5:31–34),[11] and Kant's claim in the *Groundwork* that no human being wills un-universalizable maxims but instead wills exceptions to what she sees as the only possible maxims fit for human reason (GMS 4:424). Additionally, it makes sense to ask whether the claims developed earlier in this book—including the argument of the prior chapter, which explained the mechanics of self-deception and how self-deception involves an improper usurpation of the faculty of cognition on behalf of the faculty of desire—have resources for establishing a necessary connection between self-deception and evil. I will now work through these possibilities, using them to guide us to the argument that is best capable of explaining why self-deception is a necessary condition of evil.

The Fact of Reason, Diabolical Evil, and Self-Exceptionalism. We can begin with Kant's doctrine of the fact of reason. It has been vociferously condemned by at least as many commentators as have defended it,[12] but we can put aside many of the more controversial issues[13] and focus

11. Although the second *Critique* remains the essential text for Kant's fact of reason, this fact is referenced directly at 6:50n in the *Religion*.

12. Sympathetic defenses of the fact of reason can be found in Kleingeld, "Moral Consciousness and the Fact of Reason," and Owen Ware, "Rethinking Kant's Fact of Reason." For some of the most well-known and fiercest criticisms, see Wood, *Kantian Ethics*, 134–135, and Guyer, "Naturalistic and Transcendental Moments in Kant's Moral Philosophy," 462.

13. Some of these issues are: whether the fact of reason can or cannot address skepticism, what Kant means when he claims that the fact of reason serves as a "credential"

simply on how the moral psychology informing Kant's account bears on our inquiry into self-deception. To start, while some, including Ameriks, have noted that Kant can be accused of relying on a contentious moral psychology when advocating that the moral law functions as a fact of reason,[14] I want to grant Kant the claims he makes about what we grasp when we are conscious of the moral law as a fact of reason. I will grant, then, that we become aware of our own proximity and vulnerability to the moral law when we deliberate about our actions,[15] that we retain awareness of the law's purity or strictness as a standard to which our own actions should conform (KpV 5:32), and that we know we have the ability to execute the law's demands (KpV 5:30).

Now, Kant's only goal—or at least his only express goal—is to secure our unceasing awareness of these aspects of moral obligation. And it would easily follow from this that self-deception is necessarily at work in any case where an agent explores grounds for concluding that she isn't adequately aware of the law's presence or demands, or searches for evidence that she might lack certain moral capacities. But it would outstrip the needs of the text to see Kant's doctrine of the fact of reason as implying anything stronger about self-deception. Even though certain attempts to demonstrate to oneself moral uncertainty or possible moral limitations are necessarily self-deceived, it does not follow that other instances of practical failure—including those where, in a manner that parallels Holton's and Sanford's examples, agents acknowledge their own rational and justificatory failure—require self-deception.

A similar point can be made in the context of Kant's stipulation against diabolical evil. Now some, such as Pasternack, argue for the necessity of self-deception in evil on grounds that it would be "devilish" to admit that agents "could will a principle which they know to be contrary to the law."[16] Yet this attributes to Kant a bolder and more far-reaching argument than

but not a "deduction" of the moral law, and what kind of fact the fact of reason is. On these issues, see especially Kleingeld, "Moral Consciousness and the Fact of Reason"; Ware, "Rethinking Kant's Fact of Reason"; Tatiana Patrone, "What Sort of Fact Is Kant's Fact of Reason?"; and Ameriks, *Interpreting Kant's Critiques*, 249–262.

14. On this aspect of Kant's view, see *Interpreting Kant's Critiques*, 258–262.

15. As Kant says, "It is therefore the *moral law*, of which we become immediately conscious (as soon as we draw up maxims of the will for ourselves)" (KpV 5:29). In light of this parenthetical clause, it is unsurprising that some commentators have addressed the aforementioned question of what kind of fact the fact of reason is by arguing that we must extend our sense of *Faktum* so that it includes the notion of a deed or activity. On this point, see Kleingeld, "Moral Consciousness and the Fact of Reason," 61–62.

16. "Can Self-Deception Explain *Akrasia* in Kant's Theory of Moral Agency?," 92. I return to the topic of diabolical evil later in this chapter.

Kant himself provides, as the argument against diabolical evil is not meant to function as an argument in favor of the necessity and thoroughgoingness of self-deception in evil agency. Kant's points against diabolical evil are meant to affirm our vulnerability to the incentive of respect, as well as the impossibility of rejecting the moral law without recourse to self-love (RGV 6:35 and 6:37). The latter point, which concerns the motivational underpinnings of evil, is far removed from the topic of self-deception, and the former point, insofar as it concerns access to respect, only shows that no agent can sincerely claim to be unaware of the law or know herself as unable to execute it. The discussion of diabolical evil is simply not designed to rule out knowledge of oneself as acting immorally or show that evil is impossible unless an agent finds possible grounds for thinking that she has acted appropriately.

We can now turn to the aforementioned passage in the *Groundwork*, as this too may seem to lend support to the idea that self-deception is a necessary condition of evil. In this passage, we find Kant explaining that no agent with an ill-formed maxim actually wills that her maxim should hold as a universal law of nature. Instead, Kant claims that transgressing agents intend to uphold the law's claims to universality, "take the liberty of making an *exception* to it for ourselves," and thus settle on the position of finding a "half way" point between one's self-exceptionalism and the demands of pure practical reason (GMS 4:424).

I want to make two points about Kant's remarks. First, at least one of the moral psychological claims made strikes me as faulty. While Kant is correct that the notion of making exceptions is an important one to highlight in a theory of immorality, he overlooks how often we approve of other individuals making themselves an exception. Human beings routinely counsel other people to lie, or to put their own interests above the needs of others—just so long as the person lied to or neglected is not oneself. As such, the kind of exception-making we engage in is not always or even often one of claiming that I, and only I, can make exceptions to the categoricity demanded by the law. Rather, the kind of exception-making we engage in is regularly one where we claim that exceptions can be made, so long as *I* am not harmed by them. Second, even putting this worry aside, it is still not clear exactly what we ought to conclude about self-deception. Perhaps Kant intends to imply, with this "half way" remark, that a person can only be evil if she self-deceptively tries to convince herself that her exception or deviation might enjoy some moral support, but alternative and even opposed readings are available. To name just one, it is possible that the half way point is met by someone who refuses to claim that she can find any justification for her immoral action. Just as the meat eater described by Holton operates under no such pretenses, it is not clear that evil agents in a Kantian framework must be self-deceptively hubristic. Since we can meet the half way mark either through moralistic self-deceit or by declining to paint moral failure as justified, these comments from the *Groundwork* cannot establish what Kant's view is on self-deception as a necessary condition of evil.

Self-Deception as Truth Preserving and Rationalization as Distraction. If these aspects of Kant's moral theory—the fact of reason, the stipulation against diabolical evil, and his comments about self-exceptionalism—cannot yet justify the claim that self-deception functions as a necessary condition of evil, we must look elsewhere if we wish to advance our argument. I will now move toward what I take to be the most promising way to demonstrate the necessity of self-deception in evil. I'll begin by referencing a point about self-love made in Chapter 1 and then proceed to focus on important features of self-deception that we can recall or, with a little work, extract from our discussion of it in Chapter 3.

To start, I want to point out a thus far overlooked reason to think that that evil at least often involves self-deception. Given the characteristics of self-love discussed in Chapter 1, it should be no surprise that an agent with an impure faculty of choice will try to find grounds for thinking that deviation from the moral law can be given some defense. A person who incorporates self-love into her fundamental maxim is someone striving to feel a lack of hindrances or obstacles. Thus, she will very likely try to minimize friction between those elements of her moral psychology—such as her cognition of the moral law—that discomfit her and those actions and intentions that she wills for the sake of pleasure. So long as self-love provides guidance, we put enormous pressure on ourselves to search for reasons in favor of our deviant actions. The likelihood of this only increases once we observe that in a Kantian model of motivation, knowledge is intrinsically motivating, even if it is not determinatively so. When reason is already a force or a moving power, it makes sense that an agent will rely on it to supplement that which she wants to do under the heading of self-love. And a person can do this best if she acknowledges the demands of reason at least somewhat on their own terms, and thus finds considerations in support of her desires so that they more resemble the kinds of intellectually grounded concerns the faculty of cognition is typically responsive to.

Though this is an important observation and one that can help explain the frequency with which self-deception accompanies evil, it is again insufficient to establish a necessary connection or, for that matter, to address those Kantians and other philosophers, such as Holton or Sanford, who provide reasons to be skeptical about this position. The difficulty we are presented with is not a new one, though it is helpfully crystalized by the above consideration. The worry is that the above consideration would, at least if taken alone, appear to imply that evil always assumes a particularly intellectualized form, one wherein we cloak our practical failures with some sort of partial excuse or justification. But again, since the cases of the meat eater or the smoker appear to defy this characterization, the observation that the faculty of choice will be inclined to exploit the power of reason is an inadequate basis on which to forge a necessary connection between evil and self-deception. Furthermore, though there are moments where Kant inches closer to addressing whether there is a precise way that an evil agent must conceptualize her action and what, if anything, she must will herself to believe, he ultimately does not offer any firm opinion. One such moment is a footnote of the second *Critique* where Kant briefly notes an ambiguity in the expression *sub ratione boni* and the thesis that we desire nothing that does not fall under the heading of the good. As he explains, this may mean:

> We represent to ourselves something as good when and *because we desire* (will) *it*, or also: we desire something *because we represent it to ourselves as good*, so that either desire is the determining ground of the concept of the object of the good, or the concept of the good is the determining ground of desire (of the will); so in the first case *sub ratione boni* would mean, we will something *under the idea* of the good; in the second, we will something *in consequence of this idea*, which must precede volition as its determining ground. (KpV 5:59)[17]

The first option Kant describes is the one relevant to our discussion. For if Kant thought it viable to argue that in willing or acting to bring about some end or object, our willing is such that the end or object in question requires conceptualization under the guise of the good, then this would avail us of further materials for understanding how to handle examples that—like the smoker and the meat eater—appear to external observers to depict immorality without the trappings of intellectual pretense or self-deceptive moralization. But since Kant's main goal in the text surrounding this passage is to explore a different and, for his purposes, more pressing ambiguity with respect to the term "*bonum*"—which, Kant claims, can mean either *das Gute* (the good) or *das Wohl* (well-being)—we are given no direct guidance concerning what implications these comments on *sub ratione boni* should have for a Kantian account of the intellectual pressures that accompany evil willing. While Kant does make it known that we must get something

17. I am indebted to Sonny Elizondo for bringing this footnote to my attention. See "Reason in Its Practical Application," 7n15.

good or *wohl* out of the distance we put between ourselves and the law, he outlines no reasons for thinking that we must also—and always—cognize ourselves as pursuing *das Gute* or rationalize that what we do enjoys some rational justification or objective support.

However, if we revisit some of the insights developed in Chapter 3, we can clear this impasse and see that Kant's silence on this matter presents in the end no barrier to the conclusion that self-deception functions as a necessary condition of evil. As we may recall, what characterizes Kantian rationalization is its indirect quality. We do not try to contradict what is true; we try instead to reframe it or distract ourselves from it. The agent who wishes to avoid cognition of her debt stays on the lookout for alternative grounds of belief that will allow her to trivialize the weightiness of her debt, and she must remain on the defensive against evidence that would emphasize her original cognition regarding how the sum owed exceeds what is in her coffers. By taking a fact, and surrounding it with hopes, speculations, diversions, and mere possibilities as opposed to objectively well-grounded probabilities, an agent shields herself from, but never diametrically undermines or challenges, the truth within view.

If self-deception actually preserves, and does not try to contradict, what is true, then we might be able to have our cake and eat it too. Because self-deception is truth preserving, the self-deceived person can grasp the truth of his own actions. Thus, it is not surprising that with respect to Sanford's carnival participant, or Holton's meat eater or smoker, many will be inclined to say that they can act while having clear vision of what they are doing. To show that such agents can nonetheless be characterized as self-deceived from a Kantian point of view, we would not need to argue that such individuals refuse to acknowledge their actions or that they are unjustified. We would only need to make the case that these individuals do not continually attend to that knowledge. And when we picture the life of Holton's smoker, it is most plausible to think that he recognizes that he shouldn't smoke but spends his time distracting himself from this fact. Again, what is decisive regarding self-deception in a Kantian framework is not whether an agent has a cognition of what is true but whether she vigorously attends to this truth. Thus, unless someone would be bold enough to venture that the smoker, the meat eater, and the carnival participant spend their days actively considering the true, the good, or the practically necessary, then a Kantian can establish that such individuals are indeed self-deceived.

What, though, of the fact that the smoker and the carnival participant— at least as Holton and Sanford sketched them—do not pretend that their ends or actions are justified, whether on intellectual, moral, or prudential grounds? When they have no such pretenses, some will protest that it is not appropriate to describe these agents as self-deceived or rationalizing. Even if they rely on distraction, and even if they busy themselves with other concerns, it may still be questioned whether it is appropriate to pair recognition of these faults with the seemingly more serious charge of self-deceptive rationalization. I take it that this is the kind of worry animating Kantians like Formosa or Rukgaber, and I think such skepticism can and must be addressed by those who wish to argue for the indispensability of self-deception in evil. There are two points to make in response.

One point is that these seemingly lesser vices are motivated on the same grounds that more intellectually sophisticated acts of rationalization are: both stem from a willingness to corrupt the moral incentive with self-love, and a willingness to subordinate the true to the comfortable. The other part of the answer is that Kant seems extremely ecumenical regarding what kinds of reasons or rationalizations can be relied on to shift focus away from what we know to be true or just. In the logic lectures, Kant focused on an agent's attempt to find alternative cognitions that were objectively possible but inadequately grounded. In the second *Critique*, much of Kant's discussion of *sub ratione boni* leaves us guessing as to how volition pressures cognition, and yet, and as noted earlier, he does take care to tell us that "*bonum*" can mean either *das Gute* or *das Wohl*. Now, a belief that an action promises *Wohlgefallen* constitutes, at least minimally, a reason in the sense that it is a consideration in favor of that action. Thus, so long as the belief that pleasure is on the horizon is operative in an agent, and so long as she turns to it when she looks away from what she knows to be true or good, then, crucially, the agent can be said to engage in rationalization even if she in no manner takes her actions to be justified, forms a judgment that her action is good, or tries to see her actions as reasonable. Kant leaves ample space for the idea that rationalization need not have intellectual or moral pretensions in order to count as such. Holton, and those who question whether Kantian evil is tied to self-deceit, are absolutely right to see this; the only point that seems overlooked is that even without any such moralistic or self-serious posturing, and even if mere pleasure is the only source of distraction, self-deception—at least as Kant would define it—is still at work.

In addition to accommodating examples from contemporary philosophers such as Sanford and Holton, we can see self-deceptive rationalization, or a truth-preserving pattern of distraction, as necessarily at work in the other cases noted earlier in this book. It was established in Chapter 1 that Eichmann's behavior can be properly interpreted as motivated by self-love, and we can now add that even though it is impossible and a bit ridiculous to try to say much about the inner life of someone like Eichmann, it is fairly clear that his evil relies on self-deception. It is only reasonable to assume that his compliance with positive law was a reality capable of diverting attention away from his personal moral corruption. Moreover, in Chapter 2, I differentiated between two ways that one's moral disposition can become impure: in addition to those who prioritize self-love in order to attain what is pleasing, there are those who, in an attempt to take both self-love and respect as authoritative guides, overdetermine the faculty of choice. To establish the presence of self-deception in these cases, little additional commentary is needed. To recall, attempts to overdetermine the will are characterized by compromises that secure neither what gratifies nor what is good. The Milgram participants were our prime example, but in other cases as well we should expect overdetermination to involve a similarly perilous epistemic position. Not only is the very structure of an overdetermined will possible only for those who refuse to appreciate fully the obvious folly of this enterprise. As pointed out in Chapter 2, since compromises between self-love and respect result in a material failure to get pleasure, overdetermination leaves a person well-equipped to continually reframe the significance of her own moral shortcomings. Instead of acknowledging directly how corrupt her decision-making is, she can refocus her rational powers on how unhappy she is and indulge ratiocinations regarding how those who try to do some justice to moral demands encounter suffering. Finally, since the prospect of gratification is a focal point for those who give direct priority to self-love, Kant's framework can explain how even in the most psychologically uncomplicated profiles of evil, the presence of self-deceptive rationalization can be presumed.

Now, for all that has been said above and for all the different examples we have tried to shed light on, a critic might push here and insist that, given certain concessions I have made in their direction, more still needs to be done to conclude that evil requires self-deceptive rationalization. After all, I allowed in my discussion of Holton and Sanford's examples that an evil agent can grasp clearly with her mind's eye the lack of justification for her ill-formed maxims. Given this, the critic might insist, why can this agent get a glance at this failure but not steady her gaze on it in a long-term way? It is important to question why we can presume in evil the presence of some distraction, whether intellectual or sensual, that diverts attention to the point that one is prohibited from also having a sustained cognition of her or his own moral failure. In responding to this challenge, we can bring this section to a close.

There is a difference between what at a given moment is possible within a Kantian account of the mechanics of agency and what is possible within the life of a person attuned to demands of truth, knowledge, and the moral law. An awareness of one's own evil can be secured in the former, but a sustained understanding of oneself as evil is ruled out by the latter. Thus, a Kantian should be prepared to concede—as I think common sense demands—the possibility of an agent knowing her own evil in a sporadic or piecemeal fashion while arguing that this hardly counts as an epistemic or practical credit. To see the essential role of self-deceptive rationalization with respect to evil, we must shift away from the possibility of an episodic cognition of oneself as evil and toward the question of whether one can steadily balance the virtue of self-knowledge with the vice of evil. This seems to me implausible. For as already shown, a Kantian should not try to read the co-presence of self-deceit with evil as a universal descriptive claim, one that eliminates the possibility that an agent can have any cognition of her own evil. Instead, we should interpret the idea that self-deceptive rationalization necessarily conditions evil as, first, an acknowledgment of the ubiquity of distraction alongside evil, and, second, as endorsement of a modest Socratic thesis that in casting off distractions and developing self-knowledge, one is led to knowledge of the good,[18] and that, moreover, knowledge of the good reliably—even if not immediately or invariably—produces motivation and conviction to be good. When we shift to a more extended perspective, no grounds remain for disputing that evil necessarily presupposes a self-deceiving character.

SELF-DECEPTION AND ROOTEDNESS AS THE ENTRENCHMENT OF EVIL

How Self-Deception Entrenches Evil: Two Proposals. The next question we must consider is whether self-deception can explain how evil becomes entrenched in a human being. To begin, it seems fairly clear that many commentators are comfortable assigning this role to self-deception and that self-deception is thought to accomplish this by enhancing an agent's comfort level with her own evil. We see this in Allison's explanation of how self-deception helps an agent avoid introspection and evade coming

---

18. In the *Critique of Pure Reason*, we see a somewhat similar coincision between knowledge of the self and a knowledge that refers to something other than the self. As Kant routinely notes, in clarifying how reason must not overstep the bounds of experience in its claims about knowledge of objects, we develop self-knowledge. Thus, in the A Preface, the task of reason that is "the most difficult of all its [reason's] tasks" is "that of self-knowledge" (Axii). See also KrV A366, B421, A481/B510, A735/B763, A745/B773, and A849/B877.

to terms with one's own responsibility, and we see it also in Grenberg's account of how self-deception can quiet the voice of the moral law, which always insists on making itself heard.[19] And yet there is at least one serious philosophical difficulty with the idea that self-deception serves to entrench evil.

Earlier in this chapter, we discussed that what we are looking for in an account of evil's rootedness is a richer or fuller explanation of the specific deeds that a human being commits from self-love or of that which we see at the more superficial level of action. Self-deception, simply insofar as it points us to a distinctive mental phenomenon, to some degree provides this. But insofar as any act of self-deception must be rooted in the same motivational structures that underwrite these more specific evil deeds, we seem to lose much of the explanatory power we just gained. On a Kantian account, we cannot say that self-deception is wholly unintentional, or that it is governed or put into action by some motive distinct from self-love. An agent engages in self-deception because she is committed to self-love more generally, and once we note this, it becomes unclear what sort of new explanatory light self-deception can really shed on self-love.[20] If self-deception gets its motivational teeth from self-love, then in what sense can self-deception really give self-love sharpened fangs in return? If the inadequately grounded cognitions I entertain about, for example, my moral capacities or the moral law stem from a broader commitment to self-love, then what is the philosophical status of these diversions? If they are mere instruments to help me get the things I want, then how could they actually entrench evil or the endorsement of self-love? And again, if the voice of conscience is self-deceptively quieted only because I have desired and willed it to be so, then how does self-deception really find a meaningful role to play in an account of the root of evil?[21]

There is more than one way one might try to answer such questions. For example, in a different context, some commentators have argued that Kant allows that agents can destroy, at least temporarily, certain of their own practical capacities. If, as some have argued, Kant conceives of moral weakness as a self-wrought inability to execute good maxims,[22] one could

19. See again page 68 of Chapter 3.
20. Thanks to Michael Nance for raising this issue. A very similar worry can be found in Pasternack, "Can Self-Deception Explain *Akrasia* in Kant's Theory of Moral Agency?," 93.
21. Unfortunately, these complications are not addressed by Nelson Potter when he claims that self-deception is "the major, perhaps the sole source of evil" ("Duties to Oneself, Motivational Internalism, and Self-Deception in Kant's Ethics," 386).
22. Both Frierson and Mariña offer this view, which I discuss at length in Chapter 7. See pages 184–185.

perhaps argue that self-deception likewise puts certain features of an agent's inner life out of her own reach. If the parallel to this reading of moral weakness were to hold, then self-deception could at some point become so firmly established that it would, in fact, cut off the introspective access needed to see and overcome one's own evil.[23] Now, in Chapter 7, I will show that there are some difficulties with this approach to moral weakness. But even before we lay out these difficulties, it is clear that this strategy for understanding self-deception or how it entrenches evil cannot be quite right. While Kant insists on the opacity of introspection (MS 6:411), and while Kant allows that we can train ourselves to not heed the voice of conscience (MS 6:438), he does not allow that a lack of self-awareness can become as thorough as what is required by this suggestion.

There are further reasons for putting aside the above proposal. As should be clear from earlier work in this chapter and Chapter 3, one of the characteristic features of self-deception is its instability.[24] A person laboring under a self-deception interacts with herself and the world around her in a remarkably different way from the ignorant. Someone convincing herself that her beloved has no faults must engage in a constant and deft avoidance of divergent evidence, which shows the extent to which a more adequate truth looks both within her easy reach and within her capacity for self-awareness. Thus whatever self-deception involves, and whatever explains its ability to entrench evil, it cannot be that self-deception, in fact, eliminates our sensitivity to what is true or what we ourselves have knowledge of. Moreover, even a weaker version of this view, one according to which self-deception makes introspection more difficult, though not impossible, is still not satisfying. Since self-deception forms part of an ongoing strategy to actively suppress awareness of, for example, one's moral potential and the law's demands, an agent's self-deception presupposes an already existing and steady commitment to self-love. This again makes it difficult to explain how self-deception entrenches evil.

I will now try to articulate how I think we should respond to this objection, though I will do so in a way that builds on and does not refute the core of Grenberg and Allison's insights. Thus, I begin by affirming the obvious point that self-deception lends ease to evil. Self-deception can help an agent quiet the painful claims of conscience, focus on that which puts herself in a

23. In such a case, one could still argue that an agent was responsible for this entrenchment of evil on grounds that she herself eliminated the introspective access required to make any moral progress.

24. On the instability of rationalization and self-deception, see Robert Audi, "Self-Deception, Rationalization, and Reasons for Acting," 109.

better or more pleasing light, and sidestep the humiliation and displeasure that we feel through the incentive of respect for the moral law (KpV 5:77–78). Drawing on Chapter 1, we could also note that an agent who puts out of view these hindrances to her self-esteem and her desires secures a stronger revelation of vitality and a greater sense of subjective flourishing. And in light of these observations, we begin to see how self-deception can entrench evil. Roughly put, while an evil disposition results from the fact that an agent wants to secure some end she desires and chooses under the incentive and principle of self-love, self-deception pushes evil to exceed its strategic purpose. In other words, an evil disposition or a commitment to self-love will, by virtue of its reliance on self-deception, over time establish access to new domains in which pleasure can be acquired. It seems there are at least two ways that self-deception facilitates this.

(1) First, a self-deceptive mindset is generally more pleasing than a mindset underwritten by full epistemic sensitivity to the norms of truth, evidence acquisition, and honest or sustained comparison of ourselves with the moral law. Given this, self-deception promises to deliver something of personal value, even apart from our initial reliance on it when we try to secure the ends or objects of our immoral maxims. If this is correct, then we could say that insofar as evil is coupled with self-deception, self-deception allows evil to become *liked*, or subjectively valued, in a manner that is distinct from its raw instrumental power to bring about our personal, morally impermissible ends. Thus, the more extensively an agent self-deceives, the more she transforms her evil disposition or action into something that is at least somewhat pleasing *in its own right*, pleasing to some extent that is independent of the ends or inclinations she initially wanted to secure or satisfy. Self-deception allows evil to increasingly take on the character of something valuable independent of its obvious utility for securing specific goods. Or, in other words, self-deception allows evil to partly shift its axiological status so that it becomes increasingly more a state that is in itself valued, as opposed to a mere instrument or tool for securing the objects of our desires. Of course, an agent need not have this transformation in view or foresee it from the start. At the outset of action, self-deception simply enables the acquisition of those ends sought under the principle and incentive of self-love. But over time, that self-deceptive activity increasingly allows our own immoral condition to become an object of comfort. In short, self-deception increases the pleasurability of impurity itself.

To clarify this proposal, it is important to note that I have been careful to stress above that, through its coupling with self-deception, one's evil can become intrinsically pleasing only partly or only to some extent. Such qualifiers are included because they allow us to adhere to Kant's repeated insistence that our consciousness of the moral law and our vulnerability to the voice of conscience are ineradicable. We can say that an evil disposition can partly transform into a state that is in itself valued, and that offers us something that is independent of and different from the specific inclinations we initially intended to have satisfied, so long as we take care to emphasize that this transformation can only be partial and never complete. Moral failure must remain painful, humiliating, and something that registers some internal disapproval within the agent herself. Given this, Kant's stipulation against diabolical evil is, in fact, fully compatible with the suggestion that an evil disposition, through its connection to self-deception, can offer intrinsic pleasure. As others have likewise pointed out and as we emphasized earlier in this chapter and in Chapter 2,[25] this stipulation is meant only to eliminate the possibility that an agent can remove herself from the reach of the law. But since access to the law remains throughout any self-deceptive act or state, and even when that act or state promises to deliver its own source of pleasure, then one's own evil can be (partly) valued for its own sake without there being any threat of diabolical evil on the horizon.

This point is further confirmed by the specifics of Kant's remarks on diabolical evil. Kant argues that there can be no "evil reason," in which resistance to the law is "itself elevated to incentive," and that it is impossible to "incorporate evil *qua evil* for incentive into one's maxim" (RGV 6:35 and 6:38). These claims eliminate a very specific and narrow type of moral psychology, namely, one in which an agent can find reason or cause to disobey the moral law simply out of direct, uncomplicated, and thorough hatred for or resistance to the law or the incentive of respect. But though it is widely overlooked in the literature, this restriction clearly leaves intact the possibility of a moral psychology wherein an evil disposition becomes at least somewhat intrinsically pleasing to the agent who bears it.[26] For the claim

25. See also Louden, "Evil Everywhere: The Ordinariness of Radical Evil," 106, and Allison, "Reflections on the Banality of (Radical) Evil," 176 (cited in Louden).

26. I am at other points in broad agreement with reconstructions of Kant's rejection of diabolical evil. For helpful, representative reconstructions, see Anderson-Gold, "Kant's Rejection of Devilishness"; Caswell, "Kant on the Diabolical Will: A Neglected Alternative?"; and DiCenso, *Kant's Religion within the Boundaries of Mere Reason: A Commentary*, 59–60. In an attempt to offer a different approach, Formosa argues that Kant could allow for "evil qua evil" or action done out of "hubristic hatred of the law" ("Kant on the Limits of Human Evil," 195 and 197, respectively). However, while Formosa makes interesting arguments about how evil qua evil mirrors action done from duty, he does not explain how his interpretation of diabolical evil can be reconciled with Kant's practical psychology and his theory of the incentives. Thus, I put aside his challenge to Kant's rejection of evil qua evil.

that evil can partly transform into an end in itself is in no manner equivalent to the claim that there can be evil qua evil. The notion of evil qua evil should bring to mind an evil disposition that somehow relies only on itself to get motivational strength or to supply the ends at which one will aim. The impossibility of such a disposition is not invalidated by the idea that one's own evil can be not merely a means to a pleasing end but (partly) pleasing in its own right.

(2) Second, through the pairing of evil and self-deception, it also becomes the case that a person will become pleased by and reliant on the marginalization of knowledge and self-knowledge to an extent that does not track what would be needed to ease her comfort in the willing of immoral ends. In other words, the improperly grounded cognitions we rely on can become ones that we identify with or are invested in directly, that is, independently of their initial affiliation with particular contexts of action and choice. I might initially work myself up over the possibility of future bankruptcy to justify shoplifting, but this self-deceiving speculation can gradually become an independent object of attachment.

To continue to develop this second proposal, we can draw from both broader philosophical resources and Kant's own corpus. Beginning with the former, the shift I have in mind is often referenced in discussions of racism and how racisms relate to ideology. Several philosophers have emphasized how the material benefits of chattel slavery precipitated the racialization of black and brown persons, and further how an irrational racist ideology was developed to give the system of slavery that offered these material benefits a moral sheen and foundation.[27] But as is quite clear, especially in certain contemporary settings, someone who does not stand to make material gains by virtue of her antiblack sentiments can still hold on tightly to a racist ideology. Thus, while the initial acceptance and maintenance of a racist ideology bear a clear relationship to material goals, the commitments constitutive of any such ideology can outstrip their initial purposes and become objects of attachment and affection in their own right.

Moreover, this dynamic aligns neatly with that outlined by Kant in his discussions of passions, which were only briefly discussed in Chapter 1. In the *Metaphysics of Morals*, passions are introduced into Kant's theory of wrongdoing when he singles them out as an especially problematic type of vice (*Laster*). Though the concept of a vice is, to my knowledge, never carefully expounded by Kant despite his extremely frequent use of the term,

27. See Tommie Shelby, "Ideology, Racism, and Critical Social Theory, 165"; Kai Nielsen, *Marxism and the Moral Point of View: Morality, Ideology, and Historical Materialism*, 105; and my "Promoting Black (Social) Identity," 11.

it is clear enough that vices refer to a peculiar and distinct expression of the evil that can exist in a human being. Given vice's status as the "real opposite" of virtue (MS 6:384), we can infer that while all vices presuppose the incorporation of self-love into one's fundamental maxim, the specific vices one exhibits depend on which ends and maxims one has set in her deviation from the moral law, just as the virtues a person displays depend on having adopted certain morally required, positive ends—ends of self-perfection and the happiness of others—and corresponding maxims of action (MS 6:385).[28]

Vices can then transform into passions when we not only adopt ends based on what we desire but also will our minds to "form principles [Grundsätze]" upon certain inclinations (MS 6:408). This allows—in a nod to rootedness as entrenchment—our more fleeting wants to transform into desires that have a "lasting quality," and that have become "rooted deeply" in the mind and structured so as to permit "reflection" by rational beings (MS 6:408). These remarks are echoed in the Anthropology, where Kant engages in his lengthiest discussion of the passions and describes them not merely as "without exception evil" but as both "taking root [einwurzelnd]" through and "co-existing with rationalizing" (Anth 7:267 and Anth 7:265).[29] To illustrate how a passion develops and relies on rationalizing self-deception, and thereby enables a disposition that is already evil to further entrench itself, Kant singles out in both the Anthropology and the Metaphysics of Morals those traits described as arrogance (Hochmut),[30] ambition (Ehrbegierde), and a lust for honor (Ehrsucht). In these texts, Kant tends to describe these ills as further outgrowths of the vice of self-conceit. As noted in the prior chapter, whereas self-conceit is, in the Metaphysics of Morals, described as a particular form of myopia wherein a human being focuses on her superiority over animal nature while avoiding cognition of her smallness or imperfection in comparison with the moral law, ambition and its ilk develop when a human being sets about finding further evidence of her superiority in the interpersonal realm (MS 6:465 and Anth 7:271). We appeal, for example, to our status in public life, our money, the authority we enjoy, or

28. On this point, see Biss, "Avoiding Vice and Pursuing Virtue: Kant on Perfect Duties and 'Prudential Latitude.'"

29. Translation very slightly modified.

30. As explained in note 31 of the prior chapter, Kant treats the Latin arrogantia as interchangeable with self-conceit. The German term that is translated as arrogance in the Cambridge edition of Kant's works—namely, Hochmut—is not the same thing as the Latin arrogantia. Hochmut is described as a "vice" at MS 6:465 and as a "passion" at Anth 7:272–273, and thus Kant tends to treat Hochmut as a further offshoot of self-conceit or arrogantia.

the way other people look up to us, as these are some of the hallmarks of ambition (Anth 7:266 and 7:289). In arrogance or *Hochmut*, which is characterized by an "inappropriate desire for honor," I surround myself with "flatterers" and "yes-men," that is, those willing to heed my demand that others think less of themselves than they do of me (Anth 7:272; see also Anth 7:203).

Regardless of which specific form of evidence someone tends to seek out—Kant also lists intellectual merit and an abundance of "trifles" or unnecessary material goods as what the haughty or socially ambitious person may crave (V-Mo/Collins 27:457–458)—a passion thrives on and seeks out those cognitions that most reinforce one's superior position. These passions thus initially develop to bolster a feeling of superiority and thereby entrench the more basic vice of self-conceit, but as Kant's discussion makes clear, a person can become independently attached to the selective self-image she develops. Much like how racial ideologies undergo a metamorphosis in which beliefs that initially promoted material pleasure can outstrip their initial purposes, so too can we develop passions whose connection to our more basic material interests becomes increasingly attenuated. With the passions of ambition and honor-seeking, for instance, persons can become obsessively focused on maintaining an interpersonal advantage over others. One can omit to ask herself how acquiring one more trifle really helps secure her status, and she also may pursue the singular pleasure of dominance even though it compromises her ability to get other things she wants or to satisfy "the totality of *all* inclinations" (Anth 7:266).[31] In either case, when a self-deceived state has occasioned specific new outgrowths of pleasure and self-love—outgrowths that are distinct from and in addition to the uses to which self-deception was initially put—then we can rightly say that evil has entrenched itself through self-deception.

Further Clarifications and Objections. To vet and clarify the two suggestions being offered, there are several additional points to be made. First, I should go back to our initial setup and explicitly address how my approach can explain the entrenchment or rootedness of evil. Recall that we were initially trying to determine how self-deception can bring about

---

31. As Kant puts it, a person afflicted with a passion will "please one inclination by placing all the rest in the shade or in a dark corner" (Anth 7:266; see also Chapter 1, page 27). For excellent discussions of this claim and the passions more generally, see Morrisson, "On Kantian Maxims: A Reconciliation of the Incorporation Thesis and Weakness of Will," 85–87; Sussman, *Kant's Idea of Humanity: Anthropology and Anthroponomy in Kant's Ethics*, 198–203; and Frierson, *Kant's Empirical Psychology*, 228–232.

evil's entrenchment. We then encountered the difficulty of having to explain how self-deception can lead to evil's entrenchment when the self-deceiving agent must always be motivated by self-love. Now, the centrality of self-love has not been disputed by my account. The entrenchment of evil through self-deception still presupposes that an agent has a fundamental maxim that is underwritten by a prior commitment to self-love. I have also fully agreed with those commentators who argue that we must highlight and emphasize the ease that self-deception can bring to evil. In short, then, my argument for the rooted entrenchment of evil through self-deception works by supplementing these points. Roughly put, to develop this supplement, we must see that whereas evil begins merely as a means to pleasing ends, self-deception makes it such that evil need not be bound to this condition. Self-deception leads to new attachments to both our own impurity and to specific departures from what is most evidently true. Thus, devotion to self-love becomes entrenched insofar as self-deception enables self-love to stake out new territory that it did not previously have and that outstrips our initial commitment to securing more banal and immediate objects of desire. Though my argument has been that an evil disposition can, through its reliance on self-deception, become subjectively valuable and satisfying apart from the specific ends that we initially seek under the principle and incentive of self-love, this still means that self-love, or a commitment to one's own pleasure, remains the motivating and sustaining force behind the new pleasures that we find in our own self-deceived state. Self-love also remains the principle we must reference in order to explain not only the specific ends we seek but also why certain self-deceived thoughts, such as those incorporated into the passions, have come to provide so much comfort apart from their initial instrumental utility.

We should next reflect more on why the acquisition of new territory for self-love should serve to entrench evil. We should think more about this in any case, but the need to do so only increases when we consider Kant's repeated use of battle metaphors throughout his discussion of evil in the *Religion* and how these metaphors both help and hinder our understanding of evil.[32] He discusses how we need to take care to discern what the enemy of virtue is and how there is a "human moral battle" that each of us has to fight (RGV 6:57 and 6:59), as well as how human beings need to stake out a victory for the good principle and a new type of moral kingdom (RGV 6:68 and 6:93). Additionally, Kant's opaque remarks about how a person effects a revolution in the will and thus overcomes the evil principle show

---

32. Phillip Rossi also calls attention to the motif of war in Kant's *Religion*. See *The Social Authority of Reason: Kant's Critique, Radical Evil, and the Destiny of Humankind*, 77–80.

a distinctive flirtation with the notion of political conflict. For example, when Kant puzzles over how someone can institute a revolution in his will despite being thoroughly "corrupt in the very ground of his maxims" (RGV 6:47), it seems implied that one key element of pulling off such a revolution is to engage in certain preparations somewhat quietly and behind the scenes. This is the only way a revolutionary faction in the public sphere can have any hope of success, and such discreet efforts also seem required if a person is to "bring about this revolution [of goodness] *by his own forces* [*Kräfte*]"[33] and make himself "ripe for a revolution" (RGV 6:47 and 6:80).[34]

I return to this point later, but as this example should show, such references to war and other elements of fractive political life can at least sometimes help us think more richly about the dynamics between moral goodness and evil. Indeed, one of the benefits of my argument that we can think about the entrenchment of evil in terms of the acquisition of new domains of pleasure is that this notion of expanding territory fits so nicely with Kant's more general reliance on battle metaphors. But these metaphors will reach their limits. Even though we readily understand how the acquisition of new geographical territory is a hallmark of success in political struggles, it is not quite clear why new turf matters in the case of evil and moral struggle. How exactly does the new territory secured by self-deception entrench self-love? Why would having more potential sources of pleasure enhance the position of the evil principle vis-à-vis the good principle? We might be concerned that the worry articulated at the beginning of this section would reemerge. Just as we asked at that point in this chapter why self-deception should be thought to entrench evil when a commitment to self-love must be presupposed by any instance of self-deception, we must again ask how self-deception and the changes it fashions in the landscape of self-love serve to entrench evil and change its root structure in

---

33. My italics.
34. As is well known, Kant is conflicted about political revolutions, as he simultaneously criticizes them in exceptionally strong terms and expresses approbation for them in practice, particularly insofar as they affirm faith in human progress (see his comments about the American Revolution in KU 5:375n). While Kant's critical remarks about political revolutions might lead one to conclude that he simply could not have them in any manner in mind when discussing a moral revolution in a human being, it is important to note that certain features of an intrapersonal moral context would remove criticisms that he articulates regarding political revolutions. For example, while the secrecy shrouding political revolutions clearly violates publicity conditions regarding social conduct, this worry cannot apply in an intrapersonal moral context in which the ruling sovereign (the evil principle) and the faction attempting to usurp that sovereign (the good principle) are seated in the same personal identity. In an intrapersonal moral context, one cannot hide intentions in the exact way that a revolutionary faction can withhold its aims from the head of the state.

some meaningful way. If a commitment to self-love is already in place, what does it matter that an agent may develop more domains that can serve as sources of gratification or pleasure?

Three points of response are in order. First, we can note that our goal has been, as noted directly above, to explain how self-deception meaningfully changes the root structure of evil. The goal has not been to strip self-love out of an account of the root of evil and replace it with a story about self-deception. As such, what we needed was a more systematic account of the effects of self-deception on self-love and the life of an agent with impure will. This has been secured insofar as we have moved beyond the simple point that self-deception facilitates or eases the difficulty of evil and have instead established that self-deception creates opportunities for pleasure and gratification in new places. In other words, we have seen that there is a real qualitative change underway in the lives of agents whose evil is necessarily connected to self-deception. Self-deception creates desires and pleasures that are distinct, as specific rationalizations can become unique sources of attachment and those who turn increasingly more to self-deception may develop a sensibility or, as Kant himself says, a "liking"[35] for evil.

Next, we can appreciate how the new territory that self-deception carves out for self-love protects a commitment to self-love from meeting with disappointment. I have tried to argue that even though self-deception initially aids the attempt to acquire particular goods in the mode of sense, over time we should expect agents to become independently attached to both their own impurity and to the specific half-truths they tell themselves, even if those deceptions no longer serve their initial instrumental purpose. Now, if this is correct, then one feature of this territorial acquisition is that self-deceived agents will be uniquely able to withstand and distract themselves from the disappointments that typically accompany dedication to self-love. If we can find pleasure or subjective value in our own impurity, and if specific distortions or misrepresentations can please us independent of their having any immediate use or value, then the failure to accomplish those ends we initially set in self-love's name will become less distressing or painful. By diversifying the pleasures available to self-love, self-deception insulates us from the vicissitudes of nonmoral life.[36] Thus, self-deception

---

35. Kant references someone who had once developed a positive liking or fondness for evil (*das Böse . . . lieb zu gewinnen*) at RGV 6:68.

36. Granted, self-deception cannot immunize against all possible disappointment or risk. As noted at the outset of this chapter, self-deception is intrinsically unstable because it presupposes a fundamental acknowledgment of the evidence available to us. We see this most strikingly in a brief remark about servility at MS 6:466, where Kant notes that the arrogant person, despite his persistent marginalization of other

shelters us, partly, not only from our own vulnerability to the law and the full truth about ourselves; it also helps shelter us from the inanity implicit within many forms of self-love.

Finally, we must note that the territorial transformation of pleasure should be understood with an eye toward Kant's remarks about the importance of avoiding temptation. Just as a person should avoid poverty and any other such "temptation to vice" or "obstacles to his morality" (MS 6:388), it is highly problematic if we put ourselves in a position where we develop distinctive, new enjoyments that are incompatible with, and that serve as a similar obstacle to, the establishment of a good fundamental maxim. Now, while we can say with confidence that Kant obviously regards it as crucial that we minimize this vulnerability to temptation, we must appreciate the full extent to which Kant fails to clarify how these obstacles hinder moral goodness. That is, it remains unclear exactly how human beings, who must take themselves as transcendentally free and thus immune from determination by natural forces, can understand their vulnerability to material conditions. Even though we can easily appreciate the sensual experience of the temptations discussed in this chapter—feeling enticed by certain external goods, enjoying the contentedness that accompanies one's own self-deception, and indulging our deep attraction to certain ill-formed beliefs—it remains uncertain how such experiences should be factored into a Kantian account of rational agency.

First, we could simply insist that such experiences have no deterministic causal power with respect to the faculty of choice. While this point would clearly be correct from a Kantian point of view, it nonetheless fails to explain even minimally how a noumenally free being should understand

---

persons' demands for equal respect, is, in fact, always on the cusp of servility (for an excellent discussion, see Dillon, "Kant on Arrogance and Self-Respect," 201). If the metrics one focuses on to acquire further evidence of one's own value bring an unexpected result—if, for example, a person finds that her neighbor suddenly enjoys more trifles—then, when the evidence becomes overwhelming, one might find that she has to now "grovel and waive any claim to respect from others" (MS 6:466). Of course, there are ways the self-deceived mitigate this vulnerability. The rationalizations characteristic of arrogance contain, like any ideology, not a rigid set of false propositions or beliefs but a distinctly patterned way of seeing the world (see Nielsen, *Marxism and the Moral Point of View: Morality, Ideology, and Historical Materialism*, 105, and Shelby, "Ideology, Racism, and Critical Social Theory," 165). Since distortion and bias fuel sins like arrogance, the arrogant person can be flexible: when trifles are no longer a conducive measure of one's worth, he can switch to some more intellectual merit. If that doesn't work, perhaps one's allotment of political power will suffice. Whatever the case may be, self-deception can go a long way toward assuring gratification and comfort in one's morally and epistemically illicit diversions, as well as in one's morally disordered character.

the moral relevance of temptation. Next, we could try to do justice to temptations by at least allowing that they can incline, push, or draw us toward acting in certain ways. But it will be difficult to stop this concession from snowballing. Once we allow that temptations in general have this power to incline, it will become difficult to explain why there cannot be a given temptation with respect to which the inclining would be so great that it turns into shoving. Or, as one philosopher has put it: "Would it not be strange if there were motivational forces that were nearly unbearable but none unqualifiedly so?"[37] Another option still for dealing with Kant's remarks on temptation may be to emphasize, as Kant himself occasionally does, how the temptations that beckon us to resist the moral law are produced or created by the human being herself (MS 6:394 and 6:405). But this strategy too will fail to explain exactly why the specific temptations we face in the empirical realm matter, as these remarks direct us to consider the agency responsible for these temptations more than they clarify the threat posed by temptations as we encounter them.

Thus, it seems at this point in the argument we can understand what Kant's views are but not how he intends to defend them. Self-deception entrenches evil by setting up new territory for self-love, and this should concern us for much the same reasons that an agent increasing her vulnerability to material deprivation, infidelity, addiction, and shady characters concerns us. What exactly these reasons are, though, is a question that numerous commentators have struggled with to little avail and with even less consensus,[38] and in the context of this discussion, we can do no better. Yet as we may recall from the outset of this chapter, this deficit may not indicate any real failing in Kant's account of the roots of evil. As warned, an explanation of a root structure has a very specific task. To ascertain how self-deception roots evil by entrenching it is part of that task, but explaining Kant's theory of freedom is not.

37. Gary Watson, *Agency and Answerability*, 64.

38. Following Frierson, recent and influential commentary that either is relevant to or directly tackles the issue of how empirical forces can fit with Kant's commitment to transcendental freedom includes Herman, *The Practice of Moral Judgment*, 77–93; Nancy Sherman, *Making a Necessity of Virtue*, 141–157; Louden, *Kant's Impure Ethics*, 143–159; G. Felicitas Munzel, *Kant's Conception of Moral Character: The "Critical" Link of Morality, Anthropology, and Reflective Judgment*, 321–345; Wood, *Kant's Ethical Thought*, 296–298 and 314–317; and Frierson's own *Freedom and Anthropology in Kant's Moral Philosophy*, 95–104. I should note that while I find Frierson's criticisms of these other views sound (see *Freedom and Anthropology in Kant's Moral Philosophy*, 68–91), I do not think Frierson's own attempt to reconcile empirical influences with Kant's theory of freedom is successful. For criticisms of Frierson's view that I largely endorse, see Ariela Tubert, "Review of Patrick R. Frierson, *Freedom and Anthropology in Kant's Moral Philosophy*," 771–772.

CONCLUSION

We have thus far discussed two ways that self-deception sits at the root of evil. As just concluded, self-deception is capable of entrenching evil. Self-deception is also properly viewed as a necessary condition of evil agency, a conclusion that was reached once we appreciated how in self-deceptive rationalization, an agent need not align herself with a moralistic or intellectual pretense for her action. Having explained the ways that self-deception enables and facilitates evil, the final question regarding the root of evil can be addressed in the next chapter. There, we will ask whether an account of self-deception can help explain Kant's argument in the *Religion* concerning the universal entwining of evil in human nature.

CHAPTER 5

Self-Deception, Dissimulation, and the Universality of Evil in Human Nature

In the mainstream literature on self-deception, one occasionally finds the suggestion that self-dishonesty is inextricably woven into human existence.[1] Prima facie, there is something highly compelling and attractive about the suggestion, as it is hard to imagine that even the morally exceptional discharge as they should the duty to be honest and transparent with themselves. For Kantians, the suggestion may be even more intriguing. As I discuss in detail shortly, because there is so little clarity in Kant's proof regarding the universality of evil, and because what little of the argument we can reconstruct has been so poorly received, it is tempting to expand our interpretive arsenal by trying to find a place for self-deception in Kant's proof for the universal entwining of evil in human nature.

This idea has deep appeal, and yet there are at least a few reasons why the intuition will be difficult to turn into a defensible argument. First, it is unclear what kind of proof could establish anything like the universal presence of self-deception. Second, it is not clear that self-deception wouldn't almost immediately lose the promise it appears to have for explaining evil's rootedness throughout human nature. Since we established in the prior chapter that self-deception is motivated by self-love, it is far from evident how a proof regarding the ubiquity of self-deception could dodge the issue

---

1. One notable Kantian who suggests this is Baron. See "What Is Wrong with Self-Deception?," 441.

of first establishing the ubiquity of wrongful self-love and impurity. In that case, the intuition noted above—that, somehow, it's easier to establish the widespread exercise of self-deception than it is the widespread endorsement of self-love—proves empty.

Third, any discussion of how self-deception relates to Kant's proof of an evil universally rooted in human nature cannot be treated as a straightforward extension of our inquiries in the prior chapter. In Chapter 4, we discussed how self-deception prompts a person to like and value an evil disposition, as well as how self-deception is implicated in the necessary conditions of a person's commitment to an immoral maxim. But when Kant discusses a universal evil throughout humanity, he often speaks in terms of an evil rooted in human *nature* or the human *species*, and this raises numerous questions. It is difficult to fathom what it could mean to think of a species as self-deceiving and what it could mean to think of a species as the kind of thing that is subject to moral evaluation. Relatedly, how the evil in a species relates to the evil in an individual is also unclear.

Fourth, even if we can shed light on the above question regarding how a species can be evil and what this should matter to an individual human being, there is a litany of other text-based problems—I outline them shortly—that emerge when one tries to develop a coherent picture of Kant's account of radical evil or an evil universally rooted in human nature. With so many obstacles preventing us from understanding much of what Kant wants to say about evil, any attempt to relate his account back to self-deception cannot avoid inheriting these difficulties.

In this chapter, I explore whether these challenges can be overcome and whether self-deception can play a role in Kant's account of an evil universally rooted in human nature. Ultimately, I argue that while Kant seems to want to retain the intuition that self-deception is a ubiquitous failure, he cannot do so if he restricts himself to the kinds of rationalizations discussed in the prior two chapters. However, in place of rationalization and self-deception as we have thus far understood them, we do find Kant alluding to a fault that bears something of a family resemblance to these phenomena, one he describes as self-concealment or dissimulation (*Verstellen*). My overall goal is to indicate where and why Kant maintains that such dissimulation is responsible for the evil in human nature, and I will try to reconstruct the argument needed to establish this conclusion as carefully as possible. I will also explain where the argument is vulnerable to objections or requires a generous reading of Kant.

To build our way up to these points, I have divided this chapter into three sections. In the first section, several preliminary issues regarding Kant's proof for radical evil have to be outlined. More specifically, we need to review three crucial difficulties that surround Kant's stated conclusion that "the human being is by nature evil" (RGV 6:32). First, we must consider what element of human agency or moral psychology must be understood as implicated in this evil. As we will see, Kant refers to evil as both a propensity (*Hang*) and a product of human choice, and it is not clear how these points fit together or in virtue of which Kant derives his conclusion regarding the universality of evil. Second, and as already noted, we need to address how the relationship between an individual human being and her species membership factors into his proof. Kant begins the *Religion* by discussing when an action or one's own character is evil as opposed to good, but we also need to explore his transition to the claim that our species, or human nature as such, is evil. Third, in addition to these issues, we need to consider what type of philosophical method Kant relies on when he offers his proof for the universality of evil. Commentators have long offered divergent answers to the question of whether Kant's proof is an empirical one that appeals to our anthropological and social character, or whether the proof is supposed to be an *a priori* one that emphasizes evil's noumenal or transcendental origin. We cannot avoid discussing this foundational dispute if we wish to proceed closer to an understanding of how self-deception or a nearby failure such as dissimulation figures into the (alleged) universality of evil.

Our task in the second section of this chapter is to extract from this discussion a set of interpretive constraints for a reconstruction of Kant's proof of an evil universally rooted in human nature. Here, my chief goal will be to explain how the different claims Kant makes concerning radical evil—how it is both a propensity and a chosen disposition, how it pertains to both an individual and a species, and how Kant seems inclined to both empirical and *a priori* proofs—can be woven into a coherent framework despite appearing at odds or at least in tension with one another. In explaining how Kant can bring together such varied claims, we will be able to anticipate and narrow the path by which his conclusion regarding a universal evil may be established. To facilitate this narrowing, I will throughout this section give a bit of a preview of how I think Kant's argument regarding a universal evil in human nature proceeds, even though a full discussion of this argument is reserved for the final and third section of the chapter.

In the final section, I give an explicit account of how, within the framework Kant sets up for himself, we are led to the conclusion that there is an evil universally woven into human nature. This is the stage at which I also return to the question motivating this chapter and revisit the intuition that self-deception or some similar failure is universal in scope and thus responsible for radical evil. While I will discuss objections to which the argument developed is vulnerable, we can establish strong evidence that Kant puts dissimulation at the root of evil and that there are good reasons for doing so.

As we work through these three sections, it is important to emphasize that there are, from a broad point of view, different goals I hope to accomplish. First, and at a minimum, I hope to explain how reconstructions of Kant's proof for the universality of evil must proceed. I aim to turn Kant's seemingly conflicting points into a coherent set of interpretive constraints on an account of a universally rooted evil, and I do this both to guide my own efforts in the final section of this chapter and to assist other commentators interested in trying to reconstruct Kant's views. On its own, developing this set of interpretive constraints is an important goal and one that can stand independently of my attempt to explain the connection between radical evil and dissimulation. As should be clear from my comments thus far, I recognize that some readers may be conflicted about whether we should embrace Kant's final conclusions regarding the universality of evil and whether the controversial points needed to develop this argument should be granted. For these reasons, I want to emphasize the extent to which the success of my first goal can stand independently of my subsequent goals of providing a precise reconstruction of Kant's proof and putting that reconstruction in as favorable a light as possible.

DIFFICULTIES WITH KANT'S PROOF FOR THE UNIVERSALITY OF EVIL

Radical Evil and the Human Species. I've already mentioned that Kant's discussions of evil in the *Religion* often make reference to its presence in the human species, and for a representative comment, we can point to Kant's remark that evil "belongs to the human being universally (and hence to the character of the species)" (RGV 6:29).[2]

Given this quick transition from a reference to universality to a reference to our species, Kant's remarks about the latter may simply seem a way of glossing a point that holds with respect to each (and any) distinct human individual. This is also the reading usually endorsed in the literature, since we find numerous commentators relying on the idea that

---

2. For the sake of clarity, I am treating separately the question of how to understand Kant's concept of the human species in the *Religion* and the question of whether Kant wishes to offer an *a priori* or empirical proof of radical evil. However, as we will soon see, these issues are related.

a reference to our species just functions as a shorthand for a straightforward type of universality.[3] But at least one rather significant drawback of this interpretation is that it would leave Kant's invocations of the species in the *Religion* strangely isolated from his other texts. Even more importantly, this interpretation would not enable us to recognize the provocative ambiguities that run throughout talk of our species.[4] I'll expand on these points so that we can get a sense of what feels missing and what, at least in part, motivates the account of evil I'll be developing in this chapter.

To begin, even though Kant speaks of the human species or our species membership in texts such as *Idea for a Universal History* or the *Anthropology*, it is left unclear, both by the text of the *Religion* and commentary on it, whether these remarks can be brought to bear on Kant's account of radical evil. In these other texts, the term "species" or *Gattung* is routinely used, yet generally within a naturalistic framework that is difficult to align with moral theory. For example, in *Idea for a Universal History*, Kant describes the species as a higher-order concept that can be used to lend narrative order to events that are otherwise governed in the manner that all natural events are, that is, deterministically (IaG 8:17). But since individual human beings tend neither to notice nor to care about this narrative connection, it is unclear how a reference to one's species character can be understood by a given human being in contexts of choice and action (IaG 8:17). We also, then, remain uncertain how Kant's more typical usage should inform a reading of the *Religion*. Now, even though it will likely prove difficult to bring Kant's many references to the species in line with one another, we should strive to find at least some common ground. The standing literature, insofar as it tends to collapse the notion of the species into a fairly ordinary notion of universality,[5] fails to do so.

Furthermore, if the biological and naturalistic undertones that would ordinarily attach to references to a species are forced to vanish into the background, this may cause us to overlook how deeply weird it is to talk about a defect that pertains to a species as such. In ordinary discourse, the species generally provides a perfected benchmark against which individual variations can be considered defects. For example, when a person describes

---

3. See, for example, Daniel O'Connor, "Good and Evil Disposition," 296; Morgan, "The Missing Formal Proof of Humanity's Radical Evil in Kant's *Religion*," 68; Formosa, "Kant on the Radical Evil in Human Nature," 239; Miller, Kant's *Religion within the Boundaries of Mere Reason*: A Reader's Guide, 37; and Allison, *Kant's Theory of Freedom*, 158.

4. Muchnik is another commentator who emphasizes the need to comment on Kant's references to our species membership. He also rightly criticizes several commentators for failing to do so. See *Kant's Theory of Evil*, 47–50.

5. I note some exceptions in the literature later in this chapter. See note 44.

a three-legged dog as defective, she is implicitly referencing how members of that species are held to the standard of four-leggedness. But the idea that a deformity is written into, and vital to, the very starting point of an account of a given species is extremely strange. Kant seems, counter-intuitively, to be suggesting that a defect should count as a norm, or that what is aberrational with respect to a species is also standard and typical. If we couple this with the fact that our human deformity is cast not just in evaluative terms but in *morally* evaluative terms—that is, if we note that attributed to the human species is not badness but *evil*—then the peculiarity of the biological reference becomes even more striking.

Along very similar lines, it's important to acknowledge that in many remarks in the *Religion*, Kant seems to discuss our species membership in a way that makes it perfectly reasonable for commentators such as Goethe and Schiller, whose criticisms about radical evil were reviewed earlier in this book, to have reacted as fiercely as they did. Maddeningly, in the very same breath that Kant tells us not to view his account as a rehashing of the notion of hereditary sin, he claims that his goal is to illuminate the germination, growth, and transmission of evil throughout the human species (RGV 6:40). Kant speaks of evil as "spreading" and "propagating" through "all generations," and how the presence of the evil principle in human life makes it such that the "germ of the good" cannot "develop unhindered" (RGV 6:40 and RGV 6:57; see also RGV 6:122). And precisely because these references are so vulnerable to being taken in a manner Kant does not want us to take them—that is, in the manner that Goethe and Schiller took them—we can see why it is important to develop an alternative explanation of how contagion, mutual infection, and collective disease belong in a discussion of Kantian evil. We need some way of making sense of these organic metaphors.

I will note one final reason to be cautious about the idea that Kant's references to the species are nothing more than references to a straightforward understanding of universality. When Kant explains why the human being is "by nature" evil, he is clearly trying to bridge distinctions that would otherwise remain exclusive. Nature, Kant insists, should not be taken as antithetical to freedom. As he puts it, the natural or "innate" component of evil consists in the fact that evil is "brought upon us by ourselves," and in how each human being "holds within himself" the "first ground" for the adoption of unlawful maxims (RGV 6:32 and 6:21).[6] Now, in light of this,

6. See also RGV 6:29, where Kant maintains that "a propensity can indeed be innate yet *may* be represented as not being such: it can be thought of (if it is good) as *acquired*, or (if evil) as *brought* by the human being *upon* himself."

it may be tempting to mentally substitute into the *Religion* "freely chosen" whenever we come across a reference to the species or to human nature. But if we were to read Kant in a way that eradicates all references to our species, or to a nature that pertains to human beings, that may lead us more to ignore than to grapple with Kant's thought, since it seems like the goal of his peculiar usage is to force us to rethink what the choice or acquisition of a corrupt fundamental maxim involves. Minimally, we should regard adoption of a first, original ground of evil as the institution in ourselves of something that functions as a "second nature" (RGV 6:41). But this second nature seems to refer not only to the ways that we can be accustomed to or comfortable with our own evil. It also suggests that the evil a person chooses cannot be regarded wholly as a product of her own idiosyncratic choice. Consider Kant's insistence that "by his maxims," the human being "expresses [*ausdrückt*] at the same time the character of his species" (RGV 6:21). This claim appears stronger than the mere point that the materials of an evil choice are available to each human being. Instead, this remark prompts the reader to consider how the human being constructs the first ground of his maxims in such a way that the evil expressed transcends that person's individuality or personal character. There seems to be a kind of dynamic quality that this second nature takes on, one wherein the actions of any human being have ramifications for the character of the species as such.

Unfortunately, we won't at this point be able to say much more about these peculiarities and nuances regarding Kant's references to the human species. Only after we have a full sense of the other relevant issues—namely, Kant's discussion of evil in terms of both a propensity and a disposition, and debates regarding whether Kant sought to offer an empirical or *a priori* proof of evil—can we take a synoptic view of our interpretive options regarding how to understand the human species and Kant's claim that there is an evil entwined in it.

Radical Evil as Both a Propensity and a Deed. Throughout the *Religion*, Kant repeatedly refers to the evil rooted in human nature as a propensity (*Hang*) (RGV 6:28–30.) In doing so, Kant appears to affirm that this evil consists of a *willingness* to be moved by self-love at the sacrifice of respect for the law. As a willingness or propensity, it would seem that the propensity to evil "*precedes every deed*, and hence is itself not yet a *deed*" (RGV 6:31),[7] and an obvious advantage of speaking about evil in this way is that it preserves an agent's freedom to abstain from immoral choices and

---

7. This passage is also cited in Allison, *Kant's Theory of Freedom*, 152.

instead orient her life around the moral law. But it must be acknowledged that at crucial points throughout the *Religion*, Kant makes or implies a very different, and much stronger, kind of claim regarding the evil in human nature. In short, he at points argues that evil does not consist in a mere propensity; rather, our evil consists in a deed because the propensity to evil is itself chosen.

Now, it should come as no surprise that Kant sees the need for this argument. Without it, there would be something wrongheaded about the idea that a propensity itself can be an object of moral evaluation. We would have guessed that the goodness or badness of any capacity or propensity depends strictly on its use, much like how the talents and traits noted in the very beginning of the *Groundwork*—wit, intelligence, and courage—are good or bad only under certain conditions or in certain employments (GMS 4:393). Moreover, unless Kant can argue that the propensity to evil is itself chosen, then this propensity will seem no different from those merely natural propensities—propensities to enjoy alcohol and intoxicants, for example (RGV 6:29n)—that plague all human beings and that precede imputation. While I am responsible for introducing intoxicants into myself and for the enjoyments, addictions, and actions I experience or take after becoming acquainted with them, I am not responsible for the bare subjective possibility of enjoying these intoxicants.

Thus, Kant is eager to demonstrate that the propensity to evil is a subjective ground of desire that can on its own be thought of as chosen and imputable. We see this in his affirmations that the *very propensity* to evil "may be represented" as brought upon the human being by herself (RGV 6:29), and that it is "through one's own fault" that this propensity exists (RGV 6:32). Quite explicitly, he argues for the imputation of radical evil on grounds that it consists of a disposition or *Gesinnung* "adopted through the free power of choice" or "grounded in freedom" (RGV 6:25). He also, shortly after noting that propensities generally precede human deeds, argues that evil be thought of as a kind of *peccatum originarium*, or original fault or sin through which a person forms a supreme maxim (RGV 6:31). Finally, the very first time that Kant uses the notion of radicality in the text[8] of the *Religion* occurs in the context of him stressing that this propensity is self-wrought:

> so we can call this ground [of willing maxims contrary to the law] a natural propensity to evil, and since it must nevertheless always come about through one's

8. As opposed to the chapter and section headings.

own fault, we can further call it a *radical* innate *evil* in human nature (not any the less brought upon by ourselves). (RGV 6:32)

In short, Kant aims to show that the propensity to evil in a person is itself an evil not because of what this tendency inclines a human being toward—namely, the endorsement of self-love—but because the propensity is itself the product of an evil maxim or choice: "This propensity must *itself* be considered morally evil" and "something that a human being can be held accountable for" (RGV 6:32). And yet in making this argument, the distinction between a propensity to evil and a commitment to or choice of evil threatens to vanish.

This upshot is, as we've just seen, confusing enough on its own, but it turns into troubling when we appreciate how this unclarity will make it difficult, if not impossible, for Kant to explain the possibilities of moral conversion or revolution, moral progress,[9] or the possible "victory" of the good principle over evil (RGV 6:68 and 6:93).[10] After all, if the propensity to evil is underwritten by a choice, the universality of the former will be underwritten by the universality of the latter, that is, a universal commitment to evil.

For these reasons, many commentators have questioned whether Kant intends to prove that we are universally disposed to subordinate the moral law to self-love or that, universally, all human beings, in fact, do so. Responses to this question vary widely. Some, such as Morgan, maintain that we must abandon any attempt to argue that all human beings are in actuality evil or have chosen evil as a disposition, claiming that the most Kant can prove is that we are quite drawn to evil.[11] Muchnik argues that we should align the propensity and the choice of evil with different aspects of the human being.[12] In this view, the propensity to evil belongs to each

9. I discuss the distinction between revolution and progress in Chapter 7.

10. As Palmquist and Steven Otterman note, the objection that Kant fails to explain how the propensity to evil is compatible with moral progress goes back to the earliest critics of the *Religion*. The anonymous reviewer to which Kant responds in the second edition of the *Religion*, published in 1794, himself raises this objection. See "The Implied Standpoint of Kant's *Religion*: An Assessment of Kant's Reply to (and an English Translation of) an Early Book Review of *Religion Within the Bounds of Bare Reason*," 90.

11. "The Missing Formal Proof of Humanity's Radical Evil in Kant's *Religion*," 100. Duncan likewise maintains that Kant is unable to show that evil is a "necessary feature of human beings" and that we should not attempt to find or reconstruct any such proof ("'There Is None Righteous': Kant on the *Hang zum Bösen* and the Universal Evil of Humanity," 138). Formosa also ends up quite pessimistic about the prospects of a proof regarding the universality of evil. See "Kant on the Radical Evil in Human Nature," 245.

12. *Kant's Theory of Evil*, 48.

human being and thus pertains to us universally, that is, qua our species membership, whereas an evil disposition, or the choice to commit oneself to self-love, is a decision made or not made by specific individuals.[13] Allison responds with an argument meant to minimize the distance between an evil propensity and an evil disposition. Allison argues that as unholy creatures, we are by definition willing to resist the moral law and instead pursue self-love. Furthermore, unholy creatures will commit some transgression, and since even the slightest transgression makes a person evil, each human being thus adopts an evil disposition.[14] Finally, Irene McMullin argues that we should understand Kant as working with a distinctive sense of responsibility and imputation when he discusses each person as having brought a propensity upon herself. In typical cases, our responsibility for deeds corresponds to some act on behalf of the agent. But in the case of our responsibility for the propensity to radical evil, McMullin argues that "we must treat this condition *as if* it were the consequence of an act."[15] Without this, we cannot, in her view, see ourselves as *agents*, as individuals who approach life guided by an "overarching maxim" and aim to have a coherent moral experience.[16]

These views have strengths as well as weaknesses. Each view has as a virtue that it confronts directly the tension looming in Kant's remarks about evil as both a propensity and a disposition. But the weaknesses are significant. Morgan essentially gives up on Kant's remarks about the propensity to evil as itself a chosen evil. Muchnik seems to end up in a similar position, as his account depends on a hard line being drawn between the propensity to evil and individual human choice of evil, with universality characterizing only the former. Allison's argument is also unsatisfying for at least three reasons. First, it rests on the empirical assumption that each human being will, in fact, choose to subordinate the moral law at one point or another, and it is highly controversial whether Kant can concede this empirical claim.[17] Second, since in Allison's view evil is found only in the

13. I discuss further aspects of Muchnik's account of evil later in this chapter.

14. *Kant's Theory of Freedom*, 156–157. Allison's view seems the same in "On the Very Idea of a Propensity to Evil" and "Reflections on the Banality of (Radical) Evil."

15. McMullin, "Kant on Radical Evil and the Origin of Moral Responsibility," 54.

16. Ibid. Note that McMullin's argument seems identical to one offered by Palmquist in both "The Implied Standpoint of Kant's *Religion*: An Assessment of Kant's Reply to (and an English Translation of) an Early Book Review of *Religion Within the Bounds of Bare Reason*," 89–90, and "Kant's Quasi-Transcendental Argument for a Necessary and Universal Evil Propensity in Human Nature." Thus, the criticisms I'll shortly note concerning McMullin's argument apply equally to Palmquist's.

17. Muchnik makes roughly the same point. See "An Alternative Proof of the Universal Propensity to Evil," 131.

maxims a person adopts, the argument does not really address or try to make sense of the evil that Kant describes as pertaining to the incurring of the propensity itself. Third, Allison makes demands on Kant's rigorism that go beyond what many of us would be willing to grant. Kant, as noted in Chapter 2, is obviously committed to the idea that both a given action and a human character must be evaluated as either wholly good or wholly evil. But Allison's argument relies on a rigorism whereby evil extends throughout an agent's *entire life*; for Allison's alignment of a propensity and a disposition to work, a human being counts as having an evil disposition even after she has carried out a moral revolution, steadfastly and success-fully committing herself to taking the moral law as her sole incentive.[18] Now, Kant does sometimes suggest that we think about rigorism in just this manner.[19] But it is possible to retain much of Kant's rigorism, as well as his ideas about how repentance for past evil deeds is a life-long project, without thinking that because a person was evil once we should also think her disposition or character as evil throughout her life. And yet without this stronger claim, Allison cannot explain why Kant is inclined to treat the propensity to evil as tantamount to an evil *Gesinnung* that applies univer-sally to any possible human being.[20]

McMullin's view, which is the last I will consider in this subsection, is one with which I have some sympathies. I will discuss these shortly, but right now the important point is that her argument is untenable in the terms it is offered. Let's reconsider her claim that we will be unable to think of ourselves as moral agents unless we view our propensity to evil "as if" it is something we incurred. To begin, we should note that McMullin's

18. As noted earlier, I explore Kant's account of moral revolutions and moral progress in Chapter 7.

19. See, for example, RGV 6:66–67.

20. Many of the difficulties that plague Allison's view likewise rule out an interpre-tation of radical evil advanced by Stephen Grimm in "Kant's Argument for Radical Evil" and Sussman in *Kant's Idea of Humanity: Anthropology and Anthroponomy in Kant's Ethics*. Grimm and Sussman each offers what Formosa describes as a "developmental argument" (Formosa, "Kant on the Radical Evil in Human Nature," 240). In this view, radical evil reflects the fact that human beings start out their lives beholden to sen-sual desire and only, over time, mature from heteronomy into a state where they are capable of autonomous rule (see Grimm, "Kant's Argument for Radical Evil," 243, and Sussman, *Kant's Idea of Humanity: Anthropology and Anthroponomy in Kant's Ethics*, 18 and 256–264). But as Formosa notes, Grimm and Sussman both rely on empir-ical assumptions regarding how human development proceeds (Formosa, "Kant on the Radical Evil in Human Nature," 243). Moreover, as Formosa points out, Grimm and Sussman rely on the assumption that the life we begin with as immature children is necessarily reflected in the choices we make as mature adults or individuals with a de-veloped capacity for practical reason (Ibid.). Since these assumptions—particularly the latter—are controversial, the developmental approach to radical evil can be put aside.

position does not follow immediately from Kant's commitment to transcendental freedom. When Kant stresses the necessary presupposition of acting under the idea of freedom for human beings, it is always within a context that emphasizes how an agent must regard her choices and the alternative possibilities that face her.[21] In other words, the "as if" in Kant's theory of freedom prompts us to assume responsibility for one's maxims, one's choices, or one's fundamental maxim or disposition; it does not require us to assume responsibility for every given propensity or willingness.

Moreover, one can easily reply to McMullin that we can best make sense of our moral standing if we *limit* an account of what features of practical agency are attributable to us. That is, it is not unreasonable to think that we should restrict ourselves to taking responsibility for the specific choices we make and that we should abandon attempts to see ourselves as in control of each fundamental aspect of our personhood. Often, we see this position in the mainstream analytic literature as one that stresses how we "can be accountable for playing the cards that are dealt us, even if we did not manufacture the cards, write the rules of the game, and so forth."[22] Philosophers sympathetic to this view would insist that mature moral agency involves seeing ourselves as in control only of our discrete acts, and they would rightly worry that McMullin doesn't explain why, in attributing to ourselves responsibility for a propensity, we are not implying that a person cannot be responsible unless she can view herself as a *causa sui* with regard to all fundamental aspects of her moral being.[23]

Finally, it is not clear how a person can reasonably view herself as responsible for a propensity to evil without some meaningful, personal story about her own role in the generation and maintenance of this propensity. McMullin emphasizes that the grounds on which we assume responsibility for the propensity to evil are "prescriptive" as opposed to "descriptive" grounds.[24] But in urging us to think of responsibility for a propensity to evil as a kind of "as if" responsibility—one that emphasizes *taking* responsibility for one's self in order to claim a sense of "self-ownership"[25]— McMullin fails to sufficiently explain why this assumption of ownership is rational. An agent needs a narrative that both addresses how she can justify to herself this assumption of responsibility and explains why her agency

21. See, for example, KpV 5:42–44, KpV 5:100, and GMS 4:452.
22. See John Martin Fischer, "The Cards That Are Dealt You," 129.
23. Ibid. Galen Strawson discusses the idea that moral responsibility involves being a *causa sui* with respect to fundamental aspects of who one is, "mentally speaking." See "The Impossibility of Moral Responsibility," 6.
24. "Kant on Radical Evil and the Origin of Moral Responsibility," 50.
25. Ibid., 60.

is indeed on the line if she seeks only to attribute to herself her maxims and chosen disposition. Without this narrative, the agent lacks a serious connection between herself and the wrong attributed to her. And without this connection between ourselves and our doings, the assumption of responsibility might be experienced as an excessive kind of self-punishment or self-flagellation, one that puts at risk the very kind of moral maturity McMullin wants to secure.

Perhaps this is all to say that Kant's decision to describe the propensity to evil as a type of choice has put his interpreters in a seemingly impossible position. I will address this worry and explain shortly how I propose making sense of Kant's claim. But first, we must outline the final issue complicating an assessment of Kant's argument for radical evil. That final issue, as noted earlier, concerns what type of proof Kant intends to rely on to demonstrate the universal entwining of evil in human nature.

An *A Prioi* or Empirical Proof of Radical Evil? As is widely recognized, Kant is thoroughly unclear about how he intends to prove an evil rooted throughout human nature. He comments that we can "spare ourselves the formal proof that there must be such a corrupt propensity rooted in the human being, in view of the multitude of woeful examples that the experience of human *deeds* parades before us" (RGV 6:32),[26] and this would seem to indicate his preference for an empirical proof. Yet at other points in the *Religion*, Kant inveighs against both empirical proofs in moral philosophy in general[27] and an empirical proof of the universal evil in human nature in particular. Kant notes, for example, that empirical judgments regarding human beings can only "corroborate" the proof he both needs and sought to give in order to demonstrate the universality of evil (RGV 6:39n). We also see his preference for a non-empirical approach when he maintains that in order to understand how the power of choice finds grounds for resisting the moral law, we must attempt to cognize this *a priori* and by way of pure, intellectual concepts (RGV 6:35).

Since the conflicting evidence regarding Kant's proof strategy cannot be explained away, my approach here and in the following section is to make at least some concessions to one side while nonetheless pushing us toward the other direction. To those who would endorse an empirical reading of the proof for radical evil, I grant that it is important to account for certain

26. This passage is also noted by others, including Muchnik, "An Alternative Proof of the Universal Propensity to Evil," 126.
27. For example, he argues that we cannot rely on empirical proofs when we are trying to form a judgment about the good or evil character of a specific human being (RGV 6:25 and 6:71). Such proofs are also out of place in trying to assess whether latitudinarianism or syncretism about good and evil character is possible (RGV 6:22).

themes stressed by empirical proofs. As we will soon see, empirical proofs often emphasize interpersonal relations, and I will likewise—albeit in a very distinct manner—explain how, in a Kantian account of evil, the way agents are situated vis-à-vis one another is morally relevant. I also grant that Kant never seems to offer an *a priori* proof in anything approximating a clear fashion, and furthermore that commentators interested in an *a priori* proof have not yet offered a compelling account of how this proof can or does proceed.[28] However, these concessions do not force us to abandon all attempts to consider the *a priori* foundation of an evil universally woven into human nature. Several commentators have instead tried to reconstruct the *a priori* proof that seems implicit in but officially "missing"[29] from the text of the

28. I have already explained why Palmquist and McMullin's proofs are problematic, and I address why Morgan's account of radical evil is unsuccessful in note 47. I also pointed out, in the previous section, difficulties with Allison and Muchnik's arguments, though it might help some readers if I note additional criticisms their views are vulnerable to. First, as both Wood and Morgan point out, Allison's proof lacks the explanatory power that we want and that was discussed at the outset of Chapter 4. In order to explain why all human beings choose evil, Allison more or less points out that evil is available to be chosen. This is obviously correct, but it is also trivially correct and unilluminating (Wood, *Kant's Ethical Thought*, 287, and Morgan, "The Missing Formal Proof of Humanity's Radical Evil in Kant's *Religion*," 81). On the basis of Allison's argument, we do not explain why evil is so attractive to all possible human beings or other factors implicated in evil. Second, in the section of Muchnik's book dedicated to his own proof reconstruction, he argues that the root of evil consists in our propensity to mistake subjective conditions of practical reason for objective conditions. More specifically, Muchnik highlights the "error of subreption" discussed in the second *Critique* (KpV 5:116) in order to argue that human beings are inclined to evil insofar as they mistake the pleasure felt in following the moral law as the source of moral goodness itself. Though this argument dodges many of the problems Allison's view suffers from, this discussion of subreption seems unable to help us explain the universality of evil or why it is entwined with human nature most generally. Kant neither appears to make the argument that all people are inclined to commit this vice of subreption, nor does he seem to argue that the vice of subreption is always present in those who adulterate respect with self-love. Indeed, the very use of the term "subreption" must prompt us to wonder how ubiquitous a failure of this type can really be, since in the nonpractical writings a subreption is generally described by Kant as a kind of "error" and thus, as opposed to an illusion, something that we can readily avoid if we are cautious (see Michelle Grier, *Kant's Doctrine of Transcendental Illusion*, 149 and 284).

29. As should be expected, it is not always clear when a commentator is offering a missing proof of his or her own as opposed to a reconstruction of Kant's stated thoughts in the *Religion*. Morgan explicitly and boldly identifies himself as offering a missing proof reconstruction, and this designation is the only one that makes sense since he doesn't attempt to connect his reconstruction to Kant's own words, either in the *Religion* or elsewhere (on this point, see Muchnik, "An Alternative Proof of the Universal Propensity to Evil," 128n22; again, I discuss Morgan's proof in note 47 of this chapter). Other commentators, such as Palmquist and McMullin, seem aptly described as either reconstructing Kant's own claims or offering on his behalf their own proofs in light of what is missing in the *Religion*. Muchnik's work (*Kant's Theory of Evil* and "An Alternative Proof of the University Propensity to Evil") also exists at this border, since he pulls both from the preface of the *Religion* and also from the second *Critique* to

Religion itself, and the argument I will develop is likely best regarded as working within this mode of Kant interpretation.[30]

To explain why I am more inclined toward an *a priori* proof for radical evil, it will help to say more about the difficulties with existing empirical proofs and what characterizes such proofs. Beginning with the latter point, the literature has tended to put in this category any proof that offers a social or anthropological account of the origin of evil. Such proofs are also described as historical, evolutionary, or teleological in method,[31] and all these descriptions are apt insofar as these proofs typically appeal to those structures of social life—humankind's need to advance culture through competition, or the need to use interpersonal comparisons in order to gauge one's own level of happiness[32]—that do not follow analytically from the concept of a human being[33] but instead emerge from an account of either the trajectory of the human species or the "natural desire"[34] for happiness.[35]

While it is beyond question that Kant thought social forces must be discussed in an overall theory of evil, it is less clear whether these forces can play a foundational role in his attempt to establish an evil universally present in the human species. More specifically, such proofs seem vulnerable to at least the following objections, some of which are already offered

complete Kant's proof in Part One of the *Religion*. Finally, Allison seems best described as simply attempting to reconstruct Kant's argument itself, as he sticks narrowly to the text of the *Religion* to explain how Kant would prove a radical evil in human nature.

30. In saying that my strategy is "best regarded" as offering an *a priori* proof reconstruction, I have chosen my words carefully. Though I think my view is most properly described in this manner, there are grounds to challenge this claim. I discuss this point in note 40 of this chapter.

31. See Wood, "Kant and the Intelligibility of Evil," 170–171.

32. I discuss these interpersonal comparisons in pages 28–29 of Chapter 1.

33. See RGV 6:32.

34. Wood, "Kant and the Intelligibility of Evil," 159. For criticisms of Wood's empirical proof, see Grenberg, "Social Dimensions of Kant's Conception of Evil," 173–182.

35. In addition to Wood, anthropological accounts of evil are also offered by Anderson-Gold, *Unnecessary Evil*, 33–52, and Louden, *Kant's Impure Ethics*, 132–133. Note that I do not mean to suggest that anthropological proofs are the only type of empirical proof one could reconstruct on Kant's behalf. As discussed in note 20 of this chapter, a type of empirical proof often referred to as a "developmental" proof is offered by Sussman, *The Idea of Humanity: Anthropology and Anthroponomy in Kant's Ethics*, 256–264, and Grimm, "Kant's Argument for Radical Evil." In addition, Grenberg develops a psychological proof, arguing that evil stems from a human being's anxiety about whether she can secure her own happiness in conditions of dependency and scarcity (see "Social Dimensions of Kant's Conception of Evil," 174n6). I have already noted my concerns about Sussman and Grimm, but insofar as the goal of this section is more to motivate a non-empirical approach to Kant's proof of radical evil than to refute every instantiation of empirical proof strategies in the literature, I will simply note Grenberg's view and put it aside.

by the literature. To begin, a proof for radical evil needs to establish more than the strong likelihood that a given person has incurred evil debts, but empirical proofs repeatedly encounter the objection that they are unable to establish a conclusion about the human being that holds universally. As Morgan has argued, such proofs seem to establish only that evil is "common and widespread."[36]

In addition, I want to suggest that a shortcoming regarding empirical proofs—particularly ones that stress a teleological angle—concerns the specific way they depend on Kant's remarks regarding human history. My worry is that these remarks often feel ad hoc in the way that a theodicy does, and I'll try to explain exactly what my concern is. When someone gives an account of God's wisdom or His design, she will run up against phenomena that seem counterpurposive, such as the presence of evil or the ability of the wicked to escape worldly punishment.[37] As a response, she might be tempted to engage in "ratiocinating (speculative) reason" (MpVT 8:264), coming up with contrived explanations that are unconvincing and subject to clear rejoinders. As Kant himself notes, a theodicy that responds to the presence of pain by arguing it is a necessary condition of animal existence faces the obvious reply that this makes God both an omnipotent creator and deeply limited in power—He can somehow create animal life but not shape the possibilities of its existence (MpVT 8:260). My concern is that if we try to make Kant's teleological account of human history up to the task of proving a universal propensity to evil, then his proof will come up short in a manner that resembles how a theodicy comes up short. Very clearly, Kant does maintain that the forces of social competition are a blessing and a curse, as they both advance culture and promote the proper ends of civilization while also threatening them. But it is not clear why, though the natural end or goal of the human species has enough purpose and force to effect at great temporal distance the competitive drive necessary for the cultivation of culture, nature did not or could not work by any other mechanism. Given this, there would be something undermotivated about an appeal to our teleological aim in an account of a universal evil. Such an appeal would give us insufficient insight into history, human life, or, of course, evil because we would remain thoroughly in the dark concerning why sociocultural forces work as they do. Now this is not to deny that, in other contexts, Kant's reliance on teleological arguments may be unobjectionable. If we are trying to explain what we may reasonably hope,

36. "The Missing Formal Proof of Humanity's Radical Evil in Kant's *Religion*," 65.
37. Kant discusses such counterpurposive phenomena in *On the Miscarriage of All Philosophical Trials in Theodicy*. See especially MpVT 8:257.

or attempting to shore up a morally laudable optimism regarding the future prospects of humanity, then, since these ends are clearly recommended by reason, it may be more justifiable to advance teleological explanations that are less than convincing from a theoretical point of view.[38] But since Kant does not offer the argument that reason has a need to morally evaluate the human species, even otherwise generous readers will worry that Kant has made an unnecessary, unsympathetic, and suspect judgment regarding the evil in human nature. In the context of an inquiry into evil, it is reasonable to demand that any teleological appeal be sufficiently well grounded and offer convincing insights into human life, and yet Kant's philosophy of history comes up short on this front.

Finally, to conclude this discussion of empirical proofs, I will briefly comment on a common path by which empirical reconstructions of radical evil are developed. Empirical approaches to evil often work both from the problem end and the solution end, so to speak. Such approaches frequently locate the cause of evil in unsocial sociability, and this point about the importance of empirical social relations is thought to gather strength from Kant's claims in Part Three of the *Religion* regarding the ethical community and its role in resolving evil. Kant frames this part of the text as an overview of how "the victory of the good principle over the evil principle" is secured (RGV 6:93), explaining that this victory depends on an "ethico-civil state" in which human beings are non-coercively united under laws of virtue for the sake of reciprocal moral advancement (RGV 6:95). If a more harmonious social life is part of the solution, this would seem to affirm that antagonistic social relations deeply inform the problem and are thus an essential component of Kant's demonstration that humanity is radically evil.[39]

I treat at length Kant's account of the ethical community in Chapter 8, and it would take far too long to re-create that discussion here. But for present purposes, it will suffice to note that in this later chapter, I develop a reading of the ethical community that effectively rules out the proof strategy described above. According to the view I develop, the ethical community functions in the *Religion* not as an indirect commentary on either unsocial sociability or the evil in human nature. Instead, and as I will later explain in detail, Kant turns to the ethical community to develop his

38. For an argument along these lines, see Adam Cureton, "Reasonable Hope in Kant's Ethics."

39. This is Wood's way of explaining the matter. See "Religion, Ethical Community, and the Struggle Against Evil," 504. Other commentators who share this view will be noted in Chapter 8.

response to a particular obstacle to moral reform, an obstacle that, while it prevents a human being from making the kind of moral progress she should, does not account for the central reason why human beings are evil as a species. If the view I outline in Chapter 8 is compelling, then Kant's reliance on the ethical community cannot be taken to reinforce an empirical proof based on the unsocial sociability of human beings.

Given the points made in this section, I doubt whether Kant really weds himself to an account of evil that emphasizes as strongly as empirical proofs do our social interactions. That said, despite the concerns and criticisms I have offered here, I do not think they are sufficient to refute decisively any and all versions of empirical proofs. My goal instead is to motivate a sustained attempt to reconstruct a formal proof on Kant's behalf. I will try to do so in what follows, and to move in this direction, we will need to revisit and take stock of the issues discussed in this section. In exploring Kant's lack of clarity regarding empirical and *a priori* proofs of radical evil, how Kant is inclined to treat the propensity to evil as also a choice or deed, and how Kant draws repeatedly on the notion of human beings as forming a species, we not only have shown how perplexing Kant's official remarks are. We have also begun to establish, at least implicitly, a set of interpretive constraints governing any reconstructive efforts made on Kant's behalf. I gather together and make explicit these constraints next, giving along the way a bit of a preview regarding how the missing proof I develop in the final section of the chapter will proceed.

A FRAMEWORK FOR INTERPRETING THE RADICAL EVIL IN HUMAN NATURE

As already noted, I will be considering the framework in which Kant can construct an *a priori* proof of the radical evil in human nature. We can now be more specific about how it seems this *a priori* proof must proceed, beginning with the fact that it should resemble transcendental argumentation. Instead of looking to experience with an eye toward the specific deeds human beings have tended to commit, the generalizations we might make about human beings on this basis, or the empirical drives and desires that an anthropologist or historian would see as governing human life, we can instead step back from these and consider those features of human agency that are necessarily operative in any context of deliberation and choice.

It also seems fair to say that Kant wants to try to isolate and attend to some non-obvious aspects of human agency. Consider Kant's claim that evil is that which "applies to him [the human being] considered [*betrachtet*] in his species; not that the quality may be inferred from the concept of his species ([i.e.] from the concept of the human being in general)" (RGV 6:32). The remark is opaque, but it seems we are instructed to do more than analyze the definition of finite rational agency that Kant usually gives. In other words, we need to consider aspects of human life that go beyond how we are inclined to self-love or how the law is objectively but not subjectively necessary for creatures like us (GMS 4:439). While not disputing that these are characteristics of the human being, we will need to take a broader view of the structures of our finite rational agency.[40] Moreover, it

40. Given these comments about how human agency will factor into my discussion of radical evil, one may challenge whether it is appropriate to describe my proof strategy as an *a priori* one. There are at least two reasons why this question arises. (1) In texts such as the *Groundwork*, Kant maintains that it is appropriate to describe the foundation of morality as *a priori* because this foundation renders morality binding for rational beings in general, as opposed to human beings in particular. Thus, it may seem that insofar as Kant's proof regarding radical evil holds only for human beings and not for rational beings of any sort, my approach can only be described as empirical. (2) In Kant's lectures on anthropology, he occasionally argues that an anthropological inquiry into human nature can treat human beings at an especially broad level of generality, one that is "constant" and not "bound to time or place" (V-Anth/Fried 25:471; for a discussion of both this passage and its relevance to Kant's theory of radical evil, I am indebted to Louden, *Kant's Human Being: Essays on His Theory of Human Nature*, 118). Kant thus appears to open up space for an empirically guided, observation-based inquiry into human nature, one that both dodges at least some of the worries that traditionally plague empirical accounts and aligns with my claim that Kant's account of human agency informs his theory of radical evil. However, even in light of these challenges, I still believe it is best, or at least less misleading, to describe my proof as *a priori* in character. Concerning (1), while Kant, in texts like the *Groundwork*, describes a moral theory limited only to humanity as one that is necessarily empirical in nature, his main worry is that we will corrupt both moral theory and our moral dispositions if we incorporate into ethics misguided assumptions or generalizations about, for example, the roles of happiness or moral feeling. His goal is not to argue that any theory developed around human beings is empirical in nature. To further substantiate this point, we need only note how the first *Critique* extracts the *a priori* elements of cognition for human beings in particular and not rational knowers as such. In this work, Kant begins with a thin account of human cognition: human knowledge is defined as having two stems—sensibility and understanding—and while these faculties may have a common root, the arrangement of intuition and intellect in human life is entirely different from its arrangement in a divine mind (KrV A15/B29). Because I argue in the remainder of this chapter that Kant relies on a similar starting point in the *Religion*—an account of human agency as opposed to rational agency most generally, and a remarkably thin description of what characterizes human agency—it is not inappropriate to argue that this text also employs an *a priori* mode of inquiry, one into human evil. Concerning (2), while Kant does maintain that there can be an anthropological account of human beings that transcends typical empirical limitations, I doubt the view I develop in this chapter aligns with what he has in mind. I have already noted that my reconstructed argument for radical evil will be developed on the basis of the dissembling character of human beings. Dissimulation is, as Kant says, "inherent in human nature itself" (Anth 7:120), but Kant also sees dissimulation less as an anthropological discovery and more as a threat or obstacle to general anthropology (Anth 7:120–121); its inherence

is clear that our inquiry must be into human *agency*, as opposed to features of our fixed physical or material existence. Unlike the bare fact that human beings have bodies, or that no person is alone in the world, we must find some universally shared element of human life with respect to which we are not passive. While I say more about this in what follows, it should be uncontroversial that we are not morally culpable for our embodiment, or for how each of us is not alone in this world. These features could never explain the self-wrought ethical wrong Kant wants to account for in the *Religion*. As Kant put it in the *Miscarriage* essay, no philosopher can chalk up evil to the mere "essence of things" while also preserving moral responsibility (MpVT 8:259).

Now, while it is crucial to avoid the idea that human beings deserve a negative moral evaluation or moral blame for features of their lives with respect to which they are wholly passive, such as their presence alongside other human beings in the spatiotemporal world, I want to explore whether there may be an interesting and overlooked moral significance in how agents necessarily respond to such conditions. If we can make the case that certain conditions of agency both obstruct the moral law and are actively sustained by a person through her deliberations and choices, then evil can be described both as universally present in all human lives and as the product of individual choice. That is to say, if reflection on experience shows that there are structures of human agency that contribute to a certain kind of moral hazard, and if no human being can deny that she uses her freedom in a way that supports and maintains these structures, then evil can turn out to be both a universal quality of human life and a deed with respect to which no individual can claim to be blameless or free of responsibility.

In the next and final section of this chapter, I will identify dissemblance or dissimulation as the only thing that seems to fit the bill for that element of human existence that Kant has in mind. Human beings across the board fail to make their motives public and available to cognition, and I also think Kant can argue that we must see ourselves as contributing to and thus bearing responsibility for this failure. But I don't want to delve into this discussion yet, and I mention it more so that the reader can have a

---

in human nature is thereby established largely in advance of anthropological research. Since Kant regards dissimulation as having a primacy that is lacking for other general anthropological findings, my own account of dissemblance and its place in a theory of radical evil thus seems to precede and work independently of a general anthropology. In light of this, I think it is probably most accurate to call my own proof regarding radical evil *a priori*, as opposed to empirical. I am very grateful to the anonymous reviewer who brought this question to my attention.

concrete concept in mind as we work through some fairly abstract points in the remainder of this section. At this stage, our aim cannot be an account of dissimulation; instead, we must explain why, given how narrowly Kant has restricted our interpretive options, we need to go in the general direction I have suggested here. In other words, we need to lay out the case for my claim that the key to reconciling Kant's varied and seemingly oppositional ways of conceptualizing radical evil and its *a priori* proof is as follows: first, we need to find an aspect of our lives as finite rational agents that interferes with our ability to act as the law demands and, second, we need to show that while we initially seem passive and innocent with respect to this feature, this veneer of passivity and innocence is at least partly illusory.

If we are able to locate this feature of human life, we will, as I establish throughout the remainder of this section, be able to address the aforementioned tensions and points of unclarity that run throughout Kant's account of radical evil.

Responsibility for Evil and Evil as Both a Deed and Propensity. If we can successfully defend the idea that some misuse of freedom is inevitable in human agency, then we will be able to improve upon the interpretation of radical evil offered by McMullin, who, we may recall, insisted that we approach the propensity to evil "as if" we are responsible for it.

As discussed, the chief difficulty with this view is that it does not try to explain why it is reasonable or personally significant to look at oneself as deserving this responsibility. Against this approach, I believe we need to show that each person can find a meaningful ground on which she can understand herself as willing her own vulnerability to evil. Now, as should be evident from the previous section of this chapter, this requirement put Kant in an incredibly difficult position, since the ground of this attribution must be found without reliance on empirical generalizations, and without us or Kant pretending to have insight into the biographical or personal history of any given human being. But we can dodge this difficulty by articulating on Kant's behalf an explanation regarding why any given person cannot sincerely deny the claim that she necessarily maintains certain problematic features of finite rational agency. If we can construct this narrative, then each person must see him- or herself as contributing to the reign of the evil principle.

I further argue that we can develop this explanation while admitting that no human being can do otherwise than make this contribution. Again, a contrast with McMullin's view can clarify my point. Whereas McMullin maintains that human beings did not, in fact, bring the propensity to evil upon themselves, I think the correct approach to Kantian evil involves arguing that human beings do indeed have a causally significant relationship to their propensity to evil, while conceding that it is a relationship they cannot avoid having. This concession is not problematic because there is no reason why the control we regard ourselves as having in ordinary contexts of practical deliberation must be echoed in every context of agency and freedom. As any number of contemporary compatibilist philosophers and Kant himself can point out, lack of control with respect to some deed does not mean that the deed wasn't willed, or that the deed isn't expressive of or a product of one's agency. What needs to be ruled out by the *Religion* is the concept of hereditary or ancestral sin, and what my argumentative strategy lets remain is a different kind of "original" sin that no individual person has the power to destroy (RGV 6:31).

Crucially, in light of this, it also becomes clear why Kant describes evil in terms that both resist and summon the notion of evil as a choice. On the one hand, evil should be thought of as a propensity because of the way it exists throughout humanity. Radical evil exists at the seat of all human activity; it is not subject to an individual's control and it remains untouched by the specifics of how a person leads her life. For these reasons, evil is similar to other stable, ineradicable propensities or abilities, such as a propensity to enjoy intoxicants. And on the other hand, Kant also speaks of how evil comes about *through* human actions, not independently of them. It is therefore a self-wrought propensity, one brought about through human deeds, whatever they may be.[41]

Moral Progress and the Species Character of a Person. If we can pinpoint those unavoidable dynamics within the exercise of finite rational agency that inform Kant's conclusion regarding the moral corruption of human beings, then we will also be able to address two other difficulties discussed earlier in this chapter: namely, how to understand the possibility of moral progress and how to make sense of the way our species membership relates to evil. As it turns out, these issues are related.

---

41. Notice that in explaining how the propensity to evil is self-wrought, it also seems that we'll be able to distance ourselves from the idea that this propensity is brought upon oneself at some specific moment in time or in a particular context. This is important for two reasons. First, Kant himself emphasizes that we should not think of evil as having an origin in time (RGV 6:41). Second, unless there is an element of ongoing failure with respect to our efforts to do what the law demands, we will not get to Kant's conclusion that there is an evil interwoven universally throughout human nature. Without this lasting quality, we would be able to root out the evil in us, and this possibility is explicitly denied by Kant (RGV 6:51). Thus, the framework I am sketching has the advantage of showing why each of us needs to be able to understand herself not only as fallen but also as *falling*, as continually implicated in a loss of innocence that results in an inextirpable form of guilt.

The only way I think we can explain the juxtaposition of progress and evil is by drawing on the traditional Kantian motif of thinking about the same object under two different aspects.[42] The object in this case is a given human being, considered both as a creature that can develop individualized or personal character and as a participant in the human species. Thus far in this book, I have not needed to use this distinction, but in order to confront squarely the question of how radical evil does not vitiate the possibility of moral goodness or moral progress, this two-aspect account of the human being is essential.

To think about myself in terms of my individualized or personal character, I must think about myself in terms of the specific practical principles I adopt. In Kant's view, such character concerns "the use of our power of choice [*Willkür*] to act according to rules or principles" (V-Anth/Fried 25:630).[43] Thus, my individual or personalized character is shaped by the moral priorities implicit in how I engage my faculty of choice, such as whether I am motivated by respect for the law alone or by some admixture of impurity that points to either an overdetermined will or the straightforward prioritization of the incentive of self-love. Now, as the *Religion* proceeds, we later learn that good character requires more than the adoption of the correct principle. Kant argues toward the end of Part One (RGV 6:47ff) that it takes effort to maintain and continually develop one's good character, and I'll discuss these important additions to his overall view in Chapter 7. At this point, however, I leave this complication aside and restrict us to the important point that individual character is governed by a person's endorsed principles.

But for all human beings, including both the best and the worst of us, there is another aspect of that life to consider, and that is its species aspect. On my reading of Kant, the species aspect of a person's existence concerns that aspect of his or her action that is identical to that of every other human being. To think about any given person qua her or his species membership or the character of one's species is to consider how, *regardless* of which practical principles any given person adopts or the decisions any given person makes, one cannot but use her or his freedom in a way

42. The clearest statement of a two-aspect approach to Kant's transcendental philosophy is Allison, "Transcendental Idealism: The 'Two-Aspect' View." As noted earlier, Muchnik likewise applies a two-aspect view to his theory of Kantian evil (*Kant's Theory of Evil*, 47–49), but I agree with Sussman that it is unclear how Muchnik relates these two aspects to one another ("Review of *Kant's Theory of Evil*.")

43. For this reference, I am indebted to Frierson, *Freedom and Anthropology in Kant's Moral Philosophy*, 62. For additional passages where Kant relies on this notion of character, see Anth 7:285 and 7:292.

that generates grounds for concluding that this person—as well as any possible person—is an active participant in a species that is evil, and that has brought upon itself a fundamental corruption. This is, I believe, the most plausible way to reconcile evil and moral progress.[44] A given human being can reform her individual character while that person's species character remains evil. I elaborate on this possibility below.

Rigorism, Good Individual Character, and Evil Species Character. I have argued that each person can be considered in terms of both his individual and species character. One way to explain and defend further this proposal is to show its compatibility with other elements of Kant's discussion of evil, including his rigorism and his stipulation against syncretism.

As we have seen, rigorism is a nuanced doctrine. Kant frames it as applying to actions and to "human characters" (RGV 6:22). Moreover, as established in Chapter 2, Kant also maintains that to apply the evaluative terms "good" and "evil," we can consider either what incentives a person has incorporated into her maxims or how that person has used her freedom (RGV 6:24).[45] Thus, there are two possible routes by which we can show that our moral concepts—good and evil—can apply to something other than individual or personal character: we can lean on how Kant restricts

---

44. The interpretation of "species" developed in this paragraph is, I believe, an advance over not only Muchnik's (see note 42 above) but also the handful of articles or books that take seriously Kant's references to the human species in his account of radical evil while ultimately failing to make good sense of these references. For example, Chris Firestone and Nathan Jacobs read Kant's references to the human species as indicating that there exists something akin to an "Aristotelian secondary substance," which substance has a power of choice "at least with regard to the determination of one's supreme maxim" (*In Defense of Kant's* Religion, 146). However, it remains extremely opaque what, according to Jacobs and Firestone, this means or how this secondary substance would relate to primary substances, that is, to individual human beings. This failure is only aggravated by the fact that the little time Firestone and Jacobs spend explaining the view is devoted to tracing its Aristotelian pedigree and to an explanation of how an Aristotelian makes sense of the distinction between primary and secondary substance. Alternatively, Tom Spencer, who takes a cue from a recent Fichtean interpretation of Kant advanced by Samuel Loncar, argues that Kant's references to the species as evil indicate that there is a kind of "shadow agent" operative in the background of human choice (see Loncar, "Converting the Kantian Self: Radical Evil, Agency, and Conversion in Kant's *Religion within the Boundaries of Mere Reason*," 365, and Spencer, "The Root of All Evil: On the Monistic Implications of Kant's *Religion*," 33). This is an interesting proposal, but since it is both highly speculative and promises to cause far more problems than it solves—it may, for example, give an explanation of what the "species" is, but it is deeply unclear how this shadow agent impacts human choice—I will not pursue it any further. Finally, Anderson-Gold notes that claims about the human species are not reducible to claims about individuals ("God and Community: An Inquiry into the Religious Implications of the Highest Good," 120), but what the species is, and how it relates to individuals, are yet again left unclear.

45. See page 57.

rigorism within "human character" and action, or we can lean on Kant's account of when the terms "good" and "evil" should be applied.

First, it's possible Kant would argue that the "human characters" he had in view when laying out rigorism early in the *Religion* were personal or individual in nature. In this case, if we wish now to consider, by contrast, the species aspect of a given human being and whether or not she is, under that species aspect, good or evil, we are permitted to develop a new and different set of criteria. It would then be open to us to establish a plausibly Kantian account of what species character is and how its moral quality is determined. Second, and as noted above, Kant gave two answers to the question of how the terms "good" and "evil" should be applied. We will call a human being good if her will is pure, *or* if it can be established that no deficient use of freedom is present in action. This disjunction preserves for Kant the possibility that in certain cases where we employ the terms "good" and "evil," we can appeal to something other than how a person has decided to arrange the incentives of self-love and respect. If there is something amiss in how a human being employs her freedom, and if that misuse takes place regardless of what practical principles are adopted, then under a certain description of that human being, evil is present.

Whether we proceed by the first route or the second, we get to the same place: if a person enjoys good character in the sense that she gives respect for the law its due and forms the appropriate moral principles, she is of good *individual character*, but, crucially, this does not mean she is good *tout court*, or good *under all possible aspects*. Since the species aspect of her existence concerns something conceptually and materially distinct from how she navigates the incentives of practical reason, a person can be considered good qua individual character without that designation seeping into an account of what her species aspect is like. Syncretism rules out good and evil *within individual character*, but this preserves the possibility that a person can have juxtaposed with respect to herself an aspect of good individual character and an aspect of evil species character.

The Significance of Species Character and an Objection. To conclude this section, I want to make sure we move forward with a firm sense of why one's species character is meaningful. As indicated above, my contention is that in considering a person qua what species she belongs to, we are attending to that aspect of her action that is identical to that of every other human being. Now, it is important to appreciate that even if my species characteristics are universally shared, this does not make them any less *mine*. The species aspect of my existence may well be described as generic, but that doesn't mean I can be indifferent to it or rationally disassociate myself from it. Since we are looking at how any human being *acts* and how she uses her freedom, a person's species aspect or membership is not something she can disidentify with or think herself passive with respect to.

As such, my species membership bears on my moral existence and my personhood in a way that certain other features of my life, ones I similarly happen to share universally with other human beings, do not. Again, unlike the bare fact that every person is physically born from other human beings, or that every person takes up some amount of space in this world, the evaluation of the species aspect of a person as good or evil is based on something we all *do*, some way that each of us finds ourselves using our freedom or our capacity to set ends. Our species membership is therefore not a biological or natural given but a way of living and acting that every person—even "the best of us," to draw on a phrase Kant uses repeatedly (MpVT 8:258, 8:261; RGV 6:31, 6:32, 6:33, 6:36)—constructs and willfully participates in. As Kant says in a section of the *Anthropology* titled "On the character of the species," "in order to assign the human being his class in the system of animate nature, nothing remains for us than to say that he has a character, which he himself creates" (Anth 7:321). The character of the human species arises from how human beings act.

To summarize, because it pertains to each and any possible person, and because it concerns the use of freedom, Kant can argue that our species aspect has moral relevance and is subject to moral evaluation, even though it does not pertain to an account of individual moral character and is not a matter of adopted ethical principles or the purity of one's will.[46] This is, I believe, the only way Kant's argument can proceed, though I want to acknowledge that this reconstruction will leave at least some readers ill at ease. Readers will rightly worry that Kant's argument proceeds by virtue of a bait and switch tactic: he leads us into a discussion of evil by stressing how it consists in personal impurity and wrongful self-love, and then, in order to justify the bold claim that evil is rooted in human nature, must switch to what some will see as a comparatively emaciated notion of evil, one that, insofar as it must pertain to any human being whatsoever, consists in how

---

46. Though there are limits to the analogy, it should now be clear that there is a sense in which the evil in the human species parallels the goodness in God. God does not enjoy a liberty of indifference or an ability to do otherwise concerning good or evil, but given the way He is governed by laws of freedom, the evaluative term "good" applies to Him. Similarly, any human being, qua her or his species membership, does not enjoy a liberty of indifference or an ability to do otherwise with respect to how he or she engages certain aspects of human freedom. Nonetheless, if this use of freedom can be shown to have a morally problematic quality, then this will substantiate the conclusion that each human being, qua her species membership, must be thought of as deserving the evaluative label "evil."

no human being can use her freedom or practical agency in quite the way that the moral law demands.

Indeed, even if we are—as I think we should be—sympathetic to Kant's claim that we bear responsibility for and must identify with certain failures regarding the use of human freedom, a critic could very easily resist extending the concept of "evil" to such failures. It may seem like a lack of moral imagination, or an invitation for equivocation and confusion, to proceed as if the concepts we use to evaluate personal character—good and evil—are the only concepts available for evaluating species character. Though I am not sure how extensively we should try to defend Kant on this point, toward the end of this essay, I will lay out some ways this worry can be addressed. Before we get to that discussion, however, it is important to explain why dissimulation is a good candidate for the failure of agency Kant has in mind. As we consider this, we'll also be able to address how dissimulation relates to the self-deceptive activity described in earlier chapters of this book.

DISSIMULATION AND KANT'S MISSING PROOF OF AN EVIL ROOTED IN HUMAN NATURE

I have so far tried to explain how Kant can redeem the concept of a species-wide original sin, and how he can do so without revoking the possibility that any given person can commit to the good principle or make moral progress. I have also given a rather substantial preview concerning how we must complete this missing proof, arguing that it requires explaining why "even the best" human being employs her capacities as a finite rational agent in a problematic way, and in a way that seems continuous with Kant's preoccupation with self-deception. To complete this proof, I will begin with an observation about the *Religion* as a whole.

While one of Kant's chief concerns—particularly in the first two parts—is, in general, an individual's propensity to corrupt respect for the law with self-love, a specific image of corruption looms especially large throughout the text as a whole. Without denying the heterogeneity of evil we can see at the surface level of human existence, the shape of evil that seems most salient to Kant is one where a person relies on action in accord with duty as a substitute for action from duty. This is evident in, for example, Kant's impassioned concerns about external or counterfeit service to God (RGV 6:151–180), the idea that a forced profession of commitments under oath can indicate heartfelt moral commitment (RGV 6:159; see also MpVT 8:269), or the general prospect of mere outer compliance with moral requirements replacing sincere faith and respect for the moral law (RGV 6:30–31, 6:36–37, 6:47).[47]

This emphasis is significant because it provides a clue to something deeper about Kant's theory of evil. Building off this concern in the *Religion* that an individual human being will exploit the gap between external action and internal principles of volition, Kant's *Anthropology* similarly emphasizes that the human species continually reinforces a division between outer action and inner motives or intentions. One of Kant's clearer statements in favor of this position, and an indication of why such practical reticence or, as Kant calls it, dissimulation, is troubling, is as follows:

> [I]t already belongs to the original composition of a human creature and to the concept of his species to explore the thoughts of others but withhold his own: a neat quality which then does not fail to progress gradually from *dissimulation* [*Verstellung*] to intentional *deception* [*vorsetzlichen Täuschung*] and finally to *lying*. (Anth 7:332)

Several points are needed in order to understand the import of this passage and how it relates to a proof for radical evil. To begin, though Kant does not explicitly define dissimulation either here or elsewhere, we can confidently extrapolate several features of it. Dissimulation involves, as Kant says within this same page of the *Anthropology*, "a concealment [*Verheimlichung*] of the good part of one's thoughts." To dissimulate is to hold something

47. In making this point, we can now, as promised earlier in this chapter, explain what is problematic about Morgan's missing proof reconstruction for radical evil. Morgan argues that radical evil stems from how human beings take a legitimate criterion for freedom—namely, "the absence of interference in one's choices by the agency of another"—as the whole of what freedom consists of ("The Missing Formal Proof of Humanity's Radical Evil in Kant's *Religion*," 81). However, the idea that the persistent threat to moral goodness rests on an interest in "untrammeled license" suffers from at least the following flaws ("The Missing Formal Proof of Humanity's Radical Evil in Kant's *Religion*," 84). First, and as Muchnik has already noted, Morgan's proof lacks any textual support whatsoever ("An Alternative Proof of the Universal Propensity to Evil," 128n22). Given this, Morgan's proposal could function only as a last-ditch effort to make sense of Kant. Second, and perhaps more importantly, if Morgan were right that maximal license and a desire for freedom from constraint were the root of all evil, then we would expect to see Kant emphasizing proposals for moral reform that focus on the advantages of social cooperation, the right of the state or other communities to regulate external actions, and the importance of recognizing that your right to be free from constraint must be balanced against the rights of others to be similarly free from interference. But as we can now see, these proposals are incongruous with and antithetical to Kant's stated recommendations. Kant's concern is not lawlessness or maximal license; rather, he is troubled by how people can use lawfulness as a substitute for moral goodness.

about ourselves back, and to put forward an appearance of oneself that is not fully accurate or representative of one's motives, intentions, or inner life more generally.

Moreover, whereas such misrepresentation[48] of oneself is sometimes purposively undertaken, Kant makes it clear that some dissimulation is invulnerable to personal control.[49] We see this, for example, in Kant's juxtaposition of dissimulation, intentional deception (*Täuschung*), and lying. Though Kant does not elsewhere restate this threefold set of failures, lying (*Lüge*) most plausibly involves trying to convince another person of a specific falsehood, whereas the other faults are different in kind. *Täuschung* seems to involve putting on a specific seeming or semblance, one that is intentional (*vorsetzlichen*) but not solely or primarily aimed at depriving other persons of truths to which they have rightful claims. Dissemblance, by contrast, seems to concern the way a person fails to accurately represent herself, whether to others or even to oneself, even if she has not formed a plan or *Vorsatz* to do so. A similar point is found in the *Miscarriage* essay, where Kant, after emphasizing that "sincerity is the property farthest removed from human nature" and that we deserve "contempt" on the basis of this, maintains that falsity (*Falschheit*) exists in us even when we are "without any intention to harm" (MpVT 8:270).

This explains what dissimulation is, but to move this account along, we need to address the potential objection that such dissembling should not be seen as inevitable or endemic to human action as such, that is, that dissimulation is something human beings can avoid with proper diligence. In response, Kant could hardly be more explicit that dissemblance is woven into the "original composition" of the human species (Anth 7:332). And given both my earlier argument about what our species characteristics involve and the broader context of this passage, we know exactly how to interpret this point. Since the species aspect of a person's existence concerns that aspect of his or her action that is identical to that of every other human being, to say that dissemblance is part of our original species composition is to say that regardless of which practical principles any given person adopts or the decisions any given person makes, dissemblance is always a component of human agency.

---

48. In the Cambridge Edition of the Works of Immanuel Kant, *Verstellen* and its variants are most often translated as "dissimulation," but "misrepresentation" (KrV A750/B778), "pretense" (KU 5:353 and Anth 7:153), and "dissemblance" (MpVT 8:270) are also used. I likewise treat these terms synonymously.

49. On this point, see Päd 9:486 and Anth 7:121. I revisit and add to these points about dissemblance or dissimulation in Chapter 6.

The reason why dissimulation or concealment is an ineradicable feature of human action can be made clearer by considering the variety of human characters that rely on it. On the one side, the worst of human beings, such as the depraved, can hide untroubledly behind external compliance (RGV 6:38), and they have this capacity only because their species character makes it available. If we were, as Kant says, some other kind of rational beings on "some other planet," then while we could act from self-love, we could not dissemble or hold back our inner thoughts and intentions (Anth 7:332).[50] And on the other side, since no morally good person can re-treat into the position of a Hegelian "beautiful soul," even the best human being must be someone who is willing to act in a public, external context and make oneself vulnerable to failure, luck, misinterpretation by others, and a general inability to translate seamlessly her intentions into em-pirical action. Thus even when an agent is not acting from self-love and exhibits purity of will, she is still exercising an agency that is tainted by dissimulation. If this is correct, then the dissemblance Kant speaks of in the *Anthropology* is not a mere capacity but an omnipresent quality of all human actions. The ineradicability of dissemblance is perhaps most neatly captured by Kant's statement that "although we are all aware of the falsity of the coin with which we trade, that coin still manages to maintain itself in circulation" (MpVT 8:270).

Had it not been for the prior section of this chapter, this would have been the moment at which some would have objected as follows: How, if we cannot avoid or eradicate dissemblance, can it be argued that we must take responsibility for it? Why isn't the demand to take responsibility for it groundless? But the answer to this question has already been secured. A person must take responsibility for dissemblance because it is a product of her agency. Each human being—again, regardless of how she manages her incentives or her specific actions—brings about seemings or appearances that fail to render fully evident the quality of her will. In other words, even the very best person *actively*—that is, through her actions—dissembles. Lack of control over dissemblance does nothing whatsoever to mitigate how the seemings a person puts forward are her own doings. Unlike those properties of human existence that we are essentially passive with respect to, such as our embodiment or the parents we are born from, dissem-blance is a person's own creation. Finally, since we established earlier in this chapter that the capacity to do otherwise is not a necessary condition

50. Cohen also discusses the possibility of "sincere aliens" in "Kant on Anthropology and Alienology: The Opacity of Human Motivation and Its Anthropological Implications."

for the attribution of a deed to a person, we can say that dissemblance is indeed an activity that any individual, when considered under the aspect of species character, must see himself or herself as liable for.

We can now begin to address remaining questions about the relationship between dissemblance and self-deception, as well as whether, in view of the species' participation in dissemblance, it is justified to conclude our missing proof with the claim that there is an evil universally present in human nature.

Concerning the former question, the alignment makes sense from taxonomical, structural, and textual points of view. Self-deception and dissemblance are both practical failures with an epistemic dimension: the former is motivated by self-love and concerns how we cognitively relate to our own immorality, and the latter involves a failed use of practical reason or agency that prevents us from making available for cognition the inner principles of volition. Structurally, there is significant overlap between what dissemblance produces and what self-deception requires. As established in Chapter 3, the self-deceptive agent directs her mental attention to some cognition that pleasingly distracts from an uncomfortable truth. Since self-deception does not manufacture pure fictions, and cannot wholly disregard epistemic norms, it requires the existence of a real, alternative, and at least minimally evidenced alternative representation, one that is comparatively more pleasing to focus on than the original object to which our attention was drawn. And since such alternatives are exactly what dissemblance makes constantly available to human beings, the self-loving agent has the materials needed for self-deception at the ready. When, for example, we can steady our focus on our external action and compliance with the law, a necessary component of self-deception is put in place. Finally, Kant himself very much stresses the proximity between dissemblance and deception, including both self-deception and deception of others. In Anth 7:332, the previously noted passage from the *Anthropology*, Kant clearly situated dissemblance as a precursor of and stepping stone to those instances in which, whether in the presence of others or alone, a person decides to put forward a more pleasing representation or semblance. Elsewhere, Kant is similarly inclined to the idea that dissemblance brings us closer to other types of moral or practical failures. The lectures on pedagogy, for instance, have Kant claiming that *Dissimulieren*, or the "holding back of one's own faults," "can sometimes be allowed, but it borders very closely on impurity [*grenzt doch nahe an Unlauterkeit*]" (Päd 9:486). The intimacy between dissemblance and further failures of practical reason is reaffirmed also by the *Miscarriage* essay, as Kant follows his remarks about the falsity that persists without any ill intent by noting that in light of this falsity, "The inclination to external deception should be all the less surprising" (MpVT 8:271).

It is important to provide further context for these comments and explain as comprehensively as possible why Kant appears to think a person might easily transition from dissimulation to self-deception and other misuses of practical reason. At least in part, the answer seems to be that for as much as Kant envisions dissemblance as a lamentable failure, he also regards it as playing an important role in helping an agent prepare for moral reform. Though he does not defend this proposal as explicitly or strongly as he should, Kant clearly sees dissemblance as a mechanism we must rely on in order to slowly acclimate ourselves to the types of demands made by the moral law; these are those behind-the-scenes efforts that take place prior to a revolution and that I noted in Chapter 4.[51] We can now add detail to this picture and conclude that before an agent can morally reform or purify her will, dissemblance is, in certain ways, necessarily indulged, exploited, and reinforced. As Kant notes in the second *Critique*:

> It certainly cannot be denied that in order to bring either a mind that is still uncultivated or one that is degraded onto the track of the morally good in the first place, some preparatory guidance is needed to attract it by means of its own advantage or to alarm it by fear of harm; but as soon as this machinery, these leading strings have had even some effect, the pure moral motive must be brought to bear on the soul. (KpV 5:152)

A similar claim, and one that connects the above observation directly to dissimulation, is made in the first *Critique*, as Kant speaks of how we must civilize ourselves before we can become moralized, and how human beings facilitate this transition in exercising a "propensity to conceal themselves," one by which we hide "true dispositions and make a show of certain assumed ones that are held to be good and creditable" (KrV A748/B776). From these points, it becomes clear that human beings are in a situation fraught with moral hazard: outer conformity must exist prior to moral development, but such conformity can also accustom us to substituting bare conformity for action from duty. In other words, an agent must leverage the dissembling feature of her agency in order to ready oneself for moral reform,[52] though in doing so, she realizes how

51. See page 111.
52. As I also note in Chapter 7, Kant does not think of this preliminary labor as *itself* a component of moral reform, as it does not necessarily bring a person closer to a decision to make the law one's sole incentive. Since the person who avoids public transgressions may settle quite comfortably into mere conformity, the behavioral work that precedes purification of the will cannot on its own be regarded as an act of moral improvement. See Chapter 7, pages 190–191 and note 23.

easily intentions can be hidden for the sake of self-love; she also learns an easy method by which she can distract herself from illicit grounds of choice, as she can rely on external action to minimize the cognitive attention she must pay to either the moral law or her own moral failure. In short, dissimulation both makes possible and jeopardizes the development of good individual character. As Kant says in a reflection noted in his copy of Baumgarten's *Metaphysics*, *Verstellung* or dissimulation allows "the circumvention of vice" and yet is also "the source of deception, hypocrisy, and cunning" (Refl 1412/15:615).

CONCLUSION

There is one last point needed to conclude this chapter, but I will preface it with a brief summary of the argument thus far. I have argued that there is a very narrow set of possibilities governing an interpretation of what exists at the root of evil: this root can only be described as a self-wrought or chosen propensity, and as pertaining to that aspect of human action that is the same for every human being, regardless of what ethical principles she adopts. Furthermore, our account of this root must do justice to the need for an *a priori* proof, Kant's interest in how our common public life is relevant to evil, and Kant's suggestion that the root of evil must refer to something different from what is typically thought to be most character-istic of the concept of the human being, namely, that we are vulnerable to both self-love and respect for the law.

Dissemblance, it seems, satisfies these constraints. It points us to a de-ficiency at the heart of finite rational agency, one that is a component of any human action whatsoever. While unavoidable in human life, dis-semblance must also be regarded as a willful and personally significant product of agency. Moreover, even though dissemblance remains a chosen and yet intractable aspect of our agency, it still has the flexibility or varia-bility we expect to see in a propensity, as individuals differ in whether they are willing to rely on dissemblance to fuel the more grievous vices of self-deceptive rationalization or wrongful self-love. Finally, dissemblance is, in Kant's eyes, closely related to self-deception. This should satisfy both our, and Kant's, intuition that an epistemic-practical shortcoming is universal in human nature. As Kant himself notes in his discussion of depravity, there is a "dishonesty . . . by which we throw blue dust in our own eyes" and which

deserves at least the name of unworthiness. It rests on the radical evil of human nature which (inasmuch as it puts out of tune the moral ability to judge what to think of another human being, and renders any imputability entirely uncertain, whether internal or external) constitutes the foul stain of our species. (RGV 6:38)

Dissimulation clearly fits the description Kant offers here of our radical evil. Dissimulation renders imputability and moral judgment uncertain because we can never be confident that the appearances a person puts forward are appropriately representative of inner volitions and intentions. Moreover, since dissimulation involves a failure of transparency with regard to not only others but also oneself, there is often an element of self-betrayal in dissimulation that is perplexing. When the transgressor and victim are present in one and the same agent, it is difficult to know at the outset exactly how this should inform our responsibility for dissimulation.

This brings us to the last issue we need to address: Even if dissimulation is a product of agency, why is the human species *evil* in light of it? An initial response to this question presents itself by way of Kant's rigorism: since dissimulation involves a failed use of agency, and since the evaluation "good" is warranted only if freedom is in every respect used properly, then a human being, considered through her species aspect, is necessarily evil. But as noted earlier in this chapter, this response would leave Kant vulnerable to the charges of equivocation, confusion, or a failure to be conceptually resourceful. Critics of the notion of a universal evil will insist that it makes little sense to describe a human being's species aspect with the same exact terms that we use to interpret her personal or individual character. Kantians, such critics will continue, should restrict the notions of good and evil to the personal character we develop by way of our chosen practical principles and find an alternative moral vocabulary for describing the faults that exist at the species level.

There is much that is compelling about this objection, but I will conclude by outlining the paths of response by which Kantians can preserve an account of radical evil. First, after noting that dissimulation is part of the original constitution of the human species, Kant claims that while this feature makes us worthy of contempt, the condemnation we heap on ourselves has a distinctive moral purpose. In having, as it were, the appropriate reactive attitude toward oneself qua her species character, she enlivens her "moral predisposition" and becomes attuned to her ability to "rise out of evil in constant progress toward the good" (Anth 7:332). Thus, the designation of evil with respect to our species is supposed to play an important moral psychological role and orient her to the possibility of moral progress. But, of course, there are weaknesses in this argument. Since Kant does not explain why good and evil form an exhaustive taxonomy of moral concepts for our species, and likewise does not entertain whether some other evaluative term could summon the predisposition for improvement in us, it is left unclear whether only the designation "evil" can have the unique exhortative pull Kant thinks is needed in human life.

Second, and more fruitfully, Kantians can stress, as Kant himself does, how the inner falsity of dissimulation is "evil and reprehensible" independently of the proximity between dissimulation and self-deceptive rationalization. Since dissimulation interferes with our ability to bring to self- or other-cognition our intentions and the inner principles of volition, such self-concealment makes it impossible for us to fully execute the "first command of all duties to oneself," namely, the command to know oneself (MS 6:441).[53] In light of this, it would seem that since any human being willfully obstructs the fulfillment of this command by dissembling, she is rightly vulnerable to the criticism that she is, considered under her species aspect, evil. As we have already seen, Kantians can insist on this while both acknowledging the ability to develop good personal character and, as I will demonstrate in the next chapter, allowing that real if limited progress can be made in the mitigation of at least some elements of self-concealment.

Third, and most importantly, to substantiate the claim that the human being is, qua one's species participation, evil, we can remind ourselves of the remarks made in Chapter 4 on the relevance of temptation to evil. Even though deep questions and problems remain for Kant's theory of temptation, we nonetheless demonstrated that a chief danger of self-deception consists in how it entrenches evil by increasing our vulnerability to further pleasures. And it is clear that Kant similarly regards dissemblance, insofar as it increases propinquity to other practical-epistemic failures, as a form of temptation. No matter how hard an agent tries, and no matter whether she has incorporated respect alone into her maxim, she cannot but make the argument that the break between external action and the quality of volition can be manipulated for the sake of one's own ends. Simply by acting, she reminds herself and others that we can easily obfuscate our intentions and hide behind mere compliance whenever it proves convenient. Dissemblance is thus a classic case of temptation, as it makes a turn to further vices both within easy reach and around every corner. Or, to return to the organic metaphors emphasized earlier in this chapter, dissemblance makes each of us patient zero for the spreading of further personological forms of evil or moral sickness. Since through our socially situated rational agency, we universally become the agents of a certain type of moral disease, constantly tempting both ourselves and others into further sin, we can hardly be a species that deserves anything other than the designation "evil."

---

53. I revisit this "first command" in the next chapter.

CHAPTER 6

Kantian Self-Cognition

I began this book by outlining some important features of Kant's non-moral and immoral psychology. In Chapter 1, we explored how concern for one's ego relates to Kant's hedonism, and on this basis generated a nuanced account of the incentive of self-love. In Chapter 2, we considered Kant's account of evil, arguing that Kant allows for different ways the incentives of practical reason can be arranged in a person with an evil will. Sometimes evil consists in the straightforward prioritization of self-love over respect for the moral law, and sometimes it can be found in an agent who strives to overdetermine her will and not give the upper hand to either of the two incentives, instead keeping them side by side. We then explored the cognitive aspects of Kant's account of evil, beginning with a broad overview of self-deception in Chapter 3 and next considered in Chapter 4 whether self-deception can shed light on the necessary conditions of evil and how evil entrenches itself in human beings. Finally, in Chapter 5, we considered how self-deception and dissemblance could be brought to bear on Kant's proof for an evil that is interwoven with human nature and that pertains to the species aspect of an individual human being.

In light of what's been accomplished, at least the following issues need to be addressed. To begin, we have not yet explored how Kant conceptualizes moral reform and the overcoming of evil, nor have we considered the achievement—namely, self-knowledge or self-cognition—that it seems should take the place of self-deception and mitigate against dissemblance. In addition, at the end of Chapter 1, I anticipated but have not yet offered my own account of how Kant's theory of moral reform turns out—pace

Hegel, Schopenhauer, Williams, and Murdoch—to require the development of a self that is interpersonally engaged, dependent on empirical conditions, and historically situated. The remaining chapters are devoted to these issues. In the current chapter—which I consider a companion to the discussion of self-deception in Chapter 3—I explore a Kantian account of self-cognition, relying on several different texts to explain our prospects for acquiring self-cognition and why Kant more than once describes the pursuit of it as leading us into a hell. In Chapters 7 and 8, I will consider Kant's views on overcoming evil and moral progress in the *Religion*. Among other goals, I aim in Chapter 7 to outline Kant's two-stage model of moral reform and show how this model is most defensible if we emphasize the self-cognitive efforts required for moral maturation. In Chapter 8, I explain why an essential component of Kant's theory of moral reform is participation in an ethical community, as well as how the ethical community relates to this book's thematic focus on the epistemic dimensions of Kantian morality.

Given this, the current chapter, with its emphasis on self-knowledge, functions as a kind of bridge between the earlier arguments of this book and forthcoming ones, as it will enable us to establish how a person can begin to transcend the epistemic failures of evil and transition to the subsequent cognitive accomplishments required for moral progress. When Chapter 6 is then taken alongside Chapters 7 and 8, they collectively explain much of what is involved in moral reform, the development of self-knowledge, and the way the latter is relevant to the former. They also document the reasons why, by virtue of my inquiry into self-cognition and moral reform, the suspicions of Kant articulated by Hegel and the other critics previously noted can be shown to be unsubstantiated.

SELF-COGNITION VIS-À-VIS SELF-DECEPTION

To begin, we should establish how the notion of self-cognition is situated vis-à-vis our earlier concepts of self-deception, rationalization, and dissemblance. For starters, this additional concept of self-cognition is required because self-cognition isn't only the counterpart of self-deception. While I certainly think that to whatever extent we avoid the self-deceptive rationalizations described in Chapters 3 and 4, we'll gain a more truthful self-cognition, not all obstacles to self-cognition derive from self-deceptive indulgence. In other words, not every deficit or lack of self-cognition stems from the positive vice of self-deception. There is much more to say about self-cognition, how to accomplish it, and why it is difficult than that self-cognition will develop as we avoid self-deception or that self-cognition is difficult because we are tempted to succumb to self-love.

To illustrate and clarify why not every lack of self-knowledge stems from self-deception, I'll note a few different cases, even though not all of these are revised to reflect our Kantian commitments and so may be only of limited use. Famously, Socrates, whom I'll mention again later, lacked much self-knowledge but was not self-deceived. We can further note a pair of cases from literature, from the writings of Jane Austen. While philosophers have widely noted that Austen's Emma provides a fine example of a person who employs self-deception—Grenberg and Nöel Carroll are among those who see this in Emma[1]—Elizabeth Bennet, on the other hand, strikes me as someone who is better described as lacking self-knowledge. Though Elizabeth does not initially grasp the extent to which she formed an overhasty judgment of Mr. Darcy, her failure does not seem to stem from an attempt to distract herself from what she herself knows to be true. She does not know herself as prejudiced and then explore possible cognitive grounds for assenting to some other interpretation of her behavior. Elizabeth, to some extent, lacks self-cognition, but she is not self-deceived or rationalizing. To set up a contrast from within a Kantian perspective, it is reasonable to think of Emma as driven by self-love or self-conceit and Elizabeth as having a remediable lack of self-knowledge and a remediable deficiency of virtue in an otherwise good character. We can also consider a more abstract case. For instance, I may not know exactly how friendship fits into a morally well-lived life, or how my friendships have impacted my moral struggles, but my lack of knowledge on these fronts does not necessarily involve self-deception or some other vice.

Finally, for further evidence that self-cognition can be hampered by something other than self-deception, we can recall from Chapter 5 Kant's concerns about dissimulation and the inevitable misrepresentation of one's intentions, as well as how Kant speaks of an inscrutability that any human being encounters when she tries to gain insight into the first subjective ground of her maxims, or tries to grasp adequately the depths of her heart (RGV 6:21). If these are grounds to expect that "even the best" human beings—a benchmark that, as noted in the prior chapter, Kant repeatedly alludes to in the *Religion*—find attempts at self-cognition difficult and to

---

1. See Carroll, *Beyond Aesthetics*, 285, and Grenberg, "Self-Deception and Self-Knowledge: Jane Austen's Emma as an Example of Kant's Notion of Self-Deception."

some degree impossible, then failures of self-cognition are not reducible to willful acts of self-deception.[2] Struggles for self-knowledge are endemic to human life. Since they will pertain to human beings of any variance of character, it is important that we explain why self-cognition is so difficult for all of us, regardless of the specific quality of one's will. In the remainder of this chapter, I will develop this explanation by working through Kant's suggestive and, ultimately, highly productive notion of self-cognition as a hell.

THE HELL OF SELF-COGNITION

This section heading, of course, refers to Kant's well-known but brief and opaque claim in the *Metaphysics of Morals* that only a "descent into the hell of self-cognition [*Selbsterkenntis*] can pave the way to godliness,"[3] which godliness I'll assume is equivalent to moral perfection (MS 6:441). The quote appears again in *The Conflict of the Faculties* (7:55), this time with reference to Johann Georg Hamann as its source but without Kant offering any immediately clear or extensive commentary. Now simply by noting this, we can see that we are going to encounter three related interpretive barriers as we get started.

First, Kant's direct references to self-cognition as it relates to morality are scattered and quick. As noted in the prior chapter, he does tell us at this point in the *Metaphysics of Morals* that self-knowledge is indispensable—again, it is the "first command of all duties to oneself" (MS 6:441)—and offers alongside this remark some examples of what we struggle to know about ourselves, such as whether the determining ground of action is pure or impure, whether my character or my heart[4]

2. As further, albeit speculative, evidence that we should consider it difficult for "even the best" persons to know themselves, we can observe that "even the wisest" human beings are said in the first *Critique* to be hindered by the inevitability of transcendental illusion (KrV A339/B397). Kant appears clearly committed to the claim that some epistemic failures haunt even the most well-intentioned persons.

3. I will use the terms "self-knowledge" and "self-cognition" interchangeably, since both are widely employed as translations of *Selbsterkenntis*. I also rely on both terms because I think each captures something a little different: "self-knowledge" sounds less technical and makes it clear that self-cognition is something human beings, in fact, care about, while "self-cognition" forces us to consider how Kant's theory of cognition more generally may relate to *Selbsterkenntis*.

4. I discuss Kant's concept of heart in "Moral Feeling and Moral Conversion in Kant's *Religion*." For our present purposes, it suffices to treat heart as interchangeable with character.

is good or evil, and the ways I am both like and unlike other agents. But there is seemingly no discussion about how I can work toward these forms of self-knowledge and little systematic effort to explain exactly what it means to call self-cognition a hell. Second, this is perhaps because Kant is not self-reliant for this idea of a hell of self-cognition but instead looking elsewhere—to at least Hamann, it would seem. Third, and to elaborate, we seem to have a case where an account of the historical record may only mystify matters further. It is extremely unclear what Kant would hope to do with Hamann's claim. Hamann's original remark is found in his brief response to Mendelssohn's review of Rousseau's 1761 novel *Julie, or the New Heloise*,[5] and Hamann's intent in his response is really to redeem emotional experience as, to quote one scholar, a kind of "existential turning point"[6] for human beings. But with Hamann seeing self-cognition as guided by more emotion or feeling than reason,[7] and with Kant's own moral rationalism being so generally at odds with Hamann's broader philosophical disposition, it's not clear how a reference to Hamann can clarify anything regarding a Kantian hell of self-cognition. There are also further unwieldy historical aspects of Kant's reference to Hamann's hell— Goldstein has argued that Hamann only came to the phrase by riffing on a random spelling mistake in Mendelssohn's review, one that enabled Rousseau's reference to a "hole" of rage to become a "hell" of feeling in Hamann, and furthermore that Kant would have been reminded of the reference when in 1796 he wrote a short declaration concerning the authorship of Theodor Gottlieb von Hippel, who also referenced this Hamann quote in a 1778 novel.[8] If we add up these points, then we can't help but feel even more uncertain of what Kant could have in mind concerning this hell of self-cognition.

5. "Chimärische Einfälle über den zehnten Theil der Briefe die Neueste Litteratur betreffend," in *Sämtliche Werke*, Band 2, 164 (N II, 164). This review from Hamann was also included in his collection *Crusades of a Philologian*.

6. Jürgen Goldstein, "Die Höllenfahrt der Selbsterkenntnis und der Weg zur Vergötterung bei Hamann und Kant," 195.

7. See, for example, Hamann's claim that Socrates's virtue of ignorance consisted not in reason but in feeling (*Empfindung*) in *Socratic Memorabilia*, N II, 73. For helpful commentary, see Gwen Griffith-Dickson, *Johann Georg Hamann's Relational Metacriticism*, 47–48.

8. Goldstein, "Die Höllenfahrt der Selbsterkenntnis und der Weg zur Vergötterung bei Hamann und Kant," 196. The Hippel novel is Volume One *of Lebensläufe nach Aufsteigender Linie*. Goldstein notes that the nod to Hamann is on page 240 of the 1859 edition, and while I am unable to confirm this, interested readers can consult the Deutsches Textarchiv to view a facsimile of the 1778 edition and a transcription out of Gothic script. In this edition, the reference to a descent into hell and its relation to self-cognition comes on page 396.

Nonetheless, we must try to clarify as much as possible the hell of self-cognition that Kant envisions, or that we as Kantians are committed to. Now, one may try to argue that the agonizing character of self-cognition stems from the discomfort that accompanies moral self-assessment. As is well known, Kant repeatedly insists throughout his ethical writings that a person should assess his moral worth not by comparing himself to other human beings but by comparing himself to the moral law (MS 6:442 and V-Mo/Collins 27:349–350).[9] Kant also insists that the moral law is a source of not only pain but also humiliation—pain insofar as the moral law has a negative effect on certain inclinations, and humiliation insofar as self-conceit and egoistic pretense are struck down by a law that engenders respect in us (KpV 5:72–74). Now, while I have no doubt that this is part of the reason why cognition of oneself is hellish, I do not think that it can be the whole story or that it is the most interesting element of Kant's story. Concerning the painfulness of comparison with the law, it is important to observe that not all hells—and perhaps not even the worst hells—stem from an encounter with something that is in itself or immediately painful. Consider, as philosophers writing on the meaning of life often do, Sisyphus. As is widely noted, the agony we feel when we contemplate Sisyphus does not stem from our imagining how terribly heavy his rock feels, how much it digs into his shoulders, or how raw his blisters are.[10] Thus, the fact that sensible desires are thwarted would not be sufficient to explain why he is in a hell. Moreover, even though Sisyphus presumably feels incomparably small in contrast to the immensity of the task before him and thus humiliated, his sense of frustration outstrips this. Even the most humble version of Sisyphus could rightly describe his situation as hellish if he were to point

9. While it is too off topic to engage the issue at length, it is important to question whether Kant really develops a full argument for this claim. At V-Mo/Collins 27:349–350, the argument seems to be that comparison of oneself with the moral law is needed because in comparing ourselves with others, we may get a false reading of how much self-esteem we ought to have. If others esteem me highly, Kant seems to argue, then I may endorse their impression of me without proper self-reflection. On its own, this is a convincing enough point. Also convincing are Kant's concerns in texts such as the *Religion* about our competitive disposition, which would make us worry that comparing oneself with others will lead to defensiveness and thus to a person overcompensating against any poor opinion they may form of her. But to get to the conclusion Kant wants regarding comparing oneself only with the law, Kant needs to discuss not only why comparing ourselves with others is problematic. He needs also to discuss whether any difficulties emerge when we try to compare ourselves with the law and how those difficulties stack up against those regarding comparison of ourselves with other people. That is, it is important to establish why the egoistic tendencies that can kick in when we compare ourselves to other persons cannot kick in when we compare ourselves with the law. I revisit this point later in this chapter (see note 24).

10. See Richard Taylor, *Good and Evil*, 322.

to additional elements of the scene, such as the unending nature of his efforts, how his task lacks a robust rational justification, and how his fate is universally threatening.

I want to submit that we will most illuminate the hell of self-cognition in Kantianism if we shift focus in a similar manner. We should distinguish between the pain and humiliation that accompanies self-comparison with the law and the hell that accompanies self-cognition as, maddeningly, a morally necessary task that is interminable, that resists decisive measurements of progress and precision, and that is morally necessary for *any* human being, regardless of her sensible desires, her character, and whether she suffers from the vice of self-deception. In other words, I'll discuss that element of agony with respect to self-cognition that stems not from being kept in check by someone or something else, such as the law, but from engaging in, voluntarily, a task that is without end and that seems to lack obvious standards for correctness. In what follows, I will focus less on hindrances, humiliation, or painfulness and more on the intellectual depths of self-knowledge and the cognitive abyss into which self-knowing puts a human being.

THE CASE FOR SKEPTICISM ABOUT KANTIAN SELF-KNOWLEDGE

Now initially, it may seem as though self-cognition puts us into an intellectual hell because Kant is deeply pessimistic about its possibility; perhaps human beings find themselves in an utterly shapeless abyss because we remain profoundly obscure to ourselves. On this interpretation, hell is about a skepticism that infiltrates self-cognition both broadly and deeply—deeply insofar as seemingly intractable difficulties are involved and broadly insofar as these difficulties pertain to every or nearly every meaningful element of self-knowledge. Though I do not believe we should endorse such trenchant skepticism about self-cognition, it's important to think about why we might be inclined to it. To lay out the case for skepticism and the textual evidence in its favor, I'll consider first its basis in Kant's ethics and then where Kant seems to affirm it in more theoretically minded writings.

The Case for Skepticism. To start, there are different aspects of moral psychology that we can think of as being resistant to cognition, most of which were explicitly noted by Kant in his reference to the hell of self-cognition in the *Metaphysics of Morals*. A person can try to know herself in terms of (1) her maxims, (2) the motive governing those maxims or the determining ground of the will, or (3) her character. If we consider each of these, we'll very likely find grounds in support of skepticism regarding self-knowledge.

(1) Kantians, simply from a scholarly point of view, have long struggled with the issue of how exactly to refer to the contents of maxims. Take, for example, disagreement about whether an agent's stated policy of trying to play tennis on Sundays at 10 a.m. when the courts are empty can even count as a maxim.[11] Given how little consensus there is in the literature concerning whether we, as wholly disinterested third parties, should see either this stated policy or some far more generic prescription about wanting to avoid long lines when possible as the person's maxim,[12] we can hardly expect that agents themselves will be adept at sifting through the variable ways they may explain—in much higher-stakes situations than tennis—what their ends and actions are.

(2) With respect to the motives that underwrite action, Kant himself points out the difficulty, so to speak, of proving a negative or trying to give decisive evidence that a certain motive is not directing action: "Who can prove by experience the nonexistence of a cause when all that experience teaches is that we do not perceive it?" (GMS 4:420). Similarly, at an earlier point in the *Groundwork*, he makes the widely cited point that

> [i]t is indeed sometimes the case that with the keenest self-examination we find nothing besides the moral ground of duty that could have been powerful enough to move us to this or that good action and to so great a sacrifice; but from this it cannot be inferred with certainty that no covert impulse of self-love, under the mere pretense of that idea, was not actually the real determining cause of the will. (GMS 4:407)

We can add to this an even more forceful point made in the *Anthropology*. Here, we find Kant expressing what appears to be an extremely strong and distinctive skepticism about the possibility of discovering, recovering, or uncovering what our motives are. He notes that often in self-reflection

> the human being comes to regard that which he has intentionally put in his mind as something that previously already must have been there, and he believes that he has merely discovered in the depths of his soul what he has forced on himself. (Anth 7:162)

---

11. This is Herman's well-known example. See *The Practice of Moral Judgment*, 139.
12. See Jens Timmermann, "Kant's Puzzling Ethics of Maxims," 46.

Complementary passages include Kant's remark that "without noticing it, we make supposed discoveries of what we ourselves have carried into ourselves" (Anth 7:133)[13] and that "he who investigates his interior easily *carries* many things into self-consciousness instead of merely observing" (Anth 7:143). These comments from the *Anthropology* would seem to paint a picture even more grim than that referenced in the *Groundwork*. Not only is it the case that the nature of motives is such that they resist cognition. It is also the case that we ourselves aggravate the degree to which they are out of reach. It seems as if despite good intentions, it is difficult if not impossible not to displace old motives and intentions with new ones and thus, to some great extent, we create for ourselves the opaque and indeterminate space of introspection.

(3) Finally, since it is difficult to see how a person could know her own character unless she understands what motives serve as the determining ground of the will or what, specifically, she aims to achieve through maximed action, it seems difficulties in self-cognition will extend to any attempt to understand herself in terms of character, or in terms of what practical principles she has wedded herself to.[14] If there is extensive overlap between these aspects of the self that we strive to know—that is, if knowledge of character would presuppose knowledge of motives and maxims—this only heightens the worry that skepticism about self-knowledge goes all the way down. Indeed, skepticism about just one element of self-knowledge will seem to be contagious and to undermine the possibility of securing other elements of self-knowledge.

The Case for Skepticism, Continued. To further articulate the case for reading Kant as profoundly skeptical regarding self-knowledge, we need only observe points from the *Anthropology* and more theoretical writings that, while framed in terms of self-cognition in general and not moral self-cognition in particular, nonetheless seem to jeopardize badly the prospects of the latter.

On Kant's view, the tools that enable access to self-cognition are limited. As he puts it, the supports that allow us to capture an image on film are much like the ones we need for self-knowledge. We need, at a minimum, bright lights and powerful cameras: we need lights because many of the representations on "the vast map of our mind" remain shrouded in darkness, and we need, as Kant says, something that can function as both a "telescope" and "microscope" so that we can both see better what's

---

13. This passage is also noted by Paul Katsafanas in "Kant and Nietzsche on Self-Knowledge," 112.

14. On this definition of character, see page 139 and note 43 of Chapter 5.

immediately before us and get a wide-angle view on ourselves (Anth 7:135). But since the tools we have are limited in power—we can only illuminate so much of the mind at once, and the telescopic and microscopic inspection of ourselves is forced to be selective in the images it "spreads out" for consciousness (Anth 7:136)—the acquisition of self-knowledge proves especially challenging.

We can also note that Kant appears to think of self-knowledge both as unnatural and in a specific sense impossible given certain features of human discursivity.[15] Different but compatible diagnoses of this failure are offered by Kant. From an anthropological point of view, we can revisit the human tendency to dissemble. In light of our discussion in Chapter 5, it should be unsurprising that Kant often notes how the workings of this tendency are particularly evident in social contexts, as we put forward, for any number of selfish or unselfish reasons, a different version of ourselves when in the company of others. But this tendency to dissemble is also highly relevant to our discussion of self-cognition because when I try to engage in introspection, I import this distinction between the observed and the observer into my own self, thus disabling my ability to notice myself in my original state (see V-Anth/Busolt 25:1437).[16] As is noted in the Busolt transcripts of Kant's anthropology lectures,

> [t]he human being, however, does not want to be observed. For as soon as one notices and sees it, he will either dissemble or deceive himself. In both cases, the human being is not the one he was at first. (V-Anth/Busolt 25:1437)[17]

The same point about our inability to observe ourselves also explains why an attempt to study the self—whether other selves, or one's own self—as an experimenter or a psychologist will necessarily fail. Kant emphasizes in the *Metaphysical Foundations of Natural Science* that we can have no hopes of ever establishing an "experimental psychological doctrine" because "observation by itself already changes and displaces the state of the observed subject" (MAN 4:471).[18] This claim aligns exactly with Kant's further remark in the Busolt lectures that

> through them [i.e. experiments] the human being can also not be observed. One can indeed make experiments with animals and things, but not with human

15. For explicit discussion of this "unnaturalness," see V-Anth/Mron 25:1218.
16. I revisit this point in Chapter 7.
17. For a similar point, see Anth 7:121 and note 40 of Chapter 5.
18. Thanks to Corey Dyck for suggesting I look at this passage.

beings, because as soon as he notices it he will do precisely the opposite of what one wants him to do. (V-Anth/Busolt 25:1437)

Given this, it would seem that self-cognition is unnatural because the character of the human species is such that it cannot really cooperate with the Socratic imperative to know thyself. And as Kant makes further clear, this inability is especially disadvantageous in circumstances where self-knowledge would be particularly valuable, such as cases where I am trying to get a handle on why some idea or occurrence has me worked up. While someone is "in the throes of affect," he cannot observe himself, and yet when "the incentives rest," "he has nothing to observe" (V-Anth/Mensch 25:857).

These problematic dynamics in self-knowing are further emphasized within the framework of Kantian epistemology. As is well known, Kant insists in the first *Critique* that all knowledge of the self can only be acquired through the self as it appears or exists in experience. But since it seems the development of moral self-knowledge needs to direct us away from the self as it appears and toward the inscrutable workings of the noumenal self—to the formulation of fundamental maxims, the determination of the will to action, or the activity of taking something as a reason—the domain in which moral self-knowledge can be found would seem epistemically off limits. We will be able to apperceive the moral self and know *that* it is active, but we seem literally out of our depths when it comes to generating robust descriptions of our motives or cognizing not merely that we act but some of the reasons *why* we so acted.

There are related ways the constraints of inner sense seem to obscure further the shape of self-knowledge. Whatever knowledge we get of the self is of the self as it appears, that is, in time. But this means I lack access to myself in pure and stable form: if I know myself only as I am mediated through time, then the grasp I have of myself will be, as Kant himself points out, constantly "in flux" (Anth 7:134). And this, he further notes, is a problem because observation typically requires "stability" and fixed conditions (Anth 7:134). Otherwise, we will be unable to isolate that which we are trying to discern from the contingent factors surrounding its observation. This is yet another reason why it is impossible for a human being to study herself in the way that she would study other objects, or as a scientist would study natural phenomena.

Finally, in light of these points, it may even seem as if Kant is inclined to, or at least must accept, the view that at least some modes of self-knowledge provide, in principle, no more access to knowledge of the self than they do to knowledge of other persons. To be sure, I'm stuck with myself in a special way, and that mere proximity may promote epistemic access to myself. But if I am restricted to knowing myself in experience, then it is unclear how knowing myself as appearance is qualitatively different from the cognition of another human being qua appearance. In other words, it may seem as though Kant will be compelled to go the route of someone like contemporary philosopher Peter Carruthers, who, very roughly, argues that there is no more transparency intrapersonally than there is interpersonally.[19]

The strain in this direction is never directly mitigated or explicitly addressed in the moral writings. When, for example, Kant discusses in the *Religion* how in lieu of direct introspective access, a person trying to confirm a moral change of heart or conversion must restrict her cognitions to those provided in the mode of sense (RGV 6:47–48), he fails to make clear how the attention I am to pay to my empirical activity is different from the attention I can pay to that of another person. I say more about this in the next chapter, but even for our present purposes, it is important to appreciate that Kant is not explicit about what it means to consider empirical conduct: Does attention to conduct involve keeping an inventory of acts that, since they are not even in conformity with duty, cannot be motivated by duty? Does it perhaps also involve keeping track of those actions that do good but are not required? Either way, since I can track empirical action with respect to both myself and others, it remains unclear why I could be equipped to make more reliable inferences about the quality of my own heart than of someone else's. It is therefore hard to see—particularly when we also consider the other issues discussed thus far—how Kant does not end up radically skeptical about the possibility of self-knowledge.

SELF-COGNITION AS SELF-INTERPRETATION

On the basis of the points just covered, it might seem Kant is highly pessimistic about attaining self-knowledge, and that this is a good explanation for why self-cognition is hellish. But in this section, I explain why I hesitate to accept this proposal and how a more hopeful interpretation of the prospects for self-knowledge can be developed.

An initial reason for rethinking skepticism is that we find in Kant a tendency toward the opposite extreme, with grounds for maintaining that we can be confident about our abilities to self-cognize. As Bernecker has

19. In making this point, I am drawing on Bernecker's claim that we should position Kant's theory of self-knowledge between that of the early moderns, who treat the self as uniquely transparent to oneself, and the Freudians and behaviorists of the twentieth century. See Bernecker, "Kant zur moralischen Selbsterkenntnis," 181.

pointed out, Kant seems to want his ethics to tell us not merely what is hypothetically acceptable or unacceptable for human beings as such. The actuality of testing one's maxims by the categorical imperative seems to require an anti-skeptical attitude toward at least one form of self-knowledge, namely, knowledge of the contents of one's maxims.[20] We can also note that in the theoretical philosophy, the stipulation against the possibility of cognizing things in themselves is fully compatible with an anti-skeptical epistemology. Thus, we must take caution before concluding that the self as it exists in experience cannot serve as a valuable source of self-knowledge. Finally, for another reason why one could rightly describe Kant as optimistic regarding the possibilities of self-knowledge, consider again self-deception. As should be clear from earlier in this book, to say that someone is self-deceived is not to say that her motives are opaque to her, or that she has trouble knowing her own thoughts and intentions. Drawing again on one of Kant's own examples, a person convincing herself that her beloved has no faults must consistently and carefully divert her attention away from particular cognitions, thus showing the extent to which a more adequate truth looks both within her clear reach and within her capacity for self-awareness. But if this is right, then self-deception *presupposes* knowledge—self-knowledge—of what it is I find adverse and wish to avoid.

Given this, Kant may seem to some to endorse views about self-knowledge at opposite ends of a spectrum. Some may see this as unfruitful vacillation or confusion, but we can read this dynamic more productively and see Kant as trying to articulate a view that draws something from the spirit of each side. On my view, then, the hell of self-cognition consists not in the deep skepticism we find at one far end but in something else. For interpreters, it's a hell of spelling out this middle ground between two extremes. For human beings striving for self-cognition, it's a hell shaped by a set of factors that make cognition of the self markedly different from other forms of cognition. As we'll now see, while we're not quite as bad off as Sisyphus, we are set rather adrift because reason cannot provide us with a fixed set of necessary and sufficient conditions for knowing the self and because of the distinctive ways self-knowledge is interminable. I'll now offer a more detailed account of where we see Kant making these points, how Kant's seemingly strong skepticism about self-knowledge can be re-read more modestly and less cynically, and how despite these first two points, we can nonetheless do justice to the notion of hellishness that pervades Kant's account.

20. Bernecker, "Kant zur moralischen Selbsterkenntnis," 164.

Earlier, we discussed how the conditions that allow objects to be known—something similar to lights and cameras in empirical cognition—impact the characteristics of a given representation. While this may initially seem to some to push Kant into an extreme skepticism, it's quite clear that implicit in this discussion is a strong sense of realism and a belief about the limits of confabulation. While poor cameras and lights might leave matters dark, and while some motive may be only obscurely represented to us, Kant does not seem to abandon the idea that there can be an independent and in principle available fact of the matter regarding the self. It may not be within our easy reach, but—and in keeping with arguments I made in Chapter 3—we are nonetheless connected to it by virtue of being creatures that are constitutively inclined to the truth.

Kant's broader theory of cognition will help us add nuance to this point. As we all know, cognition is typically of objects, objects that are independent of and that persist apart from an act of knowing. To some degree, this feature needs to extend to the case of moral self-cognition, wherein we remain tethered both practically and epistemically to the notion that it is important to try to get it right about ourselves. But notice that we can retain this end without it being our only goal, and that we can try to get it right while realizing that we will in certain ways change ourselves—change the object being cognized—as we try to grasp or make sense of ourselves. This is what makes self-cognition have such extraordinary depths, even for—or *particularly* for—the best, wisest, and most scrupulous human beings. We create these depths by being attentive self-knowers, since knowing oneself produces changes in who one is. Thus, Kant's remarks about our inability to grasp ourselves as we originally were aren't as damning as they initially seemed; we can embrace the notion that the object known is changed in the act of knowing it while resisting deep skepticism about the possibility of self-knowledge. Doing so requires thinking that self-knowledge is not merely an epistemic activity but a practical one, an activity capable of resulting in self-transformation. In trying, for example, to understand whether I have been a good friend, I can emerge from those reflective efforts meaningfully changed with respect to the kind of person I am. Moreover, we can understand self-knowledge this way because knowledge, generally, is a moving force. We typically think about this aspect of Kant in terms of knowledge of the moral law moving me to act, but we can also see it in the idea that a self-knowing agent will find herself moved or changed by her reflective labors.

Let's also revisit Kant's worry that we often "force" onto ourselves, or put into our own minds, accounts of our motives, actions, or some other element of moral selfhood. This is a concern that would seem to resist a less cynical gloss, but I propose that if we think a bit more thoroughly about why this is a risk and what causes it to occur, then we'll be able to shed new light on the structure of self-cognition in a way that mitigates this risk, while not dismissing it as a very live possibility.

I'll proceed by referencing again Kant's broader theory of cognition and start with the obvious: that in cognition, form organizes matter, and concepts provide rules for the synthesis of intuitions that would otherwise remain inaccessible to human knowers. Now, it is reasonable to think that moral self-cognition has to rely on a similar division between intuitions and concepts, or between matter and form. We want to be able to cognize the basic stuff of moral life, such as our motives, but we can't really access this raw material without conceptual assistance. At least in part, the reason for this is that there's nothing like a noncontroversial, obvious, or obviously singular description for human motives or character. What looks like an act of compassion or altruism can, in light of other considerations, seem sentimental, reckless, paternalistic or self-depreciative. And character, it is clear in the *Religion*, can be grasped only if we rely on a concept—like good or evil—that lets our temporal history be unified as a whole. I say more about this in Chapter 7, but at least one of the reasons why the goodness that follows from a revolution in the will is not immediately available for human cognition is that a self-understanding of character requires lending formal unity to, and gathering together into a whole, an extended set of experiences (RGV 6:47–48 and 6:66–67).[21] So while it is not immediately apparent to the moral self-knower what concept promises to outfit best different elements of moral psychology for self-cognition, it is nonetheless clear that human beings need to actively apply moral concepts to these aspects of themselves.

Thus, when Kant noted in the *Anthropology* how we might create, or put in ourselves, what we merely intended to discover, this limitation seems to stem from how self-knowledge is a form of self-interpretation. I settle on this language of self-knowledge as self-interpretation because Kant himself seems to rely on it, albeit very briefly. A few pages after his reference to Hamann's hell in *The Conflict of the Faculties*, and in the midst of a discussion of Moravian and Pietist interpretations of conversion, Kant mentions the epistemic quandary posed by moral conversions. Such conversions are supernatural experiences undergone by persons, and yet they cannot be

---

21. Although I disagree with Kelly Coble on numerous points, I am highly indebted to his "Kant's Dynamic Theory of Character," 59–60, because it forced me to think more about where Kant relies on an extended view of character. As noted, my own view is developed in Chapter 7.

experiences in any ordinary sense because the understanding lacks a rule or principle that can at once explain or verify their existence. Kant then explains how someone tries to come to a determination that he has become a new person, even though demonstrable proof cannot be found:

> [T]he human being has experienced a change in himself . . . which he does not know how to explain. . . . But an experience which he cannot even convince himself is actually an experience, since (as supernatural) it cannot be traced back to any rule in the nature of our understanding and established by it, is an interpretation [*Ausdeutung*] of certain sensations that one does not know what to make of, not knowing whether they are elements in cognition and have real objects or whether they are mere fancies. (SF 7:57)

Thus, though we cannot pretend to have incontrovertible evidence regarding a moral conversion, we are compelled, it seems, to engage in an act of self-interpretation to gain self-knowledge. Such self-interpreting is in one sense like empirical cognition, in that we are clearly trying to determine the truth about ourselves and taking there to be some reality to which we are answerable, and in another sense like reflective judgment, where determinate concepts provided by the understanding or reason are absent. In light of this lack, an agent simply *must* try to put something in her mind. She must search for an appropriate concept, but since reason offers no clear step-by-step manual for finding it, the attempt to self-cognize or self-interpret leaves a person in an epistemic abyss, one characterized by an absence of fixed contours and that threatens to disorient us.

Furthermore, examples of such exercises in self-interpretation may be found not only in the discussion of moral conversion shortly after Kant's reference to Hamann's hell in the *Conflict* but also, perhaps, alongside Kant's reference to this same hell in the *Metaphysics of Morals*. While it can seem as though in the latter text Kant simply fails to show what it would mean to try to self-cognize, another way to approach Kant's discussion is to recognize that the *Metaphysics of Morals* is, of all of Kant's main moral writings, the only text in which a discussion of self-knowledge as an integral component of duties to oneself is coupled with a painstakingly detailed discussion of virtues and especially vices.[22] The level of detail and

22. In the *Metaphysics of Morals*, Kant spends more time discussing vice and classifying vices—into vices of culture, bestial vices, diabolical vices, vices of savagery and of secret—than he does virtue or specific virtues. Presumably, this lopsidedness in Kant's discussion parallels an Aristotelian insight about virtue, namely, that there are many more ways to err in practical matters than there are ways to get matters right.

attention helps Kant on a number of fronts,[23] but we shouldn't overlook the (self-)epistemic benefits of this discussion of vices and virtues. In telling us, for example, that a person must strive to understand how gratitude is different from beneficence (MS 6:455), or that hatred should be analyzed more narrowly as envy, ingratitude, or malice (MS 6:458–461), Kant is essentially supplying us with thick moral concepts that facilitate self-reflection. Instead of only trying to determine whether one's heart or character is good or evil, she can *also* ask herself whether she is modest, sympathetic, ambitious, or cowardly. We can and must do this because in reflecting on myself in terms of vices and virtues, I in no way trespass on a Kantian commitment to moral rigorism. Rigorism demands only an exclusivity of good and evil, and Kant nowhere prohibits us from enriching our moral vocabulary or supplementing good and evil with additional concepts for self-interpretation. Indeed, we can't do self-interpretive work unless we have enough concepts through which we can keep trying to make sense of ourselves. Indirectly, then, the broader text of the *Tugendlehre* explains how, despite self-cognition being a hell, we can resist being disabled by this hell and proceed to self-interpret or self-cognize.

To lend further support to the notion of self-interpretation, we can consider how it may also enable Kant to address those who would protest that self-knowing is unattainable because we cannot get adequate reflective distance from ourselves. One serious worry about Kantian self-knowledge is that it seems vices or weaknesses will likely spread from the faculty of desire to the faculty of cognition. If, for example, I am generally a person who tends to be self-indulgent, it is hard to see how that failure wouldn't color my attempts to understand my actions: Won't I just indulge myself with the most favorable interpretation of my character?[24] But if I am right that

See *Nicomachean Ethics* II.1160b301–03: "[T]here are many ways to be in error. . . . But there is only one way to be correct." Note that while Kant criticizes three key elements of ancient Greek conceptions of virtue in the *Tugendlehre* (MS 6:404–405), he does not criticize the claim that vice is necessarily more multifarious than virtue.

23. For example, Kant needs an account of virtue and vice to explain how our inner freedom can be expressed, the different ways in which we can make duty an end in itself, and ways we may fail to enact duties of virtue.

24. For a somewhat similar worry, see Emer O'Hagan "Moral Self-Knowledge in Kantian Ethics." While O'Hagan puts her finger on an important problem, I worry that her own solution to it is too narrow. O'Hagan argues that the goal of moral self-knowledge is to fend off self-love and self-deception, and that in order to do so, we must attend to the "theoretical foundation of Kantian ethics" ("Moral Self-Knowledge in Kantian Ethics," 533). Her response thus resembles Grenberg's claim in her recent book *Kant's Defense of Common Moral Experience* that attention to the moral law itself is what's needed if we hope to overcome the deceptive machinations of the dear self. However, based on my arguments in this book thus far, it seems there are at

self-knowledge as self-interpretation has a provisional and experimental character, one that involves trying out different construals of ourselves, then it seems plausible that this can free self-cognition from the grips of self-love, and that defects of the will aren't necessarily transitive in a Kantian account of self-knowledge: they may or may not cloud attempts at self-interpretation. We have to go increasingly lower into the depths of self-interpretation—and this is what makes it such a hellish prospect—but if we do, Kant is confident albeit not certain we'll eventually emerge with a more adequate self-understanding, one that does not merely irresponsibly manufacture what it claims to have found or replicate moral failures as cognitive ones.

With this notion of self-interpretation in hand, we can now turn to another set of concerns noted previously, concerns that threatened to nullify any meaningful possibility of self-knowledge in Kant. Earlier, we discussed how Kant emphasizes the human tendency to dissemble and restricts knowledge of the self to knowledge of the self as it appears. We also discussed how these points might be taken as an endorsement of an extreme skepticism about the possibilities of self-knowledge, one that seems primed to lead to the conclusion that at least some forms of self-knowledge leave us opaque to ourselves in the manner that only other people are generally thought to be opaque. But in keeping with the overall strategy of this chapter, I would argue that a different reading could be pursued. It seems that instead of denying first-person authority in self-knowledge, we should take Kant to be denying that first-personal or private means to self-knowing are sufficient for self-knowledge.

least three reasons to be cautious regarding their account of the acquisition of self-knowledge. First, their argument is rather narrow due to its focus on the problems of self-deceit. But as I have established in this chapter, the needs for self-knowledge extend far past its role in remedying self-deception. Second, insofar as the moral law is the law of autonomy, O'Hagan and Grenberg are correct that knowledge of the moral law enables a form of self-knowing. But clearly, such knowledge does not provide knowledge of the self in a richly particularistic sense. To know oneself through knowing the moral law is to achieve only what Ware calls "generic self-knowledge," and such knowledge, while valuable, is only one limited type of the self-knowledge we crave ("The Duty of Self-Knowledge," 672). Third, though both rely heavily on it, neither Grenberg nor O'Hagan subject to real criticism Kant's claim that a person should judge herself or her moral worth only by way of a comparison with the moral law. As pointed out in note 9 of this chapter, Kant does not thoroughly explain why the defensive posture we assume when compared to other persons does not kick in when we compare ourselves with the law. Given his failure to argue for this point in detail, an account of self-knowledge that provides resources other than comparison with the law is essential. Such additional resources are offered throughout this chapter and the remainder of the book.

We can, for instance, insist that knowledge of the self requires thinking of self-knowledge as relational. Earlier in this chapter, we discussed how what we know about ourselves changes depending on the tools made available; I see different things, for example, when I use a telescope versus a microscope. By working further with these points, we can see the importance of knowing ourselves in different circumstances and under different conditions, and a chief way we secure this is through our interactions and relationships with others. As Kant put it in the Mrongovius lectures on anthropology, "[t]he human being must be occupied with himself the least," and "instead should be occupied with other objects, and only occasionally cast a glance at himself" (V-Anth/Mron 25:1218).[25] By considering the self indirectly and through external relationships, we somewhat disarm the tendency to dissemble and gain access to ourselves in a roundabout fashion.[26, 27] Thus, arguing that self-knowledge is restricted to knowledge of the self as it appears does not necessarily indicate a complete dismissal about first-personal privilege. Rather, knowledge of the self as it appears is knowledge of the self *in experience*, as something that is part of broader networks and something that is not well understood if viewed in isolation.[28]

This point is obviously underappreciated if not altogether missed by the rival approaches to self-cognition that are explicitly repudiated by Kant. Throughout the *Anthropology* and in other texts such as the *Metaphysics of Morals*, Kant is extraordinarily cynical about the obsessive emphasis on introspection found in Haller, Lavater, Pascal, and other thinkers guilty of what Kant sees as an unseemly form of moral hypochondria (Anth 7:133, V-Anth/Mron 15:1220, MS 6:485, and Anth 7:162). It should now be clear why they are mistaken in their accounts of what self-cognition requires. They overlook that in order for a human being to understand her life as a moral agent, she must do something other than merely try to uncover buried or lost facts about herself. Although those facts clearly matter,

25. For a complementary point, see also V-Anth/Fried 25:478.
26. This point about socially accessed self-knowledge indicates more common ground between Kant and Hamann than initially seemed available. Despite his extraordinarily difficult style, we can confidently attribute to Hamann the view that interpersonal relationships provide a route to self-knowledge that cannot be pursued on one's own. See Griffith-Dickson, *Johann Georg Hamann's Relational Metacriticism*, 62–67, and *Socratic Memorabilia* N, II 62–65.
27. For a similar view, see Makkreel, "Self-Cognition and Self-Assessment." Makkreel likewise recognizes the limits of introspection, and while he does not develop these points so that they show the importance of interpersonally situated self-knowledge, he does very briefly allude to it.
28. Here, I am influenced by Arthur Melnick, who, in *Kant's Theory of the Self*, argues that when Kant talks about knowledge of the self as it appears, we must remind ourselves that he is talking about knowledge of the self in experience. See 113ff.

self-knowledge is not in its essence a kind of internal archaeological dig but an ongoing exercise in self-interpretation. The need to look toward others as we try to discern who we are is crucial, since without it we risk incurring what Kant sees as Haller's fate. Those who rely only on introspection will likely succumb to an absorptive self-loathing opposed to respect for the law; such self-loathing is, perversely, incredibly attractive to human beings because our imaginations are most active and enlivened when faced with the obscurity of our own person, or when faced with darkness instead of "bright light" (EAD 8:327).

CONCLUSION

To conclude, I have tried to argue that Kantian self-knowledge is really a form of self-interpretation. It requires vulnerability and daringness: we must be willing to try out new understandings of ourselves, we must cultivate relationships with others, and we must be willing to find ourselves transformed through our efforts at self-cognition. We have also seen that the demands made on us are strenuous in peculiar ways, ones that can be interpreted as compelling us into a certain kind of hell. Reason cannot give us the definitive guidance we yearn for as we subject ourselves to different interpretations.[29] And because self-knowing colors the object known, it creates in us new depths in an unrelenting fashion. Finally, though I have largely emphasized the creative aspects of self-knowledge, I have tried

29. Similarly, Grenberg notes that self-knowledge is fallible and will fall short of certain knowledge. See *Kant and the Ethics of Humility*, 229. Grenberg's overall account of self-knowledge focuses mainly on the virtues needed to achieve it. While I agree that a discussion of how virtue relates to self-knowledge is important and explain my views about this relationship in this conclusion, very clearly the notion of self-interpretation is key to my account. In part, it's key because it addresses pressing questions about how, concretely, self-cognition can be achieved. However, it is also crucial because I think it helps us see how an agent can make progress in self-knowing even when she suffers from moral failings. If an account of self-knowledge has too narrow an emphasis on the fact that it requires certain virtues, self-knowledge will become restricted only to those who have already made significant moral progress. Moreover, an account of self-knowledge must give some indication of how those who are not yet good come to learn this about themselves; even if Kant's account of a revolution in the will must remain ultimately inscrutable, it's not clear that an account of how self-knowledge facilitates such a revolution should remain similarly opaque. I find the notion of self-interpretation attractive because it offers at least some clarity on this front, showing how what even the worst among us must do is break from fixed, familiar, and comfortable self-conceptions and begin trying out different self-interpretations. Because this task does not seem to require that the agent conceive of herself as striving for virtue or acting humbly, we can keep the notion of self-interpretation as morally neutral as possible when needed. For further discussion, see note 35 of this chapter.

to insist that self-knowers must remain motivated by the idea that there is some truth about themselves to which they are answerable, and that someone attempting to self-cognize cannot abandon the notion that there are ways to get himself right and ways to get himself wrong.

Now, on this last point, I want to be clear that the attempt to get it right should function more as a motivation than a prediction or characterization of what we will accomplish. This is because, as alluded to earlier in this chapter, the goal of self-knowledge is a practical one. We seek such knowledge not as part of a theoretical inquiry but for the sake of goodness; this is why in Kant's remark about the hell of self-cognition, the point is to cultivate a path to increased moral perfection, not increased knowledge. This is also why, in both our earlier discussion in Chapter 3 about how *Vernünfteln* marks a deviation of reason from its true end and again here in our discussion of self-knowledge, we find Kant noting that our goal is wisdom or *Weisheit*, a concept that has a distinctively practical cast.[30] The pursuit of Kantian self-knowledge thus calls to mind aspects of the Socratic commitment to identify with one's own ignorance. By taking his own epistemic shortcomings seriously, by striving to get it right, and by finding others to serve as interlocutors, Socrates is able to emerge, perhaps not with conclusive knowledge but at least with increased wisdom and with certain virtues, such as modesty and bravery.[31]

That Socrates is a model for the type of self-knower we should strive to emulate is particularly evident throughout Kant's logic corpus. This is likely the best set of texts for developing a sense of what Kant demands of human beings if we are to take our epistemic vocation and the pursuit of knowledge—and wisdom—seriously. From Blomberg and then through the Jäsche Logic, we find Kant lauding Socrates and emphasizing that the continued search for truth requires cultivating certain virtues and dispositions, chief among them a willingness to admit the depths of our ignorance and a sense of humility that corresponds to acknowledgment of this fact (V-Lo/Blomberg 24:72 and 24:212, V-Lo/Weiner 24:818, Log

---

30. On this point, see also note 20 of Chapter 3.

31. In the *Metaphysics of Morals*, Kant distances his account of moral catechism from Socratic dialogue (MS 6:479). This may lead us to believe that Kant would not have us look to Socrates for a model of moral progress. But as Guyer points out, the substance of Kant's discussion shows his extensive overlap with a Socratic model of moral education and transformation. Kant refers to one's teacher as a midwife, and more importantly, as Guyer points out, Kantian catechism is, in fact, deeply similar to the Socratic method in at least some Platonic dialogues. Kant relies on the idea that the pupil can be relied on to bring forward that which is already present in common human reason, and this is exactly what Socrates tries to do in *Meno* with Meno's slave. See Guyer, "Examples of Moral Possibility," 127.

9:44–45). Kant even goes so far as to say, in the Vienna Logic, that "the philosopher distinguishes himself more through the maxims of his mode of thought than through the connection of his cognitions" (V-Lo/Wiener 24:799).[32] In other words, it matters more to the pursuit of wisdom that we are guided by certain maxims—of modesty, open-mindedness, self-monitoring and self-awareness, or publicity—than that given cognitions are connected in a way that makes them true.[33] Thus, even if a Kantian approach to self-knowledge is forced to concede that despite our efforts, we may not be able to secure fully the truth, this result would not be fatal. So long as a person has been able to "uncover . . . the chasm of his

32. Similarly, in the *Miscarriage* essay, Kant emphasizes the comparative importance of being a truthful speaker over making claims that can be shown to be true (MpVT 8:267).

33. This comment about the importance of being guided by certain maxims shows that Kant is, interestingly, somewhat friendly to virtue epistemology. Now, Kant cannot be considered a pure or straightforward virtue epistemologist in light of his clear commitment to a correspondence theory of truth, a theory that emphasizes the importance of achieving an agreement between our representation of some object and that object itself (see KrV A820/B848, V-Lo/Blomberg 24:84 and 24:215, and V-Lo/Wiener 24:822–24). Nonetheless, Kant seems to lean in the direction of virtue epistemology when he attends to nonideal theory, as he spends a striking amount of time explaining how we make epistemic progress by avoiding certain vices. Thus, for example, while the discussion of error in the Jäsche Logic explains how errors happen and what characterizes them, many of Kant's remarks are about how we ought to adhere to maxims or cultivate dispositions that promote the avoidance of error. Moreover, the maxims and rules noted in the Jäsche Logic are those same maxims and rules that Kant refers us to in the practical philosophy: we are to think for ourselves, to think consistently with ourselves, and to think in the position of someone else (Log 9:57 and Anth 7:228). Thus, though the point would be too speculative to flesh out here, it begins to seem as though Kant believes in something like a unity of virtue. We must adopt certain maxims of thought in order to be good knowers with respect to the world around us, and these maxims pertain also to our efforts to know ourselves as part of a larger task of becoming or being good; increased epistemic perfection tends to go part and parcel with increased moral perfection, and epistemic and moral virtue become unified in the life of an agent who cares about her moral standing. This is just as it was with Socrates, whose sense of justice and moral rectitude seem inseparable from his intellectual talents and his dedication to reasoned debate. (Thanks to Huaping Lu-Adler for reminding me why Kant's three maxims of thought should be referenced in this chapter.)

ignorance" and has been humbled in doing so (V-Lo/Wiener 24:817–18),[34] self-knowing can meet its practically transformative goals.[35]

34. In this conclusion, I have emphasized those points where Kant's account of self-knowledge highlights the need for humility. But since I do not believe I have put excessive weight on the concept or overstated its importance in Kant's moral theory, my comments about humility should avoid those criticisms that Louden advances against Grenberg's aforementioned emphasis on this virtue. See Louden, *Kant's Human Being: Essays on His Theory of Human Nature*, 27–31.

35. One may question whether it is appropriate, as I have in this chapter, to refuse to offer specific success conditions for an act of self-knowledge. How, one may ask, can we be confident that we have achieved a correct—or at least a comparatively more correct—self-understanding? To respond to this worry, it is helpful to build on a point made in note 33 and appreciate that, according to the reading of Kant I have advanced in this chapter, any difficulties in addressing this question are similar to the ones faced by those working in mainstream virtue epistemology. Virtue epistemologists argue that a cognitive act's success derives from whether the knower is exercising the proper epistemic virtues (John Greco and John Turri, "Introduction," vii–viii). Furthermore, despite this focus on the knower's traits and her use of them, virtue epistemologists routinely agree that it would be incorrect to think that the attempt to gain knowledge can function without a desire to reach the truth (see, e.g., Linda Zagzebski, *Virtues of the Mind: An Inquiry into the Nature of Virtue and the Ethical Foundations of Knowledge*, 13). The view I have offered ends up being well aligned with these points. For even though I have tried to resist the idea that any attempt at self-interpretation requires virtues (see note 29 of this chapter), it is nonetheless the case that real improvements in self-knowledge require the development and exercise of virtues. Thus, whatever (my) Kant's prospects are for convincing us that increased success in our self-cognitive efforts will depend centrally on the presence of virtues, they can be no worse than the prospects of contemporary virtue epistemologists tackling this question with regard to cognition most generally. Indeed, the prospects for Kant's view may even be better. Kant does not, so to speak, begin with a virtue epistemology. Rather, according to the argument of this chapter, we are led to a virtue epistemic reading of Kant once we question how we can better secure knowledge of a certain kind of object, namely, knowledge of oneself. Plausibly, then, Kant is not committed to the view that the virtues are as centrally implicated in all other types of knowledge. In different epistemic domains, intellectual or practical virtues may be less salient. For example, a crucial test of self-knowledge is what we do, practically, with the knowledge we gain. It counts for little that I learned something about my character as I read a particular novel; to gain what we most properly think of as self-knowledge, I have to incorporate this understanding into daily life in a sustained, focused way. In other epistemic domains—for example, in a more ordinary context where a person simply has a cognition about a given state of affairs or an external object—it is far more difficult to demand that knowledge be used in a similarly pragmatic fashion and thus harder to displace the suspicion that virtue is dispensable to our cognitive activities. So again, because Kantian virtue epistemology is circumscribed, or deployed specifically to account for the possibility of an increased self-knowledge, it is well equipped to explain why the adequacy of a given self-cognition depends more on its being accompanied by virtues than on the particular content of that self-cognition.

CHAPTER 7

Kant's Two-Stage Model of Moral Reform

The starting point of this chapter is Kant's theory of moral reform, particularly its exposition in the *Religion*. The rough outlines of Kant's view are likely familiar to many of us. Kant argues that while a revolution consisting of a "single and unalterable decision [*Entschließung*]"[1] to prioritize the moral law over self-love is required in the mode of thought, we must expect a gradual shift in the mode of sense, that is, in a person's empirical conduct (RGV 6:47–48). In other words, moral reform must take place in two stages: a first stage of moral *conversion* in which respect for the law alone is incorporated into one's maxim[2] and a second stage of moral *progress* in which an agent attends to her behavior and actions for evidence of her new disposition. At least in part, these two stages are needed because while God enjoys a capacity for "pure intellectual intuition" that enables Him to grasp perfectly the quality of my heart, I will be able to "infer" or make a "conjecture" about my goodness only if I have evidence of a history of steady improvement with respect to my long-term conduct (RGV 6:67–68).

---

1. To further capture the drama of this revolution, Kant even refers to it in the *Anthropology* as an "explosion" (Anth 7:294).

2. I agree with Pasternack that even though he may not have held this view in somewhat earlier moral writings such as the second *Critique*, it is clear that in the *Religion*, Kant thinks a moral conversion can, in fact, be achieved and not merely increasingly approximated over time. See *Routledge Philosophy Guidebook to Kant on* Religion within the Boundaries of Mere Reason, 143–144.

The concern that drives this chapter is whether the *Religion* offers a defensible account of Kantian moral reform, and the structure of this chapter is as follows. I begin by questioning whether Kant, and his readers, have justified the claim that individual moral reform consists of two stages and whether they have explained how the stages are distinguished from one another. I show that these points have not yet been adequately considered, and I lay out three complementary arguments regarding where we can see this failure. If we try to articulate the difference between the kinds of moral efforts involved in these two stages, or if we even just try to envision the efforts within one of these stages alone, we will run into difficulties with Kant's account as it is currently understood.

In light of these problems, I then propose a way to reframe Kant's two-stage account of moral reform. I argue that Kant's account of moral conversion is most plausible if we interpret the decision (*Entschließung*) to endorse the moral law in terms of a commitment,[3] and if we interpret the progressive personal efforts brought on by a moral revolution more in terms of cognitive, as opposed to volitional, labor. I show that this reframing gives us a way to explain why there are two stages of moral reform and how these two stages differ. As such, this reframing also provides a set of rejoinders to those three arguments that initially threatened the defensibility of Kant's two-stage account. Toward the end of this chapter, I make the following additional points. I argue that while very different in tone, my reframing can be rendered compatible with standing interpretations of Kantian moral reform. I also discuss ways my argument, though it focuses on Kant's *Religion*, can gain further support from the *Doctrine of Virtue*.

To bring this introduction to a close, I will briefly note this chapter's role in this book more generally, as well as how it is connected to earlier chapters. Given this book's overall focus on evil and how an individual can overcome it, this chapter's importance is obvious. Given also certain gaps from earlier chapters, this discussion of moral reform takes on further importance. For example, in Chapter 5, I noted that while Kant, in

---

3. I explain what exactly I mean by a commitment later in the chapter, but, in brief, a main reason why I find the concept helpful is that it straddles phenomenal and noumenal perspectives on choice. As I discuss shortly, commitments are distinctive because they both require a specific temporal trajectory—we have to prepare for, make, and then follow through on a commitment—and jettison or transcend a typically linear, temporal progression in important ways. Kant himself both insists on the noumenal character of choice and demands that we also think about the dynamics of choice in phenomenal terms, and if we want this tension to be at least as productive as it is mystifying, then we need, I believe, the notion of a commitment to clarify his view. Thanks to both an anonymous reviewer and Paul Guyer for prompting me to develop this point.

the beginning of the *Religion*, tends to treat an individual's moral goodness simply as a matter of the principle she has personally endorsed, his view toward the end of Part One gets more complicated. It becomes clear that no human being can treat her attitude toward the moral law as static, and that something more is required of an individual to further her moral development; that something more must be clarified. In Chapter 6, and in light of this book's earlier discussions of self-deception and its connection to evil, we began to think through, from the position of Kant's broader corpus, the possibilities for a self-knowledge that is clearly indispensable to moral growth. We'll see that this attention to our cognitive powers is required to make sense of what Kant, specifically in the context of the two-stage model in the *Religion*, says about moral reform. Finally, at the outset of the book, I noted the frequent worry in the history of philosophy that Kant's ethics can't allow a person to develop anything other than a thin moral identity as a good person. I've already offered some arguments about the importance of social relationships to self-cognition in the prior chapter, but toward the end of this chapter and throughout Chapter 8, I offer further grounds for dismissing this recurring criticism by attending closely to how empirical, social, and historical conditions figure into Kant's account of moral progress.

THREE DIFFICULTIES WITH KANT'S TWO-STAGE ACCOUNT OF MORAL REFORM

(1) The first problem is as follows: neither Kant himself, nor many of his commentators, has been sufficiently explicit about how the moral failures that characterize an evil will, and thus precede a reversal of one's supreme maxim, are different from the moral shortcomings toward which a person's postconversion practical efforts are directed.

Taking just the briefest note of certain features of Kant's discussion, it should not surprise us that Kant is at least somewhat vulnerable to this objection. Even though we must be careful with how we interpret references to inclinations in the *Religion*,[4] we can easily note how Kant uses the language of a struggle against temptation to describe both (i) the nature of evil and (ii) how postconversion moral progress is sculpted. For example, and as emphasized in Chapter 2, when discussing (i) the nature of evil

---

4. It is standard practice to remind readers that inclinations are "in themselves" good and thus not to be identified with the root of evil (RGV 6:58). See Allison, *Kant's Theory of Freedom*, 151–152.

and the three stages of evil in Part One of the *Religion*, evil is presented in terms of a failure to acknowledge the extent to which we are inclined to adulterate the moral incentive with self-love and succumb to the "temptation of the flesh" (RGV 6:44; see also RGV 6:29). Concerning (ii), and our postconversion moral progress, we find a seemingly similar theme. In this case, after prioritizing the moral law, Kant claims that a morally reborn agent should attend to the gradual betterment of her empirical character by attempting to "gain an upper hand over the senses in time"[5] and thus demonstrate an increasing manifest compliance with the law (RGV 6:48).

In addition to this idea of a struggle with sensible inclination, Kant also seems to blur the divide between (i) and (ii) at points where the episodic or exception-making character of evil is emphasized. Kant is clear that a man is evil insofar as he asks for an exception "just this once" (GMS 4:424) and insofar as he wills only "occasional" deviations from the law (RGV 6:32). But it is not sufficiently clear how these deviations would differ from those that we should expect to persist throughout one's gradual reform within the mode of sense. Are the failures of practical reason that characterize evil qualitatively different from those failures that are compatible with an overall trajectory of moral progress? Are the failures of the same kind, but just less frequent or perhaps more honestly evaluated? Another option still would be that the failures of the evil man and the agent making postconversion progress are of the same kind, and that the two stages of moral reform are differentiated not by what agents do wrong, but by the kind of right they do or the type of goodness they exhibit in between episodes of wrongdoing. Perhaps the evil man is generally content to not violate strict duty, whereas the man who prioritizes the moral law also strives to be virtuous and to limit the maxims of imperfect duty only by practical love (MS 6:390).

Admittedly, Kant's failure to sift through these questions in the *Religion* is not decisive. Even if he fails to address these questions, and even if his remarks on moral reform emphasize an ongoing theme of temptation and fitful struggle, one can still argue on his behalf that an important distinction can be made out between the failures of evil and the imperfections compatible with moral progress. The distinction would be one of unprincipled versus principled struggle. Those who have endorsed the moral law may still struggle empirically and occasionally fail to conduct themselves appropriately, but surely we can at least insist on a distinction between the kind of principled struggle against temptation that marks betterment and

5. Translation slightly modified.

the unprincipled, haphazard struggle with temptation that characterizes evil. In other words, the difference we are looking for would be formal, with the chaotic quality of evil contrasted with the principled development of moral strength in empirical conduct. As further support for this proposal, one could point to the fact that Kant, with at least some frequency, describes the moral work done within the mode of thought and then in the mode of sense in terms of purification and strengthening, respectively. While impurity must be removed all at once so as to instantiate a will motivated by the moral law alone, *strength* of this will, or the removal of frailty or "weakness in complying with adopted maxims," seems to grow only gradually (RGV 6:29). Just as a person will talk about needing to be rid of the flu virus before she can begin to build her strength back up, so we should regard moral health: we fundamentally convert, casting off evil in a revolutionary purification of the will, and then we continue to make progress by developing strength in the mode of sense.

These remarks show a possible way of reading Kant's account of the difference between evil and the lapses permissible within progress, but I doubt this suggestion can work. There are at least two related ways my worry can be fleshed out. First, we can ask whether we, and Kant, can make sense of the concept of principled struggle. Or, in other words, can we make sense of a purity that exists alongside weakness? Second, in addition to Kant's own discussion, it is worth considering whether commentators sympathetic to what Kant has to say about overcoming evil have helped clarify the juxtaposition of conversion and progress. This will enable us to move from a consideration of whether Kant himself gave us the tools we need to make sense of his account to an assessment of whether the requisite tools have been made available to us.

The chief difficulty I want to call attention to regarding the concept of principled struggle, or a purity that exists alongside weakness, is that several of Kant's remarks indicate the concept is untenable. First, we must note that Kant occasionally discusses purification in gradualist terms in the *Religion*, as something achieved bit by bit instead of all at once.[6] This can only make us a little less confident that Kant wants to offer a revolutionary conception of purification, one that contrasts with the progressive work done in the mode of sense. Moreover, and more importantly, at several points Kant maintains that strength cannot be cultivated apart from purity. Or, to put the point more clearly, Kant maintains that moral

---

6. At RGV 6:83, the assiduous maintenance of one's purity is what characterizes the gradual work we must do. Kant also discusses the progressive purification of the moral disposition at RGV 6:197.

strength is the direct result of the purity of one's will, and that strength is had to the extent to which a will is pure. If this is correct, then it cannot be argued that a will that has been purified, or that a person who instilled a revolution in her intelligible character, can still be weak.

The point is perhaps most directly made in the Doctrine of Method of the second *Critique* and in terms that are we are accustomed to seeing in Kant's political philosophy. In the second *Critique*, Kant argues that the moral law is a power (*Kraft*) for us to the extent that it is pure and uncorrupted by any admixture of inclination or concern for one's own happiness. Any such admixture constitutes a *hindrance*, and Kant settles on this term because removing or hindering these hindrances immediately strengthens "the effect of the moving force," which is in this case respect for the moral law (KpV 5:156).[7] In light of this, it remains unclear how a will can be purified of any admixture and yet still find itself weak, fragile, or inefficacious. If an agent has stripped away her impurities, then the mechanisms that cause weakness are eradicated. In this case, the analogy to the flu, and the neat division between purification and strengthening, no longer hold. Being good would be more like laying the foundation in a house: we can construct the foundation only if we shore up its strength as we proceed, and to insist that we instead engage in a two-stage process, where we first install the foundation, and then later attend to its strength, seems unwise.

It is also safe to say that as the literature currently stands, the issue of how to explain the difference between the two stages of moral reform has not yet been adequately addressed. Mavis Biss's "Kantian Moral Striving" is one of the most sophisticated recent attempts to make sense of what exactly an agent struggling to make moral progress must do. Biss, however, accepts the two-stage account and then focuses on the question of how an agent can lessen her weakness or the extent to which she will "act on ill-formed maxims despite her good basic moral disposition."[8] Biss's account, then, assumes and starts from the idea that purity is secured independently of and prior to the mitigation of weakness. Grenberg's work, which likewise concerns Kantian moral development, also does not

---

7. See also RGV 6:71, where Kant discusses how a "good and pure disposition" carries "confidence in its own perseverance and stability." Moreover, see MS 6:217, where Kant claims that a grasp of the moral law in its purity is that "in which its [the moral law's] strength consists." The point is complemented by Kant's insistence in the *Religion* that the incentives of self-love and respect are "real," not logical, opposites (RGV 6:22n). As shown in Chapter 2, this means the two practical incentives are distinct forces in the way that negative and positive magnetic charges are: if an agent is not moved by one, she has enabled herself to resist that incentive by positively anchoring in her will its opposite.

8. "Kantian Moral Striving," 4.

address the issue we're looking to clear up. Grenberg has written helpfully about how evil is facilitated by self-deception and rationalization, which she frames in terms of an agent's willingness to make exception to the categoricity demanded by the moral law.[9] But Grenberg's account seems to reduce *all* moral failures to such quibbling. Grenberg characterizes the confused, piecemeal battle against the categoricity of moral demands as both the stuff of evil and the enemy of virtue. Given this, she leaves opaque what would mark the distinction between the two stages of moral reform that Kant outlines in the *Religion*. For in Grenberg's view, it would seem as though we should not have a two-stage account at all, and that there should be just one large movement of a decreased propensity to fight against the categoricity of the moral law. As it stands, then, it remains unclear how the work of conversion and progress differ from one another.

(2) The first objection focused mainly on Kant's distinction between impurity and weakness. My second objection concerning Kant's two-stage theory of moral reform refers to this distinction while focusing more on the latter term—weakness—and its synonyms. As noted in Chapter 2, frailty, or lack of strength, is at one point defined by Kant as "weakness in complying with adopted maxims" (RGV 6:29). It thus seems to be a cornerstone of Kant's account that even when a person has reformed her intelligible character, her empirical character remains in progress due to the lack of strength *Willkür* suffers from in complying with its newly established good fundamental maxim. Now, let me be clear that commentators are right to take these comments about long-term moral efforts in the mode of sense seriously. A failure to do so would minimize the idea that empirical character marks a site of meaningful moral labor. When Kant describes a person who has restored the moral principle as someone who must then try to infer the quality of her disposition on the basis of empirical conduct, we ought not trivialize this labor by implying that it involves no more than bearing passive witness to one's own goodness. Instead, we should see this agent as engaging in a certain type of moral work and doing something constitutive of a certain type of moral progress. I am thus in full agreement that we need some concept of progressively cultivated empirical character in order to allow for full moral development. I'm not, however, sure that Kant or his commentators should describe the work done in the mode of sense as that of cultivating executive strength in the performance of one's maxims.

9. "What Is the Enemy of Virtue?," 162–166.

A chief difficulty with this definition of weakness is its apparent incompatibility with Kant's commitment to transcendental freedom. There are metaphysical and practical vantage points to consider: the metaphysical question concerns how an agent can be both transcendentally free and unable to will her own compliance with adopted maxims, and the practical question concerns how to conceive the self-understanding of a moral agent who must act under presupposition of her own freedom and yet sees herself as lacking the strength required for compliance. Now, though Kant is frustratingly quiet about these questions, commentators have been less so. Frierson and Mariña try to explain the compatibility of weakness and freedom in similar ways, but they do not succeed in showing how their proposals avoid the denigration of transcendental freedom.[10]

Mariña's solution is to understand frailty or weakness in terms of the "volitional residues" left behind by an evil disposition.[11] Such residues are "desires" that are the "left over effects of once having adopted a fundamentally evil maxim," and these desires "frequently overpower" a person despite that person now being a "basically good individual."[12] Frierson, who has been especially sensitive to questions of how to blend Kant's libertarian concept of transcendental freedom with an acknowledgment of the importance of empirical conditions, endorses a similar solution insofar as he maintains that weakness is inflicted upon an agent by her past, preconversion self. Frierson then adds to this claim the following comment about transcendental freedom:

> The temporal extension of past decisions does not undermine transcendental freedom, because the limitations of one's ability to effect changes in oneself are self-imposed limitations.[13]

This is an inventive, but untenable, proposal. While Frierson clearly acknowledges how the concept of weakness threatens to upend Kant's commitment to transcendental freedom, he responds to this threat by restricting dramatically the scope of transcendental freedom. By allowing formerly bad character to interfere with one's ability to comply, in the present, with adopted maxims, Frierson and Mariña both retreat from Kant's insistence that transcendental freedom is an ability to determine the will

10. DiCenso's understanding of frailty appears to share much with Frierson and Mariña's. See *Kant's* Religion within the Boundaries of Mere Reason: *A Commentary*, 51.
11. "Transformation and Personal Identity in Kant," 493.
12. Ibid., 493–494. Mariña also draws on this notion of volitional residue in "Kant on Grace: A Reply to His Critics," 395–397.
13. *Freedom and Anthropology in Kant's Moral Philosophy*, 129.

independently of preceding conditions in space and time.[14] In their view, since my past deeds are given a kind of overriding power with respect to my present conduct, transcendental freedom is redefined chiefly in terms of an independence from material life and also from other persons.[15]

Now, perhaps the upshot of Frierson and Mariña's approach is that we should revise our commitment to Kantian transcendental freedom and argue that a person's past *Gesinnung* must, in fact, damage her ability to comply with her reformed maxims. This move would have the upside of clarifying the struggles that pervade the cultivation of empirical character, but other options—such as the reframing proposal that I'll offer later in this chapter—should be explored first. I say this not because of any particularly strong attachment to Kant's concept of transcendental freedom but because it would be exceptionally difficult to start and stop with the modification that Frierson and Mariña require. They would, for example, need to offer a principled reason why a human being is rendered weak by her past moral disposition, even though the capacity for transcendental freedom is in no fundamental way diminished by extremely poor formative circumstances, current material deprivations, or the manipulative pressures of other human beings. In other words, since Frierson and Mariña appear interested in making weakness, and only weakness, compatible with transcendental freedom, they would need to show, first, why no one or nothing else could *possibly* render an agent frail and, second, why a person weakens her own compliance ability *necessarily*—necessarily because otherwise Kant's insistence on a two-stage model is unjustified. Given the difficulty of this task, other interpretations of the labors of empirical character must be considered first.

(3) This brings us to the last of the three difficulties with Kant's presentation of the two-stage account of moral reform, and the problem concerns an argument that both Kant and his commentators give in its favor. As Ware puts it, we need a two-stage account because a person lacks "direct cognitive access to the ground or purity of one's disposition."[16] This then motivates Kant to propose the "inferential" or "conjectural" model of

14. This is perhaps clearest at KpV 5:96–97, where Kant argues that without the capacity to act independently of prior temporal conditions, a person would be reduced to an *automaton spirituale*, which differs from a material automaton only in that the former is driven to act by virtue of representations as opposed to material causes.

15. To be clear, Frierson and Mariña are not making the unobjectionable point that a kind of temporal extension of one's prior *Gesinnung* is needed if we are to take ownership of and make amends for past immoral conduct. The temporal extension they argue for is much more controversial.

16. "The Duty of Self-Knowledge," 671–672.

moral self-awareness noted briefly in the beginning of this chapter, a model that involves taking stock of the long-term moral patterns evident within empirical conduct and using this, as opposed to direct introspective access into intelligible character, to affirm our confidence in a moral conversion. Ware assesses this model favorably, explaining why we should endorse an inferential model:

> By focusing on one's actions and moral conduct the Inferential View avoids the many difficulties we encountered with introspection. Action-based inferences, for example, are not dependent on the agent's often-deluded psychological states or self-conceptions ("I feel like a new person"; "I consider myself restored").[17]

I, however, am hesitant to accept this rationale or Ware's account of how empirical and intelligible character are supposed to relate.[18] More specifically, I think there are at least three difficulties with the concept of an empirically grounded character inference.

The first issue is that we are not yet in a good position to understand exactly what it means to focus on one's empirical actions. If it means simply that we should keep on the lookout for actions that do not even conform with duty, this may be attainable. If, however, our ability to draw an inference based on conduct (*Verhalten*) requires an adequate grasp of the mental components noted within Kant's empirical theory of action, then this will be much more difficult to attain. Such an account would require that I understand my actions in terms of the beliefs, feelings, and desires that move me to act, and a sufficient grasp of these mental states is likely more difficult to secure than an inventory of acts that do not conform to duty.[19] Moreover, once the question of which of these two interpretations of empirical action—bare conduct, or conduct in addition to one's feelings, beliefs, and desires—is raised, it is difficult to resist the conclusion that the latter, or something quite close to it, is really what is needed. Moral progress—particularly the kind of moral progress that's supposed to occur

17. Ibid., 687. Even though these nuances won't affect our discussion, I want to be clear that Ware's view has more to it than this. Ware also insists on the importance of making crosswise inferential comparisons between segments of an agent's life. A person must not only draw an inference about her character based on current empirical conduct but compare this inference to the one she makes about her moral life prior to the moment she sees as marking her conversion.

18. This is, of course, not to say that I disagree with Ware that we are often deluded in our self-conceptions. As Kant himself notes, "one is never more easily deceived than in what promotes a good opinion of oneself" (RGV 6:68).

19. See Frierson, "Kant's Empirical Account of Human Action" and Allison, *Kant's Theory of Freedom*, 30–34.

after a successful moral conversion—would seem to require knowing not only *that* we are coming up short but also *how* we are coming up short. It would be important, for example, to know whether my thought of turning down a request for aid stems from jealousy or cynicism, as well as whether I appreciate how much my refusal could affect the person asking for help. In other words, progress seems to require some self-accounting of my feelings, desires, and beliefs. If this is correct, then it seems too quick to say, as Ware does, that an "agent's often-deluded psychological states or self-conceptions" will not figure into action-based inferences; assessing my own actions *involves* gaining access to my own psychological states.

Second, it is unclear whether an inferential model of moral reform will give us a sufficiently rich account of either what we are inferring from— empirical character—or what we are inferring to—intelligible character. To see why it will be hard to give a proper account of empirical character, note that Kant needs to do justice to two points. (i) As noted earlier in this chapter, he seems to want to offer a conception of empirical character that allows it to play a meaningful role in moral development. A revolution in the will is not sufficient for the establishment of good character, and a slow struggle to overcome frailty or weakness in empirical action is required. (ii) While empirical character plays a role in Kant's theory of moral reform, intelligible character is given pride of place. As we know from the first *Critique*, sensible and intelligible character are not merely two different aspects under which we can understand a human subject. Rather, empirical character is the appearance of, or effect of, intelligible character (KrV A539/ B567). But it is tough to strike the right balance between (i) and (ii), since the way Kant spells out the centrality of intelligible character threatens to minimize the significance of empirical character. When, for example, Kant notes that God enjoys a "pure intellectual intuition" that enables a perfect understanding of the quality of a person's heart, Kant cannot but give the impression that the inferential model is a lesser substitute for direct access to one's moral disposition. If we *could* have an intellectual intuition of a conversion, then it seems this would be an unquestionably better option than an inference. Kant at times implies that intelligible character would be, were it not for human introspective limits, sufficient for moral self-cognition and that empirical character, as a pale imitation of intelligible character, is what we need to resign ourselves to.

Third, the inferential model makes it difficult to give a proper account of how empirical and intelligible character relate to one another in moral self-assessment. Since we touched on this issue in Chapter 6, a brief setup should suffice. Recall that in the first *Critique* and Kant's theoretical philosophy more generally, Kant is careful to stress the obstacles we face in trying to bring into view those capacities or activities that are essential to our lives as knowing human beings. A person cannot, for example, cognize her capacity for spontaneous rational activity in the straightforward way that she can cognize an object of experience. David Jopling, writing on self-knowledge in Kant's theoretical philosophy, nicely explains why:

> [T]he activities necessary for self-knowledge—learning about ourselves, theorizing, describing and explaining ourselves—are always one logical step behind themselves and are blind to the very agency constitutive of and contemporaneous with them. We are unable to know ourselves in the very act of knowing. [20]

In the case of theoretical self-knowledge, when we strive to bring to cognition those capacities constitutive of the possibility of experience, we end up altering the activities we are trying to give an account of. Again, Jopling helps us with an analogy to eyesight. When one attempts to see how her own eye functions as the power of sight, this activity transforms that which she is trying to bring into view,[21] with the eye becoming more the object seen than that which sees other objects. Thus in the cases of both vision and cognitive activity, we must appreciate the limits of our ability to uncover in its original state that capacity we want to bring into focus. Now in Chapter 6, we established that Kant is primed to incorporate this insight into his practical philosophy insofar as it points to the possibility that self-knowledge can promote self-transformation. Granted, it will still be difficult to say exactly how this insight should then apply to moral self-knowledge in the *Religion*, since in this case we are seeking confidence (*Zutrauen*) in, not objective knowledge of, a newly reformed power of choice (RGV 6:71). Nonetheless, there is something compelling about the possibility that this same feature extends to the case of moral self-awareness. As we have seen, it is highly plausible that the attempt to become aware of my moral goodness (or badness) is itself an activity that changes my moral character. Such inference-drawing, it seems, should not merely reveal but impact moral character. But our current understanding of the inferential model of moral development cannot yet accommodate

20. "Kant and Sartre on Self-Knowledge," 74. The issue Jopling raises is just one of several pertaining to Kant's account of self-knowledge in his theoretical philosophy. Another crucial issue is Kant's insistence that we cannot know, or have insight into, ourselves qua noumena. See, for example, KrV B155–158.
21. "Kant and Sartre on Self-Knowledge," 81.

this insight, as it does not allow the labors of empirical character to have bearing on the content of one's intelligible character.

REFRAMING MORAL CONVERSION AND PROGRESS

We can now recap. We have noted several ways in which our existing interpretations of Kantian moral reform have fallen short: they seem unable to explain how a person's intelligible character is meaningfully shaped by a consideration of her empirical character, and they do not entertain whether inspection of empirical conduct involves something more or other than looking for actions that are not in accord with duty. Insofar as it is not sufficiently questioned whether frailty and impurity can be differentiated from one another, the literature and Kant himself do not explain exactly what marks the distinction between conversion and progress and why a two-stage account of moral reform is needed. We have also noted that any alternative approach to Kantian moral reform should try to honor Kant's commitment to transcendental freedom. Finally, it is clear that an alternative should account for some of the broader themes that run throughout Kant's discussion of overcoming evil, such as the sense of struggle and the seeming ubiquity of self-deception in practical life.

My next task is to articulate the reframing that allows us to address the above concerns. As noted in the beginning of this chapter, I want to propose that Kant's account of moral conversion is most plausible when we interpret the decision (*Entschließung*) to endorse the moral law in terms of a commitment. Alongside this, I propose that we interpret the progressive personal efforts brought on by a moral revolution more in terms of cognitive, as opposed to volitional, labor.

Conversion as Commitment. I will begin with conversion as commitment, and it will help to proceed by way of an example. The language of commitment can be used in many contexts, but the example that I think will illuminate the moral case is that of marriage. This is opposed to, say, committing to learn a language, which seems to have a broad meaning in ordinary discourse. Any number of stages in learning a language can be marked by talk of commitment, including initial stages in which a person may have a shaky grasp of her undertaking in both cognitive and volitional senses: she very well may not know what learning a language involves, she may have a poor sense of how tough this will prove, and she may not be able to thoroughly vet the strength of her initial commitment. Over time, it may even become evident that her commitment was quite weak. In contrast to this, a marriage commitment presents a more sharply defined example. A person making this commitment is generally someone with a good, if imperfect, cognitive grasp of the work that a successful marriage requires. We also readily understand the distinctive temporal dynamics at work and how a commitment to a marriage happens both all at once and over time, thus straddling in an instructive way noumenal and phenomenal perspectives on choice. It is not uncommon for people to regard the taking of marriage vows as an especially significant moment that marks a new beginning in a relationship. But even given this stand-alone element, we know that the commitment cannot exist unless it is bookended by hard work both before and afterward. We can also note that these labors are of different kinds, since it takes different efforts to position ourselves to enter a marriage than it does to sustain it or to help it flourish.

There are several parallels I think we can make between this case and the case of the moral law. The moral law, like a marriage commitment, is, of course, something that must be both lived up to over time and preceded by work that prepares one to make this commitment. The person converting, or committing, to make the moral law her fundamental maxim must be someone who already grasps the requirements of duty. She is not going to be surprised to learn, after making her commitment, that lying is forbidden or that there are moral reasons in favor of beneficence. Her moral commitment or moral conversion is preceded not by a history of rejection of the law but by some measure of distance from full respect. In other words—and as should be unsurprising given our Chapter 2 discussion of how, for Kant, agents often try to keep sincere respect for the law alongside self-love—a person will have already demonstrated partial alignment or identification with the law.

Moreover, a conversion, like any other commitment, must be preceded by a specific set of efforts: we must, as noted in earlier chapters, have discarded any self-deceptive pretext under which we presented evidence for our frailty (*Gebrechlichkeit*) and impotence (*Unvermögen*) (RGV 6:51).[22] This kind of weakness—the kind that exists not as a real limitation but as an epistemic construct, one that helps us avoid the hard "moral labor" of reflective self-criticism (RGV 6:51)—must be recognized by the agent for what it is and abandoned. We must, also, and as noted in Chapter 5, consistently exhibit virtue in a "legal" or strictly "phenomenal" sense, fully reforming our behavior so that we act in steady accord with duty, even if not from duty (RGV 6:14 and 6:47).

22. See also RGV 6:169 and note 59 of Chapter 2.

Now since these efforts might not lead to a conversion and can, in fact, lead to a further descent into evil,[23] Kant will not consider such efforts to *themselves* be an element of moral reform.[24] But only once these tasks are complete does someone gain the possibility of committing to the moral law. And even though the grounds on which an agent adopts this new maxim remain inscrutable (RGV 6:21), we can safely characterize part of what it involves. Since Kant, throughout the *Religion*, speaks of both a change of heart (*Herzensänderung*) and a change of mind (*Sinnesänderung*) to describe what happens in a conversion or commitment,[25] it is clear enough that it involves not only a shift in power from the evil principle to that of the good but also, and as a result, a reordering of one's identity and practices. As with a marriage commitment, moral goodness requires that a person view the moral law and an attitude of respect as now inviolable parts of her personal identity.

The Cognitive Dimensions of Moral Progress. I continue to discuss commitment throughout this chapter, but at this point it will help to clarify what efforts are required after a moral conversion or a commitment to the moral law. Kant grants that a person's revolution secures both "purity of the principle of choice . . . adopted as the supreme maxim of his power of choice" and the "stability [*Festigkeit*] of this principle," but he insists that this is not yet enough for a man to be properly called good (RGV 6:48). If the path of progress is not one of purifying and mitigating a weak hold on the good principle, what does this path involve? And what does the mode

23. To understand why Kant does not think of this preliminary epistemic and behavioral labor as itself a component of moral reform, consider the following. As established earlier in this book, Kantian evil is rooted in self-deception insofar as knowledge of the moral good—knowledge of a law that is the law of one's own reason and thus a form of self-knowledge—can generally and reliably produce moral motivation; Kant's view is not that the removal of a given self-deception always and invariably leads to moral conversion or the proper attitude toward self-love. Moreover, an agent needs to engage in behavioral remedies, but Kant is explicitly aware of the risk that an increased conformity to the law can become a stopping point instead of a stepping stone. Indeed, the person who avoids public transgressions may settle quite comfortably into mere compliance. In light of this, "legal" changes cannot on their own be regarded as part of moral improvement. Finally, an agent who misuses her freedom by adulterating, even infrequently, respect for the law with self-love, is, because of this willingness to misuse freedom, regarded by Kant as evil. Given this, it is unjustified to see positive goodness or authentic betterment in the efforts that precede a moral conversion. See also my discussion of dissimulation in Chapter 5.

24. This explains why it would be a mistake to see Kant's two-stage model of moral reform as downplaying the efforts that need to be done before the first stage, or before a conversion. Though some commentators overlook this (including, it seems, O'Connor; see "Good and Evil Disposition," 295), any commitment needs to be prefaced by a set of efforts that do not count as part of the commitment itself.

25. See, for example, RGV 6:47, 6:66, 6:70, and 6:72.

of sense have to do with it? Unless we can address these questions, the second stage of Kant's two-stage model will remain unclear.

This is where I want to explore thinking about moral progress more in terms of cognitive, in contrast to volitional, labor. These dimensions of moral progress are, as we'll soon enough see, related, but it will help to separate them out in our discussion.

To explain why this suggestion is worth considering, we can revert back to the example of marriage. I do not think the work involved in building a marriage is that of overcoming a lack of executive strength or weakness, or that people regard the temporal dynamic needed to develop a good marriage as one of ensuring that their commitment fares well against a steady stream of temptation or opportunities to falter. Even though we talk about making a marriage strong or stronger, we generally do so without implying that the work that needs to be done is that of overcoming weakness. This, I take it, is also why we generally do not take the dissolution of a marriage commitment to suggest that the parties were not, in fact, powerfully devoted to the marriage in the first place. If, when many marriages end, the dissolution is not well described as due to a failure to put strength where there was inefficacious resolve, then the development needed to allow the commitment to sustain itself, is, I think, better thought of in non-volitional terms. In their stead, we can consider framing the movement of progress in cognitive terms.

What the parties that enter a marriage generally seek is increased opportunity to convey in action what their commitment means and the importance of their commitment in their lives. Until one can find a more nuanced way to give voice to and conceptualize her commitment, a person has a less perfectly developed notion of what one's marriage is about. This is why temporality is so important to a marriage, since unless a commitment has time to evolve and achieve new forms of expression, then even the most sincerely undertaken commitments will be unable to mature as they should. Relatedly, it is especially hard to anticipate, at the outset of a marriage, the various ways this commitment can run up against other things we care about, such as friendships, work, children, or an evolving sense of self. Over time, we must develop insight into the creative ways different commitments can be made compatible and learn how to interpret and react to those moments where that compatibility runs out. Grasping these aspects of one's marriage commitment in increasingly rich, lived detail is the stuff of progress or of building a successful relationship.

To explain moral progress, a parallel emphasis on temporal development is indispensable. While Kant discusses in Part One and the beginning of Part Two of the *Religion* what we must do to bring about a change of heart, the central topic within the remaining sections of Part Two (RGV 6:66–78) are three great difficulties that stand in the way of one's ability to become a human being well-pleasing to God, or someone who approaches the moral ideal. The two initial difficulties concern first, how the human being's change of heart can be regarded as real or complete when the object of our reformed maxim—conformity with holiness—is "not exhaustible in any time" (RGV 6:66), and second, and relatedly, how we can have epistemic confidence in our moral transition.[26] If we approach these difficulties with the marriage example in mind, we can find a common temporal dynamic at work: the agent who commits to the moral law will find her deeds "*every time* (not generally, but at each instant) defective" because commitments need to be differently expressed over an indefinite duration in order to come closer to perfection (RGV 6:67). The person marrying knows that she'll only see her marriage unfold bit by bit and thus can never be fully certain about its precise future trajectory. It would only be from a God's-eye perspective that the qualities of a marriage would be evident, and the same point holds with respect to one's moral commitment. From the vantage point of creatures like ourselves, a moral commitment, like any other meaningful commitment, will need time to evolve and to develop more informed, experienced modes of expression.

To explain this proposal further and to establish why moral progress is about cognitive work, or increased moral knowledge, it will help to address a potential obstacle to this suggestion—namely, Kant's insistence that we always know what the moral law commands or what its requirements are. In response, I think the way we, and Kant, put this point in deontological as opposed to axiological terms is telling.[27] While we know what the moral law requires of us, I do not think that many of us have a well-perfected understanding of how the good will is the good that necessarily surpasses and conditions all other goods. It is exceptionally difficult for finite human beings or individuals who value so many different objects, activities, and ideals to grasp exactly what it means to be good until they can comprehend not only what the law requires of them but also the impoverished and yet non-illusory status of many other things that they regard as valuable. And as should be evident, the knowledge we seek unfolds chiefly in the

26. The third difficulty concerns the repayment of evil debts and, while extremely interesting and important, a discussion of how such repayment is possible falls outside of the scope of this monograph. For my account of this third difficulty, see "Moral Feeling and Moral Conversion in Kant's *Religion*."

27. See, for example, KrV A831/B859, GMS 4:403–04, KpV 5:37, MS 6:375n, RGV 6:182. For these references, I am indebted to John Hardwig, "Action from Duty But Not in Accord with Duty."

realm of appearance. It is hard to grasp the tension between being a morally good person and the best partner or artist until we are presented with a concrete situation in which it seems we cannot live up to both ideals. So again, the progress we need to make to cultivate our goodness is not one of overcoming a lack of power or frailty. Instead, we need to overcome a very specific form of moral uncertainty, though this uncertainty does not stem from the worry that the moral law is chimerical. It is more a Kantian variant of the concern expressed by philosophers such as Susan Wolf, Bernard Williams, or Harry Frankfurt. These philosophers never deny that morality makes demands on us, or even that those demands should be unrelenting, but they still wonder how moral goodness can take clear and easy precedence over other projects or conditional goods. Rather similarly, even if someone commits to the tenet that the only unconditional good is the *good will*, she can still be uncertain as to what it would mean—for her, and given the entirety of what she cares about—to be a *good person* and how to achieve this.

I discuss further aspects of this cognitive labor in the next section of this chapter and again in Chapter 8. At this point, though, we can continue to work out my reframing proposal by testing it against some of the difficulties with those standing interpretations of Kantian moral development that were articulated in the beginning of this chapter. To begin, my proposal gives proper due to the realm of sense and appearance. It is only in the mode of sense—through living out a commitment, working through tough situations, and having limited means for securing everything we care about—that we find ourselves with conflicting ends and come to terms with the implications of moral goodness. To the extent that we do not gain this experiential knowledge or find a way to express in more mature terms what our commitment means, we do not progress as we should, even if our commitments are still rightly thought of as intact. Furthermore, the work we do in the mode of sense clearly surpasses keeping tabs on actions that do not accord with our duty. This means that the progressive understanding and expression of moral commitment developed through empirical character is not a mere effect of intelligible character but is itself morally and personally impactful. Yet at the same time, it is evident that empirical progress is distinct from, and must be preceded by, the decision to commit to the moral law.

We can also consider how the proposal I've offered relates to transcendental freedom. We can begin by noting that when we see through our commitments in the empirical realm, we would describe this experience as one of learning, not one of being causally determined. There is no factor or set of factors sufficient to determine whether an individual will consider leaving her marriage, or set the law aside, when she learns more about what is needed to sustain these commitments. Rather, she will interpret the knowledge she has gotten and decide how to balance her commitments in light of it. Additionally, it is the case that no person can claim exculpatory ignorance if she decides to withdraw her commitments after seeing what these implications are. This is because, first, what goodness consists in, or what a marriage may need to survive, is not an elite form of knowledge. We can get it through discussion, imagination, literature, and film. We also, in making commitments, assume responsibility—at least implicitly, and often explicitly—for sticking them out even in light of our ignorance. This is clear when we commit to marry, and especially clear when we commit to have or raise a child.

Moreover, consider again the type of agent we are considering as she makes the progress needed to honor her commitment. I noted above that this agent is one who needs to learn about what her commitments mean to her, and whether she can do right by both her marriage, or the moral law, and the other things she views as valuable. As an example, say I am in a situation where my commitment to protect a beloved friend and my commitment to the moral law seem irreconcilable. In this case, my empirical context functions as a point of access to my willingness to rethink what it means to have committed to the law. But notice how different this depiction of moral struggle is from the picture presented to us by Frierson and Mariña. In their view, insufficient moral progress takes place when I find myself victimized by my past self and, despite a completely pure will and trying with all of my available might, unable to execute the maxims I abide by. In my view, insufficient moral progress occurs when there is a live uncertainty regarding how, exactly, moral goodness can be the sole unconditional good. In the above example, I am actively evaluating what to do in light of sincere attachment to both commitments; neither the current situation, nor some past commitment bleeding or "temporally extending" into the present, is determining my next move for me.[28]

28. Thus, we can agree with Kant that a moral conversion consists of an "unalterable" (*unwandelbare*) decision (RGV 6:47–48). To say that this decision is unalterable is not to say that a moral conversion is fixed such that no efforts are needed to sustain it, or that it is somehow impossible for an agent to reevaluate her decision in light of newfound knowledge. Rather, Kant clearly means to imply that the decision or conversion is not subject to the causal laws that govern change in the empirical world. A decision to commit to the moral law will not weaken simply by virtue of persisting in time, and it will not be passively affected by a person's surroundings in the way that an object is affected by its location in a spatial network (on this last point, see EAD 8:333). Therefore, even though a conversion is unalterable in the sense of being unable to be changed or diminished by temporal conditions, we cannot from this conclude that an

Finally, even though we set aside Kant's emphasis on overcoming weakness in moral progress to develop this view, the alternative approach to moral reform that I have offered can be translated back into volitional language to demonstrate its compatibility with Kant's own words. A person strongly considering being a good friend over being morally good can be regarded as exhibiting a lack of strength or weakness, so long as we take care to shed the physical, sweaty overtones that often attach to these concepts. To reaffirm the moral law by progressively coming to terms with the different facets of the unconditional goodness of good will is to strengthen one's commitment. To entertain seriously the idea that good will is not elevated above all other goods is, correlatively, a kind of normative defect or weakness. We can allow that postconversion moral progress requires the removal of frailty, so long as we regard frailty not as an inability to act as we have intended but as an incomplete or weaker-than-needed understanding of what we have committed ourselves to. But to repeat, an agent who lacks full understanding does not lack the wherewithal or executive power to act on her maxims. Even if I decide after extensive consideration to abandon the moral law for my friendship, or if someone decides to exit her marriage so as to reclaim a lost career, it would be unreasonable to describe us as suffering from ineffective wills or uncommitted to morality or marriage in the first place. In such cases, a person turns *toward* something else—namely, friendship—and does not merely fall *away* from the moral law. We would be better thought of as *unwilling*, not *unable*, to do what we now see is entailed by marriage or moral goodness.

To conclude this section, now that we have explained the volitional language Kant uses to elucidate moral progress, we can also clarify those references to continual struggles with sensibility and self-deception in both Kant's *Religion* and commentaries by Grenberg and others. As we can now see, a struggle in the mode of sense is exactly what takes shape after a conversion, though very clearly, this struggle is qualitatively different from the (at least) occasionally lost battles with self-love that characterize evil. To briefly review Grenberg's comments, we can recall that because she saw self-deception as hampering both a willingness to engage in a moral revolution and the work of moral progress, her account obscured Kant's claim that there are different stages of practical struggle before and after a moral conversion. Yet here again, my reframing can help because it can point us to a phenomenon that is closely related to self-deception, namely, a lack of

agent cannot revise her commitments. Indeed, Kant seems to think we must be able to revise our commitments because an individual can never rule out the possibility that she will turn back to evil.

self-knowledge. While a moral conversion can be put out of reach through self-deception, moral progress can be jeopardized if we neglect to scrutinize the true, extensive nature of our commitments. And just as sensibility is needed to prevent blindness in theoretical cognition, the gradual perfection of moral self-understanding likewise requires the lived experience of moral commitment in the empirical realm.

CONCLUSION

My focus thus far has been on the two-stage model of moral reform articulated in Kant's *Religion*. To conclude this chapter, I want to broaden my focus and consider, albeit very briefly, Kant's account of moral reform in the *Doctrine of Virtue*.

While the general structure of Kant's account in this later text is not altogether obvious, there is some consensus that he does not abandon the two-stage model. Kant does, we must note, emphasize in the *Doctrine of Virtue* how we must continually strive to improve ourselves, and for this reason it may seem that a more "gradualist"[29] view regarding moral reform is on hand, one that would eliminate distinct stages and instead put us on a singular path of betterment. But as he did in the *Religion*, Kant speaks again of an initial point in moral development where an *Entschließung* must be made "all at once and in its entirety" (MS 4:477).[30] I'll thus follow Allison and Biss, who argue that the gradual development of virtue stressed in the *Doctrine of Virtue* aligns with the second stage in moral reform, or with the progress that occurs after a moral decision—or, as I've argued, a moral commitment—is made.

If a two-stage model of moral reform is present in both texts, then the *Doctrine of Virtue* can supplement our discussion of the *Religion* in two ways: first, by potentially challenging the interpretation I've offered in this chapter, and second, by providing an opportunity to expand and clarify that interpretation. I'll briefly consider one such challenge and one such avenue toward further clarification of Kant's two-stage model of moral reform.

Strength and Virtue in the *Doctrine of Virtue*. I have criticized throughout this chapter the idea that moral progress involves the mitigation of executive weakness or incompetence in the faculty of choice. But my focus has been on the *Religion*, and one may worry that the *Religion* is not

29. Biss, "Kantian Moral Striving," 3.
30. On this point, see ibid. and Allison, *Kant's Theory of Freedom*, 169–170.

representative of Kant's considered approach to progress. It might even be argued that passages that bolster the interpretation of weakness I've tried to refute seem widely available in the *Doctrine of Virtue*.

In the *Doctrine of Virtue*, Kant connects weakness and strength to the central concept under discussion—namely, virtue—by arguing that virtue is "the moral strength of a *human being's* will in fulfilling his *duty*" and in overcoming those impulses of sensibility that "impede the law of its will" (MS 6:405). Kant also presents virtue as an executive capacity, claiming that the moral strength of virtue consists in a person's "own lawgiving reason, insofar as this constitutes itself an authority *executing* the law" (MS 6:405). Yet these points about a persistent lack of executive wherewithal threaten to erase the arguments I've made and put us back where we started: with a view of moral reform that identifies the second stage with the gradual mitigation of executive weakness in moral adherence, a weakness that—somehow—remains after an initial stage of purification is complete.

This threat, however, can be easily dismissed. There are many features of Kant's discussion of virtue I can't comment on, but it is relatively clear that throughout the *Doctrine of Virtue*, the space between weakness and strength is generally described as one between reluctance and readiness. The person who lacks virtue does not fail to execute the law; rather, she does so reluctantly (*ungern*).[31] And in contrast, the person who has strength of *Willkür* exhibits a readiness (*Fertigkeit*) and an easy frame of mind (*Leichtigkeit*).[32] Similarly, when Kant discusses the executive capacity of the will, he does not describe strength as a matter of *whether* or *how often* the will performs those demands legislated by reason. Instead, strength attaches to the quality of the will *in* this performance. Thus, Kant argues, for example, that the self-constraint that characterizes virtue consists not in the ability to carry out ethical demands but in the absence of reluctance (MS 6:380). The aforementioned claim that "virtue is, therefore, the moral strength of a *human being's* will in fulfilling his *duty*," in fact, reinforces this point (MS 6:405). On closer inspection, it is fairly apparent that in this passage, execution of the law is assumed and that strength pertains to how, not if, a human being does her duty.

From this, we can conclude that Kant quietly but clearly dismisses the notion that the slow progression of virtue involves overcoming a failure whereby, despite having a good maxim, we are still too weak to fulfill our intention to act on this maxim. Virtue is not that which exists when there

31. See, for example, MS 6:379, 6:382n, and 6:386.
32. See, for example, MS 6:218 and 6:407.

is a sufficient quantitative level or material degree of executive power; rather, virtue, as strength of will, is a quality of a given and stable executive power. Given this, there appears to be no fundamental incompatibility between the accounts of postconversion moral reform in the *Religion* and the *Doctrine of Virtue*. In both texts, moral progress is not about developing executive powers we lack. Instead, moral progress concerns the frame of mind with which someone acts and whether she displays an ease in moral affairs and a clear-eyed vision of the good.

Love and Conduct. I have argued that the decision to convert to the moral law can be understood in terms of a commitment, one that requires personal identification with the moral law. I have also argued that moral progress requires the slow, reflective development of one's commitment in the world of sense, that is, in experience. Between these claims, and my points in the prior chapter about the importance of interpersonal relationships to the development of self-knowledge, we have growing evidence that allegations that Kantian ethics relies on a socially isolated, ahistorical, and highly generic concept of selfhood are unjustified. To continue to demonstrate the distinctive ways my account of Kantian moral reform refutes this image, it may help to explain further why a person's moral identity both doesn't need to be, and likely won't be, abstract.

While we can't eliminate the possibility of devotion to morality itself, it is much more probable that moral commitment will go the way it often does in real life. Few of those referred to as moral saints or the morally exceptional approach their commitment as one to morality as such. Instead, they typically develop a more narrow practical concern, focusing, for example, on alleviating the suffering and marginalization of lepers or providing medical care to a given population of women.[33] Very occasionally, there are instances where an individual works a high-paying job so as to devote maximal amounts of money to charity, but these cases appear more rare.[34] Moreover, such cases fail to match not only the model of commitment we ordinarily expect but also, importantly, what Kant seems to envision. It is reasonable to conclude that moral commitment will tend to take shape in the manner that the field of imperfect duty takes shape in the *Doctrine of Virtue*: our sense of obligation, or our willingness to take the

33. These are some of the cases discussed in Larissa MacFarquhar, *Strangers Drowning: Grappling with Impossible Idealism, Drastic Choices, and the Overpowering Urge to Help*. See 119–152 and 13–40.

34. See, for example, MacFarquhar's *Strangers Drowning*. Of the different cases of moral exceptionalism she explores, only one features a couple that tries to donate a large percentage of their income to the most cost-effective charities (see 71–102). In every other case, individuals devote themselves to a very specific moral cause.

law itself as a reason for action, ends up directed toward a set of practical loves that give our commitment a certain trajectory and distinctiveness.[35] The type of moral agent Kant points us to in this discussion of how ethical duties become limited only by love is someone committed to a highly specific, personalized, and morally informed set of cares; she has found a cause or causes she cares about. In light of this, any worry that Kantianism forces an agent's moral sensibility into a socially isolated concern for what the law demands again seems largely unfounded.

The idea of a moral cause also offers, in my view, a helpful way to illuminate further what Kant has in mind in the *Religion* when he emphasizes the importance of conduct or *Verhalten* after a conversion.[36] In the previous section, I explained that the mode of experience or sense is morally significant because it is the realm in which we learn more about what we are committed to. Now, it may seem that this interpretation downplays Kant's emphasis on "conduct" in the empirical realm. After all, and as noted in Chapter 6,[37] the most obvious way to interpret this emphasis is to think of Kant as recommending the vigilant self-monitoring of actions, whether for actions that are contrary to what the law commands or actions that obviously speak against what we take our motives or intentions to be. Admittedly, my account of the second stage of moral reform does not emphasize this kind of self-monitoring. But the reason is that even though many commentators treat the concept of conduct as interchangeable with that of empirically manifest action,[38] such a move is at odds with Kant's own use of these terms, at least in the *Religion*.

It's crucial to note that in this text, the concept of conduct or *Verhalten* belongs clearly to Kant's theory of a moral and rational religion, whereas the concept of action or *Handlung* belongs to Kant's practical psychology.[39]

35. See MS 6:390.
36. See, for example, RGV 6:47, 6:64, and 6:66.
37. See page 164.
38. Ware, for example, treats the terms identically throughout "The Duty of Self-Knowledge." See, for example, 673, 686, and 687. O'Connor also treats these terms identically in "Good and Evil Disposition," 291. Finally, Palmquist explicitly defines a *Lebenswandel* in terms of empirical behavioral patterns, even though, as I show just below, Kant uses this term in the same manner that he uses *Verhalten*. See Palmquist, *Comprehensive Commentary on Kant's* Religion within the Boundaries of Mere Reason, 527.
39. As already noted, I restrict my claim about the distinction between *Verhalten* and *Handlung* to the *Religion*. Because of the high frequency with which Kant uses these terms, I cannot provide a thorough review of how they are employed in other texts. Nonetheless, I will quickly note that while the distinction does not appear to be replicated elsewhere, it is striking and consistent enough in the *Religion* for me to call it to our attention with confidence.

Thus, when Kant discusses empirical actions or *Handlungen* in the *Religion*, it is often in the context of reminding us how they are phenomenal happenings that do not reveal the quality of an agent's will or how "cultish" actions are not what a moral religion demands.[40] But as far I can tell, at nearly every instance that Kant speaks of conduct or *Verhalten* in the *Religion*, he is referring not to the phenomenal manifestation of the determination of the will but to those deeds through which we express a moral commitment.[41] Conduct is not a set of phenomena that we try to glean information from. Rather, conduct is about *good works*, that is, good life-conduct or a good *Lebenswandel*.

Thus, when Kant claims the second stage of moral reform concerns the gradual transformation of conduct, he is not arguing that this second stage is to be characterized in terms of the aggressive self-monitoring of external action; to see this as his argument would be to elide completely his fairly careful distinction between *Handlungen* and *Verhalten*. Instead, Kant is arguing that the reformed person must take up commitment to a moral cause in an increasingly conscientious fashion. It is on the basis of good life-conduct, not mere action, that a reformed will is empirically evidenced. This means that technically, there is no such thing as *Verhalten* before a conversion; there are only *Handlungen*. It also means that moral development involves dedication to specific good works and not a highly theoretical or academic attitude of a reverence toward the moral law.

40. On external actions as "cult"-like, see RGV 6:84 and 6:115.
41. With only two exceptions, Kant does not even use the term *Verhalten* until RGV 6:47ff., that is, until after he has introduced the idea of postconversion progress. After 6:47, and in his subsequent discussions of progress and what the reformed agent must do as time proceeds, *Verhalten* and especially *Lebenswandel* are referenced numerous times and are Kant's terms of choice for explaining what we look at to assess moral progress (see, e.g., RGV 6:143, 6:184, and 6:191 for characteristic uses of *Verhalten* and RGV 6:82, 6:105, 6:118, and 6:119 for characteristic uses of *Lebenswandel*). One exception is RGV 6:41, where Kant treats *Verhalten* as equivalent to behavior and comments on how past conduct determines nothing about an agent's present-day decisions. The other exception is RGV 6:24, but this usage occurs in Kant's discussion of how our conduct is determined by whatever incentive a human being has incorporated into her maxim. Thus even here, *Verhalten* is not used to refer to phenomenal actions.

CHAPTER 8
Moral Misunderstandings and the Ethical Community

The two-stage model of moral reform outlined in the prior chapter is not Kant's sole word on what is required to overcome evil. In Part Three of the *Religion*, and in order to secure "victory of the good principle over the evil principle" (RGV 6:93), Kant argues that an "ethico-civil state"—or an ethical community—in which human beings are freely, non-coercively united for the sake of reciprocal moral advancement is also needed (RGV 6:95). Yet the precise role the ethical community plays in Kant's broader theory of moral reform is less than clear.

In the secondary literature, interpretations of the ethical community vary widely and across several dimensions. In terms of what *importance* the ethical community has in Kant's account of evil and its overcoming, some see it as primary and unparalleled, while others think the ethical community can play, at best, a secondary or limited role.[1] With respect to what *defects* the ethical community aims to address, some view this communal relationship as facilitating our postconversion progress, while others maintain that the ethical community helps one shed the evil principle and either

---

1. Guyer, though he sees Kant as "extremely vague about its [i.e., the ethical community's] role in the perfection of virtue," argues that if Kant's views in the *Religion* are reconstructed, the ethical community can "only *reinforce* individual commitments to virtue" ("Kantian Communities: The Realm of Ends, the Ethical Community, and the Highest Good," 111; Guyer's italics.) By contrast, Wood sees the development of the ethical community as of the first importance, since, in his view, only an ethical community can properly counteract the unsocial sociability constitutive of evil. See *Kant's Ethical Thought*, 314, and "Religion, Ethical Community, and the Struggle Against Evil," 504.

purify or prioritize the moral incentive.[2] As concerns *who* is enjoined to form or promote an ethical community, certain commentators note Kant's own point that becoming a member of the ethical community is a duty of the "human race toward itself" or the "human species" (RGV 6:97), whereas others do not hesitate to describe the ethical community simply in terms of the assistance it provides to individual persons.[3] Finally, on the question of what the *goal* of the ethical community is, and, consequently, what broader practical doctrines Kant's account of this community relies on, some see the ethical community as seeking and affirming the importance of Kant's highest good,[4] even as others take the ethical community in an explicitly political and cosmopolitan direction. For this latter set of scholars, the ethical community functions as a "guide" so that we can work in concert to create global institutions and norms that protect human rights in a pluralistic, culturally heterogeneous world.[5]

2. As noted in Chapter 7, most commentators fail to adequately acknowledge or explain the difference between the two stages of moral reform. While this failure can make it difficult to isolate which type of moral defect they believe the ethical community is meant to address, some characterizations can still be made. For example, it should be clear from note 1 that Wood puts the ethical community at the center of our first-stage moral efforts. Other commentators, such as Dennis Vanden Auweele and Moran, see Kant's account of the ethical community as addressing a postconversion moral need. Vanden Auweele highlights how the ethical community has benefits for those who have adopted a good disposition in "Kant on Religious Moral Education," whereas for Moran, the ethical community helps solve a "coordination problem" that would otherwise interfere with the pursuit of the highest good (*Community and Progress in Kant's Moral Philosophy*, 78).

3. Vanden Auweele and Moran do not attend to Kant's remark about the role of the species or the human race with respect to the ethical community; Kristi Sweet likewise makes no reference to these comments in her discussion of the ethical community in *Kant on Practical Life*, 169–176. Others, such as Frierson, Palmquist, and Miller, note Kant's references to the human species but do not explain their significance (see Frierson, "Providence and Divine Mercy in Kant's Ethical Cosmopolitanism," 150–151; Palmquist, *Comprehensive Commentary on Kant's* Religion within the Boundaries of Mere Reason, 261; and Miller, Kant's *Religion within the Boundaries of Mere Reason*: A Reader's Guide, 88).

4. For Moran's account of the highest good as the goal of the ethical community, see note 2 above. Sweet likewise sees pursuit of the highest good as a goal of the ethical community, yet she also argues that the ethical community is intended to promote human relationships that foster recognition over competition (*Kant on Practical Life*, 174–175). Finally, while Anderson-Gold tends to be more interested in the political aspects of the ethical community (see note 5 below), she occasionally references the highest good as the ethical community's aim. See "God and Community: An Inquiry into the Religious Implications of the Highest Good," 126.

5. DiCenso, *Kant's* Religion within the Boundaries of Mere Reason: *A Commentary*, 137. See also Anderson-Gold, "Cultural Pluralism and Ethical Community in Kant's Philosophy of History," 66–71, and Rossi, *The Social Authority of Reason: Kant's Critique, Radical Evil, and the Destiny of Humankind*, 77. While Nicholas Tampio maintains that Kant's discussion of the ethical community is too exclusionary to do the political work it needs to, he nonetheless shares with DiCenso, Anderson-Gold, and Rossi the belief

I am interested in these debates and any account of the ethical community must take note of them. But I will not begin by addressing them one by one, in part because such a strategy would interfere with my chief aim for this final chapter. At this juncture, my main goal is to explain how the ethical community addresses obstacles to moral progress that are as yet untouched by the theory of moral reform outlined by Kant in Part Two of the *Religion* and in Chapter 7 of this book. To advance my account, I will work through the argument at RGV 6:93–102, where Kant makes the case for an ethical community by way of a political analogy: just as we ought to leave the state of nature and establish a juridico-civil society, so must we leave what Kant calls the "ethical state of nature" and form an ethical community or commonwealth (RGV 6:96). This analogy is widely noted in the literature, but I submit that it has been misunderstood or improperly appreciated. According to the view I develop in this chapter, and put as succinctly as possible, this analogy enables us to conclude that the ethical community is needed to mitigate a problem regarding discordant moral judgments.

As established in Chapter 7, a person's postconversion efforts are characterized by a willingness to work out the nature of one's moral commitment over some extended period of time. With the increasingly clear and concrete grasp of the moral law gained through devotion to some cause, concomitant progress in moral self-understanding is also secured. But—and yet again, despite certain influential caricatures of Kant—continued progress along these measures is impossible in a state of isolation. For moral and epistemic reasons alike, it is crucial that individuals develop a common vocabulary or set of touchstones that helps them articulate and share judgments about the good with others, better adjudicate moral disagreements, and envision ways to revise our judgments when presented with divergent views. In what follows in this final chapter, I'll explain why these are requisite elements of moral reform and how, exactly, the ethical community secures them. I will thereby be able to complete the book with a more thorough reconstruction of Kant's theory of moral reform.

KANT'S POLITICAL ANALOGY

I will begin this section by outlining briefly how some have attempted to understand Kant's analogy between an ethical community and a juridico-civil

that the ethical community is meant by Kant to promote a cosmopolitan peace. See Tampio, "Pluralism in the Ethical Community."

society and thus justified the need for an ethical community. This will serve as a useful foil as I develop my own account.

Particularly insofar as Kant relies on classic Hobbesian expressions regarding the state of nature (RGV 6:95–97), some have reconstructed Kant's argument along roughly the following lines. Kant attests that the "juridical state of nature is a state of war of every human being against every other" (RGV 6:96–97): we encounter actual or potential hostilities at every turn, ones that prevent us from seeing how our (provisional) property or bodily integrity can be secured. In a similar manner, the "ethical state of nature" is one in which "the good principle, which resides in each human being, is incessantly attacked by the evil which is found in him and in every other as well" (RGV 6:97). This leaves us, it would seem, in a state of ethical vulnerability. We appear surrounded by forces that threaten to "corrupt" us, and, as Frierson puts it, we exist in a "social climate that fosters vice,"[6] one marred by interpersonal jealousy, envy, avarice, and competition most generally (RGV 6:93).

Thus, just as civil society is required to provide security with regard to external freedom, an ethical community is needed to reorder those social relationships that would otherwise generate "fertile breeding grounds"[7] for the promotion of evil, therein removing those temptations that can interfere with the cultivation of inner freedom. Now, there are, of course, differences among those who endorse this general picture of the ethical community. Wood, for example, emphasizes more strongly than others the insidious nature of social dynamics, arguing that "the origin of evil is social, and so must be the struggle against it."[8] Frierson underscores how social vices stem from underlying impurities in individual wills, and DiCenso is especially concerned to stress that social influences, however worrisome they may be, cannot be deterministic.[9] Yet despite these differences, they agree that if we hope to exit an ethical state of nature—a state in which, for DiCenso, "we prioritize maxims of self-love and the unbridled competition of all against all in pursuit of dominance"[10]—then an ethical community must displace it.

This account is not implausible and, as should be clear, there is textual support that can be given on its behalf. But there are points it overlooks,

6. "Providence and Divine Mercy in Kant's Ethical Cosmopolitanism," 147. By citing this phrase from Frierson, I do not mean to imply that the account sketched here aligns with his own in every regard.
7. "Providence and Divine Mercy in Kant's Ethical Cosmopolitanism," 147.
8. *Kant's Ethical Thought*, 314.
9. *Kant's Religion within the Boundaries of Mere Reason: A Commentary*, 132.
10. Ibid., 136.

including the possibility of a different reading of Kant's analogy between ethics and politics. As these oversights are noted and an alternative reading is developed over the course of this chapter, we'll also be able to revisit and extract what appears correct in the above interpretation.

To begin, the view sketched above neglects to note that Kant relies on the concept of a juridical state of nature or *Naturzustande* at two different junctures in his political philosophy. He relies on it not only to explain the need for, and to justify the creation of, a civil society or union (e.g., MS 6:256–257 and 6:306–307). He also turns to the state of nature to explain the need for, and to justify the creation of, an international federation of states or nations. As Kant sees it, states that do not also form part of a pacifist league of nations can be described as existing in a state of nature (ZeF 8:354 and 8:356; MS 6:349) or a "state of nature among states" (MS 6:346 and 6:347).

There is reason to think that this point regarding a state of nature in an international context is especially germane to Kant's discussion of the ethical community in the *Religion*. At points in his writings, Kant emphasizes that special insights can be reached if we put inquiries into international politics alongside moral questions or frameworks. We are asked, in the *Religion*, to make sense of persons in the ethical state of nature and the ethical community by considering their parallels in a juridico-civil setting, and when Kant writes on international matters, he proceeds by envisioning states as persons and by characterizing the vulnerabilities of states in moral terms. In *Perpetual Peace*, for instance, Kant claims that "nations, as states, can be appraised as individuals [*wie einzelne Menschen*]" (ZeF 8:354; see also ZeF 8:345, ZeF 8:357, and MS 6:350), and in the *Metaphysics of Morals*, he maintains that without an international rightful order "a state, as a moral person [*als eine moralische Person*], is considered as living in relation to another state in the condition of natural freedom and therefore in a condition of constant war" (MS 6:343). In these cases, Kant appears to maintain that the moral condition of a single person unbound to others through community can illuminate what is problematic about an international order that lacks a pacifist league. And on the basis of this observation, it begins to seem likely that Kant may intend for us to gain insights about the ethical community by considering not only a pre-civil union state of nature but also a pre-federation "state of nature among states."

Now, the instructional value of this point may not be immediately apparent. One can grant that a juridical-ethical analogy is integral to how Kant structures his arguments concerning international relations, but object that whatever significance this analogy has in the reverse direction— that is, when applied to questions about the ethical state of nature and the ethical community—can be grasped without going through the above detour or making special note of the above points. It is already often enough noted that the ethical community is like a pacifist league of nations insofar as membership in neither can be coerced in the manner that individual persons can be coerced to leave the juridical state of nature and enter civil society (RGV 6:95).[11] It is also widely observed that the ethical community shares with a league of nations a universal or "enduring and ever expansive" quality (RGV 6:94; see also 6:102), as the ethical community is guided by moral principles that prevent it from being limited by a particular set of boundaries or by geographical constraints.[12] Finally, it may be pointed out that the reasons why we need an ethical community, a civil society, or a pacifist league of states are *all* closely analogous to one another. As DiCenso put it, individual human beings need the ethical community so as to escape "the unbridled competition of all against all in pursuit of dominance."[13] A similar concern motivates not only the creation of civil society but also, it seems, a league of nations. One of Kant's chief concerns in *Perpetual Peace* and sections on the rights of states in the *Doctrine of Right* is to decrease or remove the likelihood of war (ZeF 8:343–347, MS 6:350–351, and MS 6:354), and he maintains that a "federalism of free states" can facilitate this end of peace (ZeF 8:354). Thus, whether the battles we envision are interpersonal conflicts regarding property or international hostilities and threats that can lead to war, we find warning, all the same, of competitive social vices such as envy or greed.

So again, given these points, one can question whether we will forgo some real benefit if we neglect to consider the features of a pre-federation "state of nature among states" and proceed, as most commentators, to understand the ethical state of nature only by way of a parallel to a pre-civil society state of nature among individual persons. In what follows, however, I will concede something to this objection while mostly rejecting it. My view is that this "state of nature among states" is particularly useful, if not quite indispensable, for understanding what is problematic about the ethical state of nature and what the ethical community is meant to address. As this should make clear, I am therefore willing to grant that the conclusions I'll reach shortly regarding the ethical community could

---

11. Frierson highlights this point by referring to the ethical community as an "ethical cosmopolitanism." See "Providence and Divine Mercy in Kant's Ethical Cosmopolitanism."

12. See, for example, Wood, "Religion, Ethical Community, and the Struggle Against Evil," 506, and Palmquist, *Comprehensive Commentary on Kant's Religion within the Boundaries of Mere Reason*, 270.

13. *Kant's Religion within the Boundaries of Mere Reason: A Commentary*, 136.

perhaps be established without special emphasis on states in an international context. In fact, and for reasons that will become clear soon, I will concede this rather happily. But it remains the case that Kant's international political writings prove markedly helpful for illuminating Kant's account of the ethical community in the *Religion*.

A STATE OF NATURE AMONG STATES AND A LEAGUE OF NATIONS

In the previous section, I noted Kant's concern that absent a league of nations, or in a state of nature among states, war remains a likely prospect. But to understand what, on the basis of this observation, we should conclude regarding the ethical state of nature, we must explore more carefully the causes of war in an international context.

Kant emphasizes how wars are precipitated by hostilities or aggressions (ZeF 8:349–350),[14] and on occasion he also appears to delve into the motivations behind such hostilities by referencing the concept of evil and by using explicitly moral language. As Kant puts it, a "certain malevolence is rooted in human nature" and is "quite undisguisedly and irrefutably obvious in the external relation of *states* to one another" (ZeF 8:375n). It can therefore seem as though Kant provides an account of war as uniformly born from desires for conquest, exploitation, or some other clearly "lawless" or "barbaric" end (ZeF 8:347 and MS 6:351, respectively). Even if we give this picture a bit more nuance by noting that hostility can exist in a merely potential form, and that a state of nature among nations will persist simply insofar as these savage tendencies are latent (ZeF 8:344; MS 6:346),[15] we nonetheless may be tempted to conclude that, for Kant, illicit motives or goals underwrite any potential or actual war and that a "state of nature among states" reveals the same tendency toward competition and social aggression that many commentators see in a state of nature among individuals. However, it would be a mistake to draw this conclusion.

14. If a state enjoys a republican constitution, or a constitution that requires citizens to consent to a decision to go to war, this greatly decreases the likelihood of such conflicts, as the public is aware it will carry the costs of waging war and suffer the devastations that war brings (ZeF 8:350). Nonetheless, Kant does not venture to assume that hostilities will altogether cease with the adoption of a republican constitution.

15. Of course, the same point holds in the context of civil society, as individuals are in a state of natural war with each other even if no actual hostility is present (MS 6:307).

To begin, a closer look at the relevant texts reveals that Kant neither argues nor presumes that the motives behind war uniformly speak to the evil in human nature. We see this, for example, when Kant notes that actions not motivated by or intended to communicate hostility may nonetheless be perceived as such. For example, there is nothing motivationally suspect in the fact that, before humanity reaches the goal of abolishing standing armies, a country will want to maintain and perhaps increase its readiness for war, even though in doing so, it may be perceived by other states as threatening them (ZeF 8:345). Moreover, if standing armies have been abolished, states may still perceive one another as aggressive actors for any number of reasons. So that a state will not be utterly vulnerable to an external attack, occasional civilian military exercises will be desirable, but there is, of course, no assurance that such innocent measures won't be perceived as preparing for hostilities (ZeF 8:345). Kant also notes that if a nation accumulates large amounts of some treasure or valuable resource, other states may regard this accumulation as an act of war (ZeF 8:345). And even though Kant remains highly critical of war, he does, at least sometimes, stress how we cannot make generalizations regarding its motivational underpinnings or assert unequivocally its alignment with the evil in human nature:

> War itself . . . needs no special motive [*Bewegungsgrundes*] but seems to be engrafted onto human nature and even to hold as something noble, to which the human being is impelled by the drive to honor without self-seeking incentives [*Triebfedern*]. (ZeF 8:365)

While Kant often expresses the hope that certain social phenomena, such as war or commerce, will ultimately advance civilization and bring us closer to perpetual peace, this comment cannot be confined so that it pertains only to Kant's philosophy of history. Rather, Kant is clearly making a point about individual moral psychology and the motives (*Bewegungsgründe*) and incentives (*Triebfedern*) that drive us to participate in war. Wars between states, he maintains, are not necessarily or even usually born of hostility, aggression, or the political equivalent of evil. But if this is correct, we now face the question of what other conditions might precipitate conflict.

I submit that Kant's answer is convincing and consistent across *Perpetual Peace* and the *Doctrine of Right*: What characterizes a state of nature among states is that "in this condition each is the judge [*Richter*] of his own case" (ZeF 8:355; see MS 6:349 for an identical description). Conflict among states arises easily and by virtue of the fact that each nation has a distinct constitution to guide the state's actions and, crucially, its own set of courts to adjudicate decisions regarding whether some action or policy is in accordance with a given law (MS 6:306). Even if two distinct states are similarly devoted to a republican form of governance, the mere fact that they have different institutions and do not share their courts means that each country can regard as justified certain actions or policies, even if another state cannot come to this determination itself. One state, for example, may determine that the boundary it shares with another nation is to be drawn a particular way, or that a stay of a certain duration from noncitizens exceeds what can reasonably be described as a visit. Such actions can be made in accordance with republican principles and with license from a nation's own courts, but there can be no assurance that other states will regard such actions as ones they ought to comply with. Indeed, even if a state's decisions adversely and meaningfully affect another nation, such decisions "cannot straightaway be declared wrong" by this other party (ZeF 8:355).

Now, of course, decisions to expel noncitizens after a certain length of stay or redraw a geographical boundary may have problematic motivations attached to them, including obviously xenophobic or imperialist ones. And in an international context, we need to be especially alert to this prospect, since, as we are often reminded by contemporary political critics, a given state can, in at least some respects, treat its own citizens justly or internally adopt liberal or republican principles while failing to take the same stance toward external states or noncitizens.[16] But it is reasonable to conclude, as Kant seems to, that actions or policies interpreted as aggressive and imperious need not stem from malevolence or some social vice. In reference to one of Kant's more infamous turns of phrase, we could say that while a nation of devils is capable of exiting the state of nature (ZeF 8:366), even nations of angels may find themselves at odds with one another. Hostilities, both potential and real, can be born easily from disagreements between states and we are not entitled to presume that vicious motives are responsible for such disagreements.

Kant's neutrality concerning the motivations that lead to warfare and endorsement of the claim that plain disagreements between states can at least sometimes result in interstate aggressions is reflected in his description of what a league of nations tries to accomplish. Across both *Perpetual Peace* and the *Doctrine of Right*, he consistently presents a league of nations as a forum in which international disputes or disagreements can be aired and, hopefully, resolved. When Kant concludes his discussion of this league in the latter text, he argues that the league he envisions would, much like

16. Noam Chomsky is one critic who makes this point.

the assembly of the States General at the Hague (MS 6:350), allow nations to "decid[e] their disputes in a civil way . . . rather than a barbaric way (the way of savages), namely by war" (MS 6:351). And again, it is only through such a federation that we can solve the problems that would otherwise result from a state of nature among states or a situation in which "each is the judge of his own case" (ZeF 8:355). As Kant sees it, this federation provides a forum for the adjudication of disputes that inevitably arise when two or more nations, even if they are similarly committed to republic norms and principles, find themselves on a collision course due to differences in language, culture, tradition, and, among still further features, case and constitutional law. This collision course, whether latent or actual, is what characterizes the state of nature among states. And it is what a federation of states aims to steer us clear of, as the league's goal is to settle disagreements while preserving the heterogeneity of nations and national identities. The "positive idea *of a world republic*" is (ZeF 8:357), Kant insists, to be rejected, but this does not vitiate the league's ability to address the discord that can ensue from the pluralism accompanying the historical development of distinct nation-states.

It is, moreover, only with this precise framework in mind that we will best understand why a federation of nations is able to achieve its goals. Some of Kant's critics have argued that a league of nations seems able to accomplish little on the international stage, since the incentives to abandon peace agreements will often be quite high.[17] But this objection presupposes a certain view about what drives conflicts between states. If, as this criticism presupposes, wars are always characterized by greed and a desire for conquest or acquisition, then it does seem highly plausible that a federation of nations is extraordinarily limited in what it can do. Were an opportunity for ongoing exploitation or occupation of another nation to emerge at comparatively little cost, such an opportunity would likely not be turned down. In the very best cases, a league of nations among avaricious and mutually antagonistic states would function only as a bargaining site for states that would lose roughly as much as one another were hostilities to break out. But in such a setting, only actual aggression is checked, as latent aggression would remain below the surface and ready to rise if this balance of power were thought by some nation to have shifted in an especially favorable way (TP 8:312). And as Kant notes, this scenario would in no manner count as

17. See Friedrich Gentz, "Über den ewigen Frieden," 479. For this reference and a discussion of Gentz's criticism, I am indebted to Kleingeld, "Approaching Perpetual Peace: Kant's Defence of a League of States and His Ideal of a World Federation," 314–315.

a success for a league of nations, since "the suspension of hostilities is not yet assurance of peace" (ZeF 8:349).

If, however, we conceive the role of a federation of nations against the background view that international conflict can be born from mutual misunderstandings and well-intentioned differences in policy opinions, a more favorable assessment emerges, as well as an assessment that makes better sense of those texts that explore how nations exit the state of nature among states. In *Perpetual Peace*, for instance, Kant introduces the demand for a federalism of free states as the second article for perpetual peace, whereas the first article stipulates that each state must adopt and become well-ordered by a republican constitution. While we must repeat that there is a political space in which a just arrangement of power within a state exists without any external correlate, the league of nations is clearly not introduced with this particular type of state in mind. Rather, given the design of this league as a non-coercive and voluntary domain in which internally "rightful" nations come together (ZeF 8:355), hand over a measure of power, and commit to work with the judges of this outside congress, we must conclude that Kant has assumed a certain degree of sincere respectfulness and ethico-political maturity among most if not all of the league's members. By emphasizing the possible moral innocence of those disputes that can lead to war, it becomes much more plausible that a league of nations can efficaciously promote peace and provide meaningful relief from the state of nature.[18]

Now that this account of the state of nature among states and a league of nations is complete, I will briefly review the concession that, as noted earlier, would need to follow. I have chosen to emphasize how Kant discusses the concept of a state of nature in an international context, mainly since it's in this context that he tends to be especially clear that conflict can be born of mere disagreement. It is, I believe, difficult to dispute the textual evidence for this position. It is also, I believe, exceptionally difficult to dispute on general philosophical grounds that there are any number of possible causes of international strife, including distinct cultural mores, variances in religious belief or practice, language barriers, opposed opinions regarding the importance of history or custom, incompatible approaches to diplomacy, the particular evolution of case law, and so on. But it only helps my case to note an important way in which the account I have given of the state of nations among states turns out be quite close to the one Kant gives of

18. Kleingeld reaches a similar conclusion concerning why Kant's league of nations might prove more effective than often assumed. See "Approaching Perpetual Peace: Kant's Defence of a League of States and His Ideal of a World Federation," 320.

the state of nature among persons. In neither instance does Kant endorse the view that the state of nature is necessarily characterized by aggression, ill-intentioned overreach, greed, or avarice. According to the argument developed in the beginning of his discussion of public right in the *Doctrine of Right*, while we are all aware "of the maxim of violence in human beings and of the tendency to attack one another" (MS 6:312), these are not the grounds on which we are justified in compelling entry into civil society and removal from the state of nature. On the contrary, Kant insists that "however well disposed [*gutartig*] and law-loving [*rechtliebend*] human beings might be,"[19] it is still a matter of *a priori* rational necessity that we leave the state of nature (MS 6:312).

This point is often overlooked since many interpreters have read Kant as endorsing a "presumption of badness,"[20] or a presumption that because of the evil present throughout human nature, we can rightfully assume that the people surrounding us are imminent threats to our person and our property.[21] But the scholarship is increasingly coming to the understanding that we can secure Kant's conclusions about the need to exit from the state of nature without this presumption. Violence can break out even when there is no *maxim* of violence behind it. In fact, "well disposed and law-loving" people can pose threats to one another simply because in the state of nature, individual persons—and equally, Kant adds, "peoples and states"—are in a position where each party "follows its own judgment" and does "*what seems right and good to it*" (MS 6:312). This concern about discordant judgments should be no surprise to anyone familiar with casuistical questions regarding Modern conceptions of property and their Lockean elements: if, to cite an example from Kyla Ebels-Duggan, you leave an area for some length of time after planting a tree and then another person cultivates its fruit,[22]

19. I have modified Mary Gregor's translation, which renders *rechtliebend* as "law-abiding."

20. This phrase is used repeatedly by B. Sharon Byrd and Joachim Hruschka in *Kant's Doctrine of Right: A Commentary*. The phrase is also used as a foil throughout Alice Pinheiro Walla's critique of Byrd and Hruschka in "Human Nature and the Right to Coerce in Kant." As made clear by what follows in this chapter, I endorse Pinheiro Walla's criticisms of Byrd and Hruschka.

21. Now, there may initially appear to be textual evidence for this presumption. Most notably, at MS 6:307, Kant references a "presumption of evil" that is relevant to his argument that individuals can be coerced to leave the state of nature. But, as Pinheiro Walla shows, the evil we can presume in another person holds not insofar as she or he threatens us but insofar as another person refuses to form a civil society. See "Human Nature and the Right to Coerce in Kant," 132–133.

22. "Moral Community: Escaping the Ethical State of Nature," 5. Though at this and other points it seems Ebels-Duggan could endorse the claims I am making in this section,

when we come together again, we'll exist in a state of nature if we lack a common set of courts or a mutually recognized judiciary that can resolve our conflicting views about ownership. Or, to build off a well-known example from Robert Nozick, if you install a set of wooden posts in the ground, you and I can find ourselves at odds about whether this entitles you to the land encircled by posts or merely the land that exists directly under them.[23, 24] No presumption of badness is advocated by Kant or needed to make sense of either the strife individuals are vulnerable to or why we must exit the state of nature.[25] Thus, we can see that Kant, once again, has an agnostic attitude regarding what motives can be responsible for conflict. While the international context proves especially helpful for motivating and clarifying Kant's worries about a state of nature, his characterizations of *any* such state of nature uniformly emphasize neutrality about an agent's motives. The path to hell—whether in interpersonal or world affairs—can be paved with good intentions. And with this account of the state of nature now at hand, we can turn to the question of how it informs Kant's *Religion*.

it is unclear to me whether she would distance herself from the "presumption of badness" in the way that I, Pinheiro Walla, or Jeremy Waldron have. For Waldron's view, see note 25 below. I say more about Ebels-Duggan's view in notes 33 and 40 of this chapter.

23. *Anarchy, State, and Utopia*, 174.

24. The examples I have given would, in the literature on Kant's theory of the state, typically be referred to as examples of "indeterminacy" in the state of nature among persons (see, e.g., Arthur Ripstein, *Force and Freedom: Kant's Legal and Political Philosophy*, 168–176). The concept of indeterminacy is appropriate for certain descriptions of these kinds of cases, not least because it reflects Kant's own language at, for example, MS 6:266. But this introduces the question of why, in the work I've done so far to prepare us for discussion of the ethical state of nature, I have chosen to refer to the conflicts pervading the state of nature among states as matters of disagreement as opposed to indeterminacy. The reason is as follows. In exiting the state of nature among persons, one gains the right to have a court settle a dispute and issue a determinate, enforceable decision as to what the wood posts establish or who owns the fruit. Given this, the notion of indeterminacy is closely associated with rights that have no parallel in Kant's federation of states or the ethical community. Thus, it could be potentially misleading to refer to conflicts permeating the state of nature among states as problems of indeterminacy. In addition, since individual actors can't be assured of determinate outcomes in either international affairs or ethics, it is helpful to shift our emphasis from indeterminacy to the goal more within reach, namely, increased understanding of the different vantage points that lead to disagreement. I elaborate on this point in the remainder of this chapter.

25. For likeminded conclusions, see Waldron, "Kant's Theory of the State," 195–196; Pinheiro Walla, "Human Nature and the Right to Coerce in Kant," 132–134; and the work of Ripstein, who is perhaps the best known advocate of a "non-remedial" reading of Kant's theory of the state. I am indebted to Pinheiro Walla for bringing Waldron's article to my attention.

The analogy between the ethical state of nature and a state of nature in a juridico-civil context is introduced several pages into Part Three of the *Religion*, and we soon find Kant highlighting a feature that should now be quite familiar to us. For Kant, what characterizes these states of nature is that "[i]n both each individual is his own judge [*Richter*]" (RGV 6:95). Notably, both the phrasing and the term "*Richter*" directly match the language later used in *Perpetual Peace* and the *Doctrine of Right*. Kant also, in a footnote, references both the state of nature's Hobbesian lineage and how in such a state, each person "wants himself to be the judge" and to assert his own judgment in matters of "one's own affairs" (RGV 6:97n). Together, these points show that in order to understand the ethical state of nature and the ethical community, it will indeed be crucial to refer back to its analogue in Kant's political philosophy.

To fill out further Kant's characterization of the ethical state of nature, I will quote at length and work through a selection of the text:

> Just as the juridical state of nature is a war of every human being against every other, so too is the ethical state of nature one in which the good principle, which resides in each human being, is incessantly attacked by the evil which is found in him and in every other as well. Human beings (as we remarked above) mutually corrupt one another's moral predisposition and, even with the good will of each individual, because of the lack of a principle which unites them, they deviate through their dissensions [*Mißhelligkeiten*] from the common goal of goodness, as though they were *instruments of evil*, and expose one another to the danger of falling once again under its dominion. (RGV 6:96–97)

This account of the ethical state of nature is both perplexing and capable of moving our reconstruction forward. As with Kant's broader account of the ethical state of nature throughout the *Religion*, this particular passage is challenging because it is not immediately clear how we ought to characterize the risks we face in the ethical state of nature. At first glance, the risks seem to pertain to our very capacity for sustained moral motivation: Kant speaks, after all, of how human beings corrupt one another, how goodness is incessantly under attack by evil, and how we are at danger of falling under the dominion of evil's rule. Given this, the ethical state of nature can seem to highlight our tendency to adulterate the moral incentive, particularly when a person is proximate to those who lack a moral commitment. In this case, a person's central moral challenge concerns whether, in a climate of sustained mutual aggression, she will abandon the good principle for the evil one.

But at other points in this same exact passage, the vulnerabilities Kant highlights in the ethical state of nature seem either more attenuated or to lead us toward a somewhat different picture. Kant appears to affirm the goodness of individuals in the ethical state of nature and to argue that threats to them stem not from evil itself but "the lack of a principle which unites" the good in each of us. He also speaks of human beings as falling victim not to the evil principle per se but to a situation in which we will function "as though [als ob]" we were the tools, "instruments," or machinery (Werkzeuge) of evil (RGV 6:97). Moreover, while Kant does speak of mutual corruption in this passage, he also refers us to remarks he made "above," and when we turn to these earlier comments, we find this corruption framed in a peculiar way. On the first page of Part Three of the Religion, Kant notes that "envy, addiction to power, [and] avarice" tend to "assail his [man's] nature" (RGV 6:93–94), and while Frierson, Wood, and others take these comments to show that evil is characterized by unsocial sociability or that what the ethical community must do is address those "fertile breeding grounds" of social life that promote evil,[26] Kant does not present the risks we face in a way that aligns with this interpretation. In his further telling, no specific social dynamics must be presupposed in order for a threat to be present. Indeed, it seems that no particular attitudes or actions toward another human being are needed in order to have an ill effect on that person. As Kant states quite clearly, it is not necessary to assume that those around us are "sunk into evil" (RGV 6:94); instead, for persons to "mutually corrupt" another individual, "it suffices that they are there, that they surround him, and that they are human beings" (RGV 6:94).

As we begin to appreciate these details, it becomes clear that Kant's account of the ethical state of nature is not only more nuanced than it at first appears. It is also nuanced in ways that recall the complex character of the state of nature in Kant's political writings. In both cases, the causes of conflict or antagonism are different from what we initially make them out to be. In the political case, we are in a state of nature insofar as the mere potential for conflict exists. Most importantly, even the best-intentioned parties can find themselves in discord with one another. Such strife can exist without an underlying vice as its cause and can revolve around, for example, where a state's boundary lies or what installing wood posts in unoccupied land entitles a person to. Kant appears in the Religion to emphasize

26. "Providence and Divine Mercy in Kant's Ethical Cosmopolitanism," 147.

a similar neutrality regarding why we find ourselves at odds with one another in the ethical state of nature. There is no presumption that anyone around us is "sunk into evil." And even if the "good *principle*" is "incessantly attacked" by evil, this is not to say that actual *persons* threaten or intend to threaten one another. Kant's point seems rather more abstract and general, and meant to illustrate that the conflict permeating the ethical state of nature is not necessarily or even probably a by-product of a given individual's commitment to the evil principle.

This is a crucial observation. It explains how we can understand Kant's claim that the duty to form an ethical community pertains "not of human beings toward human beings but of the human race [*Geschlecht*] toward itself," or of the "human species [*Gattung*]" (RGV 6:97). In the argument regarding the radical evil universal in human nature outlined in Chapter 5, I established that when Kant speaks of our species character, he does so to highlight the aspect of a person's action that is identical to that of every other human being. To consider a person qua her species membership is to consider how she is constrained to act regardless of which practical principles she adopts. Thus, when Kant says it is a duty of the human species to leave the ethical state of nature, he is arguing that all persons—even the very best—find themselves in a state of discord with other human beings and must therefore take measures to leave this state. The duty to leave the ethical state of nature cannot be prescribed on an ad hoc basis or described as a duty that pertains to a person qua his or her individual disposition, since even if each person was to make the moral law his or her fundamental maxim, there would still be some feature of his or her action productive of conflict.[27]

So we can conclude that, in the ethical state of nature, purity of will does not rule out "dissensions," conflict, or discord. But *why* will people—even those committed to the moral law—find themselves in conflict and what, exactly, are these conflicts about? What sort of unity or collective arrangement is absent and what would it take to develop it? Again, the breadth of possible answers is clear given how variably Kant's readers have understood the goals of the ethical community. And while many of their suggestions—several of which were noted at the start of this chapter—are initially plausible, none fully convince. DiCenso, Anderson-Gold, and others argue that the ethical community is characterized by global institutions and normative frameworks that emphasize the universality of human rights.[28]

27. I build on these arguments about our species' obligation to form an ethical community in the conclusion of this chapter.
28. See page 204 and note 5 of this chapter.

But there is no evidence for this position and it takes well too far Kant's analogy between the ethical community and juridico-civil affairs. Indeed, this reading fully ignores Kant's insistence that there is merely a "certain analogy" between these two domains and instead sets up a full alignment between our ethical and political ends (RGV 6:94).[29] Alternatively, Kant does make a brief reference to the highest good in his account of the ethical community, one that has been picked up by Wood, Sweet, and Moran.[30] As Wood puts it, "true community involves the collective pursuit of ends set in common with one another,"[31] and since the only end that can be universally presumed is the highest good,[32] advancement toward the highest good must be what characterizes the ethical community.[33] There are, however, at least a few reasons why this reference to the highest good can't be as straightforward as it initially seems,[34] and the most immediate, pressing

29. On this point, I am in full agreement with Palmquist, *Comprehensive Commentary on Kant's* Religion within the Boundaries of Mere Reason, 255.

30. See note 4 of this chapter for references to Moran and Sweet's approaches. For Wood's references to the highest good, see *Kant's Ethical Thought*, 311–316.

31. Ibid., 315.

32. Ibid., 314–315.

33. Ebels-Duggan likewise emphasizes the collective pursuit of ends but offers a distinctly second-personal account of what these ends are and what is involved in sharing them ("Moral Community: Escaping the Ethical State of Nature," 8). Instead of the highest good, Ebels-Duggan focuses on ends of benevolence and argues that, in the ethical state of nature, each person lacks the ability to give another person reason to support her or his "discretionary choices" and, by extension, fails to have directly affirmed her or his status as a setter of ends ("Moral Community: Escaping the Ethical State of Nature," 8). The ethical community, by contrast, exists when the general duty of benevolence has been transformed such that persons recognize each other as authorized to make claims for assistance in the pursuit of some goal or project. As Ebels-Duggan sees it, we mutually agree upon certain projects or plans for which we will support one another, and in doing so, an end set by one individual becomes "jointly ratified" or endorsed as worthy of pursuit by both parties ("Moral Community: Escaping the Ethical State of Nature," 15). This is an extremely interesting approach, but there is very little evidence that it can really be Kant's view. There are several points at which this becomes clear, but I will limit myself to two important (and related) difficulties. First, Ebels-Duggan's emphasis on second-personal reasons is completely absent from Kant's discussion. Second, because her view requires that intimate relationships are the paradigmatic examples of moral communities, Ebels-Duggan's view evolves into one that, in fact, becomes at odds with Kant's own. For Kant, it is essential that ethical communities have an "ever-expanding" scope (RGV 6:94); we must, as I will revisit later in this chapter, approximate as closely as possible the "diffusion" of the ethical community so that it will eventually become a "universal republic" (RGV 6:94 and 6:98, respectively). Ebels-Duggan, however, leaves it unclear how the breadth demanded by a universal republic can be reconciled with the partiality or exclusivity characteristic of intimate unions. Since this problem seems unsolvable, Ebels-Duggan's view is not viable in its current form.

34. Because Kant's discussion of the highest good is unsatisfyingly quick and abbreviated, and because Kant never even refers to the proportion of virtue and happiness in this comment, some may question, with Palmquist, whether Kant has in mind

difficulty is that an enjoinder to share ends with one another is not meaningful absent guidance on how to overcome those dissensions or conflicts that stand in the way. To characterize the ethical community in terms of the highest good is to restate what is absent in the ethical state of nature, but it does not actually explain how human beings can equip or prepare themselves to exit that state or how to form, or work toward, an ethical community. Moreover, as I will argue in what follows, this problem can be addressed, but only so long as we don't neglect an opportunity to rethink the causes behind conflict and discord. I argued in Chapter 7 that it is extremely helpful to understand moral progress more in cognitive than motivational terms and that postconversion weakness results from an imperfect grasp of what a moral commitment means. In the context of the current chapter, we will see how the cognitive underpinnings of moral progress can not only help illuminate the conflicts we face in the ethical state of nature but also, and as a result, assume an even more central role in Kant's theory of moral reform.

FROM THE ETHICAL STATE OF NATURE TO THE ETHICAL COMMUNITY

As we have established and as Kant notes, what characterizes a juridical state of nature among individuals or states are divergent understandings of how external freedom may be expressed (RGV 6:98). By contrast, the ethical state of nature, according to the *Religion*, centers on a different type of conflict or disagreement, namely, a conflict concerning *inner* freedom or our capacity to be unified under "laws of virtue" (RGV 6:94 and 6:95).

Thus, given Kant's analogy between these two domains, it is reasonable to conclude that those *Mißhelligkeiten* that cause strife in the ethical state of nature are best framed not only, as the Cambridge translation puts it, as "dissensions" but also—and as a mirror to the political case—as "disagreements" or "misunderstandings" regarding the expression of virtue. As noted in Chapter 7, virtue refers to a qualitative feature of the power of choice, one that increases over time and through the reflective cultivation of a *Lebenswandel*. But the path to good life conduct can be conceptualized in different ways; people similarly devoted to moral advancement can and do clash with one another regarding what set of social

something more generic, different, and "indeterminate" than the highest good as it is fleshed out in the second *Critique* (*Comprehensive Commentary on Kant's* Religion within the Boundaries of Mere Reason, 262).

causes or what moral priorities are most fitting of that commitment.[35] For instance, poverty, racial indifference or antipathy, environmental degradation, or the deterioration of civic norms can be thought more or less salient and as demanding either higher or lower priority in the pursuit of good works. A shared, underlying moral commitment in no way resolves every ethical disagreement, whether actual or potential, that can cause strife and disharmony among persons.[36]

This much seems correct, but one might question whether such disputes are problematic. The variability of such ethical beliefs would seem to be an inherent feature of social life, and it can also seem to be a positive one. Surely, this kind of virtuous pluralism is both intrinsically interesting and, since it exposes people to a variety of moral vocations and perspectives, instrumentally valuable. If Kant's concern about the ethical state of nature is this type of disagreement, and if the ethical community is to strip away this pluralism or is otherwise insensitive to its importance, then one will ask whether this doesn't speak all the worse for the ethical community and all the better for the ethical state of nature.

This criticism is not, in the end, applicable, but only if we heed some of its insights and both limit and properly interpret the function of the ethical community. First, let's note what this criticism neglects to mention. As Kant explicitly states in the section titled "Why the Human Being Must Leave the Ethical State of Nature In Order to Become a Member of an Ethical Community," it is through our mutual disagreements or *Mißhelligkeiten* regarding the "common goal of goodness" that individuals function "as though they were instruments of evil" (RGV 6:97). I commented on this indirect language earlier, and we can understand it better now. Good persons can find themselves undermining, interfering with, and being obstructed by others despite no intention on anyone's part to do so. The pursuit of good works is a passionate exercise for an individual, but the failure to understand how others engage in it, and the failure to communicate or even

---

35. This point is overlooked by Anderson-Gold, who argues that "[g]ood dispositions are naturally in harmony. There can be no conflict between them" ("God and Community: An Inquiry into the Religious Implications of the Highest Good," 126). For reasons that will become clear in what follows, I find this view implausible, both on textual and philosophical grounds.

36. Given my emphasis thus far on how the ethical community facilitates the cultivation of virtue, it might not be clear how this community avoids functioning as a moral elite. I have argued that even the very best of persons has some aspect of her actions that is productive of conflict and thus stands to benefit from the ethical community, but how, one might ask, do those involved in more preliminary moral struggles with evil participate in this community? I address this question directly and at length in the conclusion to this chapter.

fully grasp one's *own* approach to virtue, can lead to social stagnation, confused or poorly articulated plans for action, distrust, and any number of civil conditions so divisive or problematic that we must regard them "as if" they were the handiwork or machinery of evil. The danger we must attend to is stated most sharply in the draft of the *Conflict* essay, which offers helpful insights into Kant's theory of government and his views concerning the possibility of human progress. In a set of comments that pertain to the state of nature in both its political and ethical guises, Kant notes that when a multitude comes together to form a people,

> there must therefore first of all be agitation as in the *status naturalis* because even if human beings were all good natured, the diversity of opinions would certainly bring them to violence. Then someone will certainly say: "See what comes from our freedom and equality!"[37] (VASF 23:462)

As Kant makes vividly clear, unless they exit the ethical state of nature, even the best-intentioned persons leave moral commitments—both their own and those held by others—vulnerable to being unappreciated, undercut, or otherwise viewed with suspicion. What legitimacy, it will be asked, is there in devotion to moral causes or to our liberal ideals if they do not materially facilitate moral progress and if they, worse still, can even increase conflict? The value of pluralism is no illusion, but we cannot, as Kant quite rightly recognizes, be sanguine about our moral disagreements or failures to understand one another in the pursuit of good works.

Second, the pluralism whereby good works are differently prioritized by different persons would be suffocated by the ethical community only if Kant viewed this community as a space in which a shared plan of action must be fully determined and agreed to. But there is no reason to suppose that this is the case. Dissensions or misunderstandings are abated—and meaningful unity or community is achieved—not, really, when those who have made a moral commitment agree to do the same thing but when they make sense to one another. In putting the point this way, I am leaving room for the reciprocal sharing of ends and the pursuit of the highest good to remain parts of what the ethical community aims to accomplish. My argument is only that if we focus too narrowly on these goals, then we will overlook, first, how mutual misunderstandings are the obstacle that stands centrally in their way and, second, how the mitigation of such misunderstandings is the main task for the members of ethical communities.

37. Translation very slightly modified.

As I now further explain, there is much in favor of the claim that mutual understanding, as opposed to a perfected form of collective agency, is what Kant sees, and what we should see, as the central purpose of the ethical community. To begin, an increased ability to understand another's vantage point on good works appears to be what any voluntary community can reliably achieve. If the ethical community is to be non-coercive not merely in letter but also in spirit, then heterogeneous conceptions of goods works will often be ineliminable. By contrast, the ability to understand why someone has chosen one form of conduct (*Verhalten*) or a specific *Lebenswandel* is a plausible and significant goal.

Moreover, if we turn to Kant's account of how ethical communities must be organized, we will gain additional evidence concerning the importance of increased mutual understanding. As is well known, Kant maintains that we cannot be unified "except in the form of a church" (RGV 6:100), and that individuals so unified must conceptualize themselves as a "people of God" (RGV 6:99)—that is, as carrying out ethical duties that "must also be represented as divine commands," and with hearts open to God in the most "intimate" manner (RGV 6:99). I submit that by situating the ethical community in a church, and describing its members as a people of God, Kant gives us essential information concerning the chief aim of an ethical community, precisely how such a community equips us to overcome the misunderstandings that characterize the ethical state of nature, and how we thereby develop a socially engaged, productive approach to the pluralism that accompanies good life conduct.

A church has a core set of traditions, historical practices, and documents or scriptures that Kant sees as enabling individuals to acquire a progressively more refined empirical cognition of the moral elements of a religion. There is, as he says, a "peculiar weakness [*Schwäche*] in human nature" that prevents human beings from having an immediately clear vision of those moral truths that would comprise a true religion (RGV 6:103), and specific churches frame those truths in ways that allow them to be cognized or understood more readily.[38] As Kant conceives it, this "confirmation from experience" makes our grasp of the moral law and of virtue more local, particularized, or "contingent," but also more firm or steady (RGV 6:109 and 6:105, respectively). With the aid of a church, we gain the clarity and self-understanding that accompanies being able to give more vivid expression or sharper voice to one's approach to good life conduct.

---

38. This is especially clear at RGV 6:115 and 6:117.

As such, this account of the ethical community as a church centered on a "historical" or "ecclesiastical faith" extends the emphasis on the slow development of experiential moral knowledge and self-knowledge in Chapter 7. A church's traditions, practices, and texts help an individual comprehend what virtue demands and articulate priorities in the pursuit of good works. Moreover, these practices and texts provide, crucially, a shared touchstone or common vocabulary among persons, ensuring both that moral development is not a private or solipsistic affair and that those social dynamics that impede mutual understanding are addressed. Individuals within a given church can rely on scripture and tradition to refine, through both personal reflection and collective discussion, their understandings of good life conduct and to better engage those fellow members who hold at least somewhat similar beliefs. Scripture is also particularly well suited to open lines of communication between members of different faiths or between those with more radically different approaches to good works.

Scripture has unique potential because whereas traditions can be changed somewhat easily and in ways that reflect the particular needs or interests of a given few, scripture has a more stable and transcendent character (RGV 6:107). Interpretation of scripture will vary,[39] but since the words themselves cannot, it is "only through scripture" that we find "a revelation to present and future generations" and thereby facilitate especially broad forms of dialogue and mutual understanding (RGV 6:107). Thus, even those of different faiths, and those pursuing quite disparate kinds of good works, can refer to another faith's scriptures to understand why alternative beliefs are reasonable and how other well-intentioned people can have such different moral priorities. Indeed, since all legitimate ecclesiastical faiths are guided by the same goal of improving the moral condition of human beings (RGV 6:112), we have reason to be confident

---

39. Kant's views regarding scriptural interpretation are outside the scope of this chapter, but I will briefly note that Kant's treatment of this issue is in no manner at odds with the claims I make in this section regarding ecclesiastical faiths. Kant believes that reason, which any member of the laity possesses, is the most "authentic" interpreter of scripture (RGV 6:114). In addition, so long as the laity is free to think openly and publicly about religion (RGV 6:114), then scriptural scholars are also well positioned to do their job. This latter group is charged with understanding the original language, customs, and history of whatever church community produced a given set of scriptures (RGV 6:113). On the basis of this background, scriptural scholars then find reasonable moral interpretations of religious texts and rule out those interpretations that, though plausible or desirable on moral or other grounds (RGV 6:110), must be deemed dishonest or impossible on historical grounds. Scholars must adhere to this constraint, since any attempt to disregard history so as to promote a scripture's moral lesson would backfire. For in such cases, the people of a faith would not have access to a "definite and self-maintaining system" of moral or religious thought (RGV 6:114).

that members of a given church are primed to engage in productive dialogue with other faiths. Of course, ethical communities that do not take the form of a church still contain—through their own practices, history, and mission statements—those empirical elements that promote understanding of oneself, others, and possible good works. But it should not be too controversial to say that lesser weight tends to attach to attempts to modify these documents and traditions. In Kant's eyes, a secular ethical community will likely not anchor us firmly enough in those doctrines and symbolic parables that need to be in place in order for a person to have a common set of terms and insights with others. For at least this reason—I note another momentarily—churches remain his preferred model for ethical communities.[40]

Up to this point, I have stressed how an ethical community in the form of a church can provide publicly shared resources that help individuals clarify their own moral beliefs, articulate them to those who are not inclined to agree, and appreciate the beliefs about good conduct held by others. But alongside a discussion of these advantages, it is crucial to observe that there is at least one risk incurred in these collective exercises and that Kant, correspondingly, builds into his conception of the ethical community certain safeguards.

While it cannot be emphasized enough that an individual must engage in dialogue with others as she cultivates her approach to good works, it is also the case that after sufficient self-reflection and inquiry with others, a person must—so long as her own views are reasonable—consider herself permitted to break from prevailing positions within her ethical community regarding virtue and what social works take moral priority. The need for an ethical community to preserve independence of thought is evidenced by Kant's insistence that its members are to view themselves as a "people of

40. I believe that the strategy used in this paragraph for understanding the religious elements of Kant's ethical thought is especially promising. As Palmquist notes, while commentators have tended to minimize, ignore, or portray as indefensible the religious aspects of Kant's practical philosophy and the *Religion*, there has been a relatively recent wave of scholarship pushing against this trend; Palmquist places himself, Pasternack, and Firestone and Jacobs in this new camp (*Comprehensive Commentary on Kant's* Religion within the Boundaries of Mere Reason, xiv–xvi and 4). While I share Palmquist's worries about readings that minimize Kant's interest in empirical religion, my approach is different from his and certain others in this recent wave, since I try to explain why Kant is quite reasonably drawn to religion at certain key junctures but do not and will not argue that religion must be indispensable at these junctures. By contrast, Palmquist at points argues that Kant's appeals to religion are necessary adjuncts to his moral theory. See *Comprehensive Commentary on Kant's* Religion within the Boundaries of Mere Reason, xiv, and "Does Kant Reduce Religion to Morality?"

God" (RGV 6:98–101). By framing membership this way, Kant avoids two undesirable extremes.

On the one hand, and as described above, since church members are not socially isolated but united around shared, stable documents and traditions that guide moral inquiry, the ethical community aids the development of self-understanding and mutual understanding. On the other hand, since they are a "people of God," the private relationship between an individual parishioner and the One who knows that person's heart counterbalances the accumulated weight of social opinion. This, again, is a feature of a church that is difficult to replicate in non-religious ethical communities. In a non-religious community, where one acts either for fellow humanity or for one's fellow community members, a person likely does not enjoy the freedom of thought that accompanies a mindset tasked with discharging "divine commands" (RGV 6:99). A secular organization is more inclined to be a "democratic" one, where we are expected to submit to the crude "despotism" of majoritarianism (ZeF 8:352), or, which is perhaps worse, where we become vulnerable to the "illuminatism" of "individual inspirations" and thus adopt the fantastical insights popularized by self-anointed moral visionaries (RGV 6:102). But as a people of God, church members are united to one another while given a bulwark against peer pressure and its threat to free, productive thinking.[41]

And if we revisit Kant's guiding political analogy, this point finds only further support. Since individual persons seek to exit the state of nature without forming intimate unions or special alliances with one another, we must expect a parallel respect for the separateness of persons in the ethical community. Within the international context, Kant's pacifist league preserves the heterogeneity of nations and national identities, as well as a rich pluralism of traditions, cultures, and constitutionally permissible

41. Kant struggles to explain exactly what form the constitution of an ethical community takes and what it is analogous to. He settles on the answer that an ethical community is most like a "household" (RGV 6:102), and has met some resistance to this claim. Both Wood and Ebels-Duggan, for example, argue that an intimate relationship—whether friendship or marriage—would be a better analogue (Wood, *Kant's Ethical Thought*, 316, and "Religion, Ethical Community, and the Struggle Against Evil," 508. See also Ebels-Duggan "Moral Community: Escaping the Ethical State of Nature," 15). However, I find Kant's description of the ethical community in terms of a household quite appropriate once it is observed that he does not intend for us to envision a household in any ordinary sense at this stage of the *Religion*. His ultimate aim is to convince us that a people can see themselves as strongly united even if they lack common ancestors or blood. Thus, just as those in a republic can view themselves as born of the "same mother" from the "perspective of rights" (MS 6:343), so can those in the ethical community view themselves as born of the same father—namely, God—from the perspective of virtue.

arrangements of power. As states ought not to be compelled or coerced into joining a federation that would surpass a "coalition" (MS 6:351), or whose constitution would override the fundamental "separation" that must characterize even the most closely neighboring nations (ZeF 8:367), human beings should likewise abstain from the sort of ethical community that infringes on self-determination in thought and action.[42]

CONCLUSION

To complete this chapter, I will briefly consider a few remaining gaps in my treatment of the ethical community.

To begin, while the prior section of this chapter highlighted the importance of the ethical community to those who are engaged in the pursuit of good works, we can be certain—and I have been careful to leave room to note—that this community is still meant to be an inclusive one. By this I mean that an ethical community must bring into its fold those with different, and more preliminary, moral struggles.

Kant is explicit that an ethical community cannot be exclusive in its membership.[43] As he notes, a community cannot count as such unless it contains "many human beings of equally many dispositions" (RGV 6:105). Even more clearly, when Kant compares the ethical community's structure with the end or "final consequence" it aims to realize, he remarks that

> [t]he separation of the good from the evil, which would not have been conducive to the church's end in the course of its advance to perfection (since the mingling of the two was necessary precisely for this reason, in part to sharpen the virtue of the good, and in part to turn the other away from their evil through the example of the good), is represented as the final consequence of the establishment of the divine state after its completion. (RGV 6:135)

Kant's ultimate vision for the ethical community here is clear. As a necessary goal, all human beings are subject to the command to join an ethical community, regardless of which particular stage of moral reform one is in. But

---

42. While I disagree with DiCenso's emphasis on the institutional aspects of the ethical community (see pages 218–219 of this chapter), I believe he is right to see God as preserving the autonomy of the members of the ethical community. See *Kant, Religion, and Politics*, 252.

43. Again, while I am at odds with DiCenso's account in important regards, I am in complete agreement with him that the ethical community is conceived by Kant as highly inclusive. See *Kant, Religion, and Politics*, 249–250.

beyond this, any human being must *already* be viewed as, in a meaningful way, part of the ethical community because of his or her ability to have reciprocal exchanges with those of a different moral constitution. From one side, evil can be regarded by those involved in the struggle for virtue as an opportunity to sharpen their focus, as the presence of a common enemy can only remind those otherwise falling into conflict about good works that their real opponent is evil and not each other. And, from the other side, those who are good must share a community with those who are not yet, so as to engage them, at least, with an example to strive for.

For this reason, while there is something amiss in those readings of the ethical community that see only its role in addressing a "social climate of vice" or mutual antagonism between persons,[44] we can now conclude that what is, in fact, problematic is an excessively narrow focus on the conditions of evil.[45] Furthermore, while the exact reasons for inclusive membership may not have been clear until now, this "ever-expanding" quality should not come as a surprise (RGV 6:94). As noted earlier in this chapter, the duty to join the ethical community holds "not of human beings toward human beings but of the human race toward itself," or of the "human species" (RGV 6:97). If any human being, regardless of her actions or the particular constitution of her will, is solicited to join the ethical community, then even though Kant's main focus is on the slow progression of virtue in the empirical realm and those disagreements that can render good persons the tools of evil, this focus is neither a reason to restrict membership nor incompatible with other aims.[46]

Next, given my claim that we should expect a pluralism in good works and that particular ethical communities are tasked with helping individuals understand and accept as legitimate these variable

44. This is, to repeat, Frierson's turn of phrase in "Providence and Divine Mercy in Kant's Ethical Cosmopolitanism," 147.

45. Given my attention in the prior section to how the ethical community assists those who have already made a moral commitment, my approach is thus in contrast to Wood's, as Wood credits the ethical community with "effect[ing] a fundamental change of heart or revolution in the moral disposition of its members" (*Kant's Ethical Thought*, 316). I am perhaps somewhat closer to Firestone and Jacobs, who argue that the ethical community is only for those that are "moral converts" (*In Defense of Kant's Religion*, 183). But even in this case, my view does not align with theirs. For while Kant takes care to emphasize those ethical defects that persist even for people of good will, it is also important that the ethical community not be a closed space, or a space that caters only to the needs of those who have made a conversion.

46. Because Kant couples this inclusive structure with a strong emphasis on the work constitutive of postconversion moral progress, it is not surprising that commentators have struggled to understand what moral deficiencies or weaknesses are being addressed by the ethical community. On this point, see also page 203 of this chapter.

expressions of virtue, it may seem as though my account runs afoul of Kant's apparent interest in a much stronger form of unity among those who have exited the ethical state of nature. There are two ways this objection might get cashed out. Some will object that my account fails to attend properly to the role of the highest good as a common goal for the ethical community, whereas others will worry that I have neglected Kant's claim that particular ethical communities—that is, particular churches or ecclesiastical faiths—are, eventually, to transition into a universal ethical community or a pure religious faith, one wherein the historical contingencies and statutory practices of particular faiths are abandoned (RGV 6:115 and 6:121–124).

In response to this latter point regarding the development of a universal faith, it is important to note that Kant nowhere describes this transition as an obligation that persons should attempt to carry out. When he initially introduces this idea at RGV 6:115, he describes the establishment of a universal faith as more of a factual prediction, that is, as something that simply will happen. Then, a bit later, both the reasons for Kant's interest in a universal faith and how we should envision a transition toward it become more transparent. While Kant, as discussed earlier, views historical faiths as better suited to address our ethical needs than non-religious or secular organizations, such faiths are not without their disadvantages. By virtue of their documents, practices, and traditions, ecclesiastical faiths have a stable character that can promote intra- and interfaith dialogue, but such faiths—particularly insofar as persons can be born directly into them—might also hamper our willingness to think for ourselves. There is, as it was famously put in the *Enlightenment* essay, a tendency to incur one's own minority (WA 8:35), and this insight is relevant in the context of religion as well, as an ecclesiastical faith can prove difficult to "reconcile . . . with freedom in matters of thought" (RGV 6:123n). More specifically, Kant emphasizes, repeatedly and vociferously in Parts Three and Four of the *Religion*, that we are liable to fall into a passive or servile attitude regarding faith, interpreting traditions and practices not as an opportunity for moral reflection but as invitations to the cultlike, external performance of service.[47]

This is a significant problem, and one that the moral interest "constantly urges us to resolve" through "the idea of an objective unity of religion of reason" or a universal and pure moral faith (RGV 6:123n). But as Kant makes clear, a universal faith resolves the issue not through a directive or

---

47. For an excellent discussion of Kant's worries regarding servile forms of faith, see DiCenso, *Kant, Religion, and Politics*, 266–267 and 269–277.

encouragement to displace directly ecclesiastical faiths. Instead, this universal faith functions as a "regulative practical principle" (RGV 6:123n). This is a highly unorthodox expression and not one Kant elsewhere uses,[48] as regulative principles typically help organize and promote the activity of theoretical reason, especially in the domain of scientific inquiry. But even though Kant fails to call attention to how peculiar this notion of a regulative practical principle is, his intent seems clear enough. Just as those who investigate the different powers of the human mind transgress the proper limits of reason if they take, for example, the idea of a "fundamental power" as constitutive of objects (A649/B677), so would members of an ethical community overstep if they treat a universal faith as an end to be made real by the activity of the will. A universal faith is an idea (*Idee*) in the way that a fundamental power is: persons should act *as if* a universal faith will eventually emerge. Individuals should regard those conflicts or misunderstandings that persist within and among ethical communities as if they are not intrinsically insurmountable. Through the idea of a universal faith, we gain a reminder that ecclesiastical faiths are, fundamentally, only the "vehicle" for moral truths (RGV 6:106). Given this, my account, which emphasizes a plurality of faiths, does not need to be amended in any significant way.

Finally, questions about whether I have done sufficient justice to Kant's comment that the highest good is the end of the ethical community will in some ways echo the concerns noted above. In arguing that the ethical state of nature is characterized by disagreements regarding virtue and good works, and that the ethical community's foremost task to mitigate these misunderstandings, it may seem that I've failed to account for how the ethical community is a "union" or "system of well-disposed human beings" through which "the highest good can come to pass" (RGV 6:97–98). If Kant's interest is collective action, then my account, which emphasizes how shared documents and practices can help us understand other persons, will seem off the mark.

A twofold response is in order. First, and as mentioned earlier, even if others are correct that the ethical community is characterized by "the

48. Kant does, however, come quite close when he claims in the *Anthropology* that a cosmopolitan society should function as "not a constitutive principle" of human agency but "only a regulative principle" and an "unattainable idea" (Anth 7:331). Given Kant's analogy between, on the one hand, political and ethical states of natures and, on the other hand, his analysis of how we exit these states, his claim that a cosmopolitan society should only regulate the actions of the human race affirms my argument in this paragraph that a universal church is not to be treated as a material end or object of the will.

collective pursuit" of an end "set in common with others,"[49] well-disposed or well-intentioned persons will first need guidance on how to understand or recognize as legitimate the different approaches to virtue and good works that separate them. A more robust mutual understanding is the indispensable first step to those further and deeper forms of agreement in which agents reciprocally share and align themselves toward the pursuit of common ends. Therefore, my account of the ethical community is not in any deep tension with those that highlight its orientation toward the highest good. The argument of this chapter shows only that those accounts move too quickly, and, crucially, that far more attention must be given to how failure to collectively share in one another's ends is not always born of evil.

Second, while human beings should strive to form a union that has the highest good as its aim, Kant is clear that those working toward this must recognize that it will exceed their power to realize this well-ordered whole (RGV 6:98). We are to do what we can to bring about the highest good, but what we can do must take into account not only what is empirically possible but also what is morally appropriate given pluralistic expressions of virtue and the parameters set by personal conscience. When human beings have done as best they can within these limits, they are then to adopt the "presupposition" that those striving toward the highest good are, through God, "united for a common effect" (RGV 6:98). Given this, there is no real incompatibility between my account of the ethical community and one that focuses on the highest good. We must appreciate the division of labor Kant envisions: the idea of God allows us to understand how alignment toward a common effect will be perfected, but human beings must first accomplish what they can through action and, first and foremost, social discourse.

49. Wood, *Kant's Ethical Thought*, 315. See also page 219 of this chapter.

Conclusion

This book has explored key aspects of Kant's account of evil, how evil relates to self-deception, and—with a particular emphasis on its epistemic dimensions—Kant's theory of moral reform. I have argued, first, that we can lend complexity to Kant's claims about how evil is grounded in self-love in the following ways. In Chapter 1, I showed that if we consider the presence of the self in nonmoral life, we will see that a person who incorporates self-love into her fundamental maxim may not pursue the actions and ends that we would immediately associate with hedonistically motivated behavior. In Chapter 2, I explored where in Kant's writings we see him advocating the idea that there are different ways an evil will downgrades the incentive of respect for the law. Whereas in some cases an agent gives simple priority to the incentive of self-love, an agent may also attempt to "overdetermine" her faculty of choice or keep both incentives of practical reason alongside one another. Following this, and in Chapters 3 through 5, I explored the connection between evil and self-deception. After developing in Chapter 3 an account of how Kant conceives of self-deception or rationalization, and the crucial ways that self-deceptive rationalization remains vulnerable to norms of evidence and belief formation, I then documented in Chapters 4 and 5 how this analysis enables us to explain the ways that evil is rooted in self-deception or in dissimulation. Finally, in the last three chapters, I explored how, in a Kantian framework, self-knowledge can be acquired (Chapter 6); why moral reform is divided into two stages and why it requires an empirical, temporally developed form of self-knowledge (Chapter 7); and Kant's arguments about how an ethical community can equip human beings to further refine, express, and communicate an approach to good life conduct (Chapter 8). Taken as a whole, these final chapters show that influential critics such as Hegel, Schopenhauer, Williams, and Murdoch have overlooked where Kant's ethics requires the development of a self that is interpersonally engaged, attentive to empirical conditions, and situated in a communal context that informs her particular pathways in moral reform.

As noted at its outset, one of my aims throughout this book has been to continue the recent trend of reassessing Kant's theory of evil, a particularly important task in light of earlier scholarship that tended to view his account either in generally unfavorable terms or as so inadequately developed that it discredited Kant's status as a philosopher. By uncovering a defensible and nuanced account of evil, evil's reliance on self-deception, and how the development of self-knowledge is integrated into moral reform, this book has met its stated goals. However, it is important to acknowledge potential deficiencies in the present study, and two in particular deserve attention.

First, and as shown in Chapters 4 and 5, there are junctures at which a full defense of Kant's theory of evil requires a full defense of Kant's theory of freedom. In both chapters, we saw how self-deception and the nearby defect of dissemblance increase our vulnerability to temptation. Insofar as the dissembling character of human action shows how outer conformity with the law can displace attention on one's inner motives, and insofar as self-deception enables us to form passions and a liking for impurity, the danger of both vices stems in part from how they tempt us either into, or further into, evil. But it has not only been outside the scope of this book to develop Kant's views regarding how exactly temptation functions, or how human beings, who must take themselves as transcendentally free, can in general understand the relevance of empirical conditions. There is also, in the literature, both no consensus as to how Kant resolves this issue and skepticism that this tension between transcendental freedom and material vulnerability can be adequately addressed, whether by Kant or his commentators.[1] Since this book cannot tackle this problem, I have thus far left an important gap empty while banking on the hope that it can eventually be filled.

Second, given how Kant relies on self-deception to illuminate evil and the endorsement of self-love, it may seem as though he develops a theory of self-deception that cannot be easily adapted to other contexts or inquiries. There is one particular instantiation of this worry we should linger over,

---

1. On this point, see note 38 and pages 113–114 of Chapter 4.

and it will enable us to say more about some of the above-noted concerns regarding Kant's theory of freedom as well.

According to an argument advanced by Cynthia Stark, Kant's views regarding the proximity between self-deception and self-love become untenable when we observe the full range of moral failures in human life.[2] Kant expressly supports the claim that all human beings know themselves as worthy of self-respect and fair treatment at the hands of other persons (MS 6:435–436), and on the basis of this, it seems that any individual who doubts herself as worthy of respect and self-respect would have to be laboring under a self-deception. Take, for example, a wife who claims that her own interests are always nothing in comparison with her husband's—Stark calls this the "Deferential Wife" case—or a person of color who regards himself as inferior to those who are phenotypically white.[3] Given Kant's moral psychology, it appears both persons must be seen as failing to acknowledge a moral status that is integral to one's own reason and agency and thus failing to be properly candid with oneself. But if self-deception presupposes, as it has in this book, a commitment to self-love, then we must also see a vice or character defect at work in the examples offered. This diagnosis is, for Stark, highly problematic because it seems that the drivers of fault in these examples are "perfectly obvious socio-cultural reasons."[4] After all, we could hardly make sense of such deficits of self-respect were it not for social norms regarding the second-tier status of women and persons of color.

Stark's objections go to the heart of how Kant deploys the concept of self-deceptive rationalization. Throughout this book, self-deception has been presented as an accompaniment to a deeper, more basic failure to give respect for the law adequate recognition. But this was due not only to my interest in Kant's theory of evil or my focus on the practical writings. For even in texts like the lectures on logic, rationalization and similar cognitive defects are generally described as motivated by pleasure. A person seeks, for example, to put distance between herself and some cognition—such as how much money she owes a creditor—that makes her uncomfortable, or that is comparatively less pleasing than some alternative cognition for which some, albeit less, evidence is available. Despite lengthy discussions of error, prejudice, and other intellectual vices in his logic lectures, Kant gives us no indication that self-deception can be motivated by something

2. See Stark, "The Rationality of Valuing Oneself: A Critique of Kant on Self-Respect."
3. Both examples are Stark's. See "The Rationality of Valuing Oneself: A Critique of Kant on Self-Respect," 76.
4. Ibid.

other than an arrogance, indulgence, or indolence that ultimately derives from improper self-love. And yet, as Stark's examples show, if any moral failure—including all failures of self-respect—requires an illicit self-deception grounded in self-love, then Kant's decision to circumscribe self-deception within an account of self-love has objectionable and offensive implications.

Now, because this book's main query is Kant's theory of evil, how evil relates to self-deceit, and moral reform, a full treatment of the above objection is outside my purview. That said, I submit that the arguments of this book will be an indispensable first step for determining the best way to respond to Stark's objections. As I have traced through different chapters Kant's arguments about how self-deception is put in the service of self-love, I have also laid out a theory of self-deception that, given its underpinnings in Kant's broader theory of mind, should prove valuable for dealing with the criticisms under consideration. We have seen that, for Kant, human beings are intrinsically interested in attaining evidence for their beliefs. Our cognitive attention is inherently captured by what seems true, so much so that, to recall a passage that was important to my initial discussion of self-deception, "[i]n most cases . . . a procedure of giving our approval, or withdrawing it, or holding it back[,] does not rest at all on our free choice, but rather is necessitated through and by the laws of our understanding and our reason" (V-Lo/Blomberg 24:156).

Thus, in cases where sociocultural norms present overwhelming evidence of one's diminished status—whether through insufficiently fair equality of opportunity, a lack of social respect, or some other mechanism—Kant's theory of cognition explains why it is exceptionally difficult to wrest attention away from these external markers and back toward inner consciousness of one's own worth. Even if the Deferential Wife can turn within and gain insight into her incomparable dignity, it is hardly difficult to understand why she is unable to stay fixed on it or square it with the preponderance of the evidence presented to her. Human beings are constitutively vulnerable to the truth, but this also means they are constitutively inclined to accept the epistemic manipulations produced by injustice.

This is, as noted, only the beginning of a defense of Kant against the above objections. But since these comments show not only how we may handle Stark's examples but also how Kant's practical philosophy—once supplemented with his broader theory of mind—could begin to give better acknowledgment of the importance of empirical conditions and prevailing social norms more generally, they are an especially promising note on which to end.

BIBLIOGRAPHY

Allison, Henry. *Kant's Theory of Freedom*. Cambridge: Cambridge University Press, 1990.

Allison, Henry. "On the Very Idea of a Propensity to Evil." *Journal of Value Inquiry*, vol. 36, no. 2–3 (2002): 337–348.

Allison, Henry. "Reflections on the Banality of (Radical) Evil." *Graduate Faculty Philosophy Journal*, vol. 18, no. 2 (1995): 141–158.

Allison, Henry. "Transcendental Idealism: The 'Two-Aspect' View." In Bernard den Ouden and Marcia Moen (eds.), *New Essays on Kant* (New York: Lang, 1987), 155–178.

Ameriks, Karl. *Interpreting Kant's Critiques*. Oxford: Oxford University Press, 2003.

Ameriks, Karl. *Kant and the Fate of Autonomy: Problems in the Appropriation of the Critical Philosophy*. Cambridge: Cambridge University Press, 2000.

Anderson-Gold, Sharon. "Cultural Pluralism and Ethical Community in Kant's Philosophy of History." *Graduate Faculty Philosophy Journal*, vol. 9, no. 1 (1982): 67–78.

Anderson-Gold, Sharon. "God and Community: An Inquiry into the Religious Implications of the Highest Good." In Philip J. Rossi and Michael Wreen (eds.), *Kant's Philosophy of Religion Reconsidered* (Bloomington: Indiana University Press, 1991), 113–131.

Anderson-Gold, Sharon. "Kant's Rejection of Devilishness." *Idealistic Studies*, vol. 14, no. 1 (1984): 35–48.

Anderson-Gold, Sharon. *Unnecessary Evil: History and Moral Progress in the Philosophy of Immanuel Kant*. Albany: State University of New York Press, 2001.

Anderson-Gold, Sharon, and Pablo Muchnik. "Introduction." In Sharon Anderson-Gold and Pablo Muchnik (eds.), *Kant's Anatomy of Evil*. Cambridge: Cambridge University Press, 2010.

Arendt, Hannah. *Eichmann in Jerusalem: A Report on the Banality of Evil*. New York: Penguin Books, 2006.

Aristotle. *Nicomachean Ethics*, translated by Terence Irwin. Indianapolis: Hackett, 1999.

Audi, Robert. "Self-Deception, Rationalization, and Reasons for Acting." In Brian P. McLaughlin and Amélie Oksenberg Rorty (eds.), *Perspectives on Self-Deception* (Berkeley: University of California Press, 1988), 92–120.

Baron, Marcia. "Freedom, Frailty, and Impurity." *Inquiry*, vol. 36, no. 4 (1993): 431–441.

Baron, Marcia. *Kantian Ethics Almost Without Apology*. Ithaca, NY: Cornell University Press, 1995.

Baron, Marcia. "What Is Wrong with Self-Deception?." In Brian P. McLaughlin and Amélie Oksenberg Rorty (eds.), *Perspectives on Self-Deception* (Berkeley: University of California Press, 1988), 431–449.

Barry, Peter Brian. *Evil and Moral Psychology*. New York: Routledge, 2013.

Baumgarten, Alexander. *Metaphysics: A Critical Translation with Kant's Elucidations, Selected Notes, and Related Materials*, translated by Courtney D. Fugate and John Hymers. London: Bloomsbury, 2014.

Beck, Lewis White. *A Commentary on Kant's* Critique of Practical Reason. Chicago: University of Chicago Press, 1960.

Berkowitz, Roger. "Misreading 'Eichmann in Jerusalem.'" http://opinionator.blogs.nytimes.com/2013/07/07/misreading-hannah-arendts-eichmann-in-jerusalem/.

Bernecker, Sven. "Kant zur moralische Selbsterkenntis." *Kant-Studien*, vol. 97, no. 2 (2006): 163–183.

Bernstein, Richard. *Radical Evil: A Philosophical Interrogation*. Cambridge: Polity Press, 2002.

Biss, Mavis. "Avoiding Vice and Pursuing Virtue: Kant on Perfect Duties and 'Prudential Latitude.'" *Pacific Philosophical Quarterly*. doi:10.1111/papq.12141.

Biss, Mavis. "Kantian Moral Striving." *Kantian Review*, vol. 20, no. 1 (2015): 1–23.

Byrd, B. Sharon, and Joachim Hruschka. *Kant's Doctrine of Right: A Commentary*. Cambridge: Cambridge University Press, 2010.

Card, Claudia. *The Atrocity Paradigm*. Oxford: Oxford University Press, 2002.

Carroll, Noël. *Beyond Aesthetics*. Cambridge: Cambridge University Press, 2001.

Cassirer, Ernst. *Kant's Life and Thought*, translated by James Haden. New Haven, CT: Yale University Press, 1983.

Caswell, Matthew. "Kant on the Diabolical Will: A Neglected Alternative?" *Kantian Review*, vol. 12, no. 2 (2007): 147–157.

Caswell, Matthew. "The Value of Humanity and Kant's Conception of Evil." *Journal of the History of Philosophy*, vol. 44, no. 4 (2006): 635–663.

Chignell, Andrew. "Belief in Kant." *Philosophical Review*, vol. 116, no. 3 (2007): 323–360.

Clark, Robert Thomas. *Herder: His Life and Thought*. Berkeley: University of California Press, 1955.

Coble, Kelly. "Kant's Dynamic Theory of Character." *Kantian Review*, vol. 7, no. 1 (2003): 38–71.

Cohen, Alix. "Kant on Anthropology and Alienology: The Opacity of Human Motivation and Its Anthropological Implications." *Kantian Review*, vol. 13, no. 2 (2008): 84–104.

Cureton, Adam. "Reasonable Hope in Kant's Ethics." Paper presented at the 2016 Southern Study Group of the North American Kant Society.

Dalferth, Ingolf. "Radical Evil and Human Nature." In Gordon Michalson (ed.), *Kant's* Religion Within the Boundaries of Mere Reason: *A Critical Guide* (Cambridge: Cambridge University Press, 2014), 58–78.

Descartes, René. *The Philosophical Writings of Descartes Vol. II*, translated by John Cottingham, Robert Stoothoff, and Dugald Murdoch. Cambridge: Cambridge University Press, 1984.

DiCenso, James. *Kant, Religion, and Politics*. Cambridge: Cambridge University Press, 2011.

DiCenso, James. *Kant's* Religion within the Boundaries of Mere Reason: *A Commentary*. Cambridge: Cambridge University Press, 2012.

Dillon, Robin. "Kant on Arrogance and Self-Respect." In Chesire Calhoun (ed.), *Setting the Moral Compass: Essays by Women Philosophers* (Oxford: Oxford University Press, 2004), 191–216.

Doris, John. *Lack of Character*. Cambridge: Cambridge University Press, 2005.

Duncan, Samuel. "'There Is None Righteous': Kant on the *Hang zum Bösen* and the Universal Evil of Humanity." *Southern Journal of Philosophy*, vol. 49, no. 2 (2011): 137–163.

Ebels-Duggan, Kyla. "Moral Community: Escaping the Ethical State of Nature." *Philosophers' Imprint*, vol. 9, no. 8 (2009): 1–19.

Elizondo, Sonny. "Reason in Its Practical Application." *Philosophers' Imprint*, vol. 13, no. 21 (2013): 1–17.

Engstrom, Stephen. "The *Triebfeder* of Pure Practical Reason." In Andrews Reath and Jens Timmermann (eds.), *Kant's* Critique of Practical Reason: *A Critical Guide* (Cambridge: Cambridge University Press, 2010), 90–118.

Enoch, David. "Agency, Schmagency: Why Normativity Won't Come from What Is Constitutive of Action." *Philosophical Review*, vol. 115, no. 2 (2006): 169–198.

Fackenheim, Emil. "Kant and Radical Evil." *University of Toronto Quarterly*, vol. 23 (1954): 339–353.

Firestone, Chris L., and Nathan Jacobs. *In Defense of Kant's* Religion. Bloomington: Indiana University Press, 2008.

Fischer, John Martin. "The Cards That Are Dealt You." *Journal of Ethics*, vol. 10, no. 1–2 (2006): 107–129.

Formosa, Paul. "Kant on the Limits of Human Evil." *Journal of Philosophical Research*, vol. 34 (2009): 189–214.

Formosa, Paul. "Kant on the Radical Evil in Human Nature." *Philosophical Forum*, vol. 38, no. 3 (2007): 221–245.

Frierson, Patrick. "Character in Kant's Moral Psychology: Responding to the Situationist Challenge." *Archiv für Geschichte der Philosophie*, forthcoming.

Frierson, Patrick. *Freedom and Anthropology in Kant's Moral Philosophy*. Cambridge: Cambridge University Press, 2003.

Frierson, Patrick. "Kant's Empirical Account of Human Action." *Philosophers' Imprint*, vol. 5, no. 7 (2005): 1–34.

Frierson, Patrick. *Kant's Empirical Psychology*. Cambridge: Cambridge University Press, 2014.

Frierson, Patrick. "Kantian Moral Pessimism." In Pablo Muchnik and Sharon Anderson-Gold (eds.), *Kant's Anatomy of Evil* (Cambridge: Cambridge University Press, 2010), 33–56.

Frierson, Patrick. "Providence and Divine Mercy in Kant's Ethical Cosmopolitanism." *Faith and Philosophy*, vol. 24, no. 2 (2007): 144–164.

Garcia, Ernesto. "A Kantian Theory of Evil." *The Monist*, vol. 85, no. 2 (2002): 194–209.

Gentz, Friedrich. "Über den ewigen Frieden." In Kurt von Raumer (ed.), *Ewiger Friede: Friedensrufe und Friedenspläne seit der Renaissance* (Freiburg: Karl Alber, 1953): 461–497.

Goethe, Johann Wolfgang. *Briefe, Bd. 2 (Briefe der Jahre 1786–1805)*, edited by Karl Robert Mandelkow. Hamburg: Wegner, 1962.

Goldstein, Jürgen. "Die Höllenfahrt der Selbsterkenntnis und der Weg zur Vergötterung bei Hamann und Kant." *Kant-Studien*, vol. 101, no. 2 (2010): 189–216.

Greco, John, and John Turri. "Introduction." In John Greco and John Turri (eds.), *Virtue Epistemology: Contemporary Readings*. Cambridge, MA: MIT Press, 2012.

Grenberg, Jeanine. *Kant and the Ethics of Humility*. Cambridge: Cambridge University Press, 2005.

Grenberg, Jeanine. *Kant's Defense of Common Moral Experience*. Cambridge: Cambridge University Press, 2013.

Grenberg, Jeanine. "Self-Deception and Self-Knowledge: Jane Austen's Emma as an Example of Kant's Notion of Self-Deception." *Con-Textos Kantianos*, no. 2 (2015): 162–176.

Grenberg, Jeanine. "Social Dimensions of Kant's Conception of Evil." In Pablo Muchnik and Sharon Anderson-Gold (eds.), *Kant's Anatomy of Evil* (Cambridge: Cambridge University Press, 2010), 173–194.

Grenberg, Jeanine. "What Is the Enemy of Virtue?" In Lara Denis (ed.), *Kant's Metaphysics of Morals: A Critical Guide* (Cambridge: Cambridge University Press, 2010), 152–169.

Grier, Michelle. *Kant's Doctrine of Transcendental Illusion*. Cambridge: Cambridge University Press, 2001.

Griffith-Dickson, Gwen. *Johann Georg Hamann's Relational Metacriticism*. Berlin: De Gruyter, 1995.

Grimm, Stephen. "Kant's Argument for Radical Evil." *European Journal of Philosophy*, vol. 10, no. 2 (2002): 160–177.

Guyer, Paul. "Examples of Moral Possibility." In Klas Roth and Chris W. Supranant (eds.), *Kant and Education* (New York: Routledge, 2012), 124–138.

Guyer, Paul. *Kant*. New York: Routledge, 2006.

Guyer, Paul. *Kant and the Experience of Freedom*. Cambridge: Cambridge University Press, 1996.

Guyer, Paul. *Kant on Freedom, Law, and Happiness*. Cambridge: Cambridge University Press, 2000.

Guyer, Paul. "Kantian Communities: The Realm of Ends, the Ethical Community, and the Highest Good." In Charlton Payne and Lucas Thorpe (eds.), *Kant and the Concept of Community* (Rochester, NY: University of Rochester Press, 2011), 88–137.

Guyer, Paul. "Naturalistic and Transcendental Moments in Kant's Moral Philosophy." *Inquiry*, vol. 50, no. 5 (2007): 444–464.

Hamann, Johann Georg. *Sämtliche Werke*, edited by Josef Nadler. Vienna: Verlag Herder, 1949–1957.

Hardwig, John. "Action from Duty But Not in Accord with Duty." *Ethics*, vol. 93, no. 2 (1983): 283–290.

Herman, Barbara. *Moral Literacy*. Cambridge, MA: Harvard University Press, 2008.

Herman, Barbara. "On the Value of the Motive of Acting from Duty." *Philosophical Review*, vol. 90, no. 3 (1981): 359–382.

Herman, Barbara. *The Practice of Moral Judgment*. Cambridge, MA: Harvard University Press, 1996.

Henson, Richard. "What Kant Might Have Said: Moral Worth and the Overdetermination of Dutiful Action." *Philosophical Review*, vol. 88, no. 1 (1979): 39–54.

Hippel, Theodor Gottlieb von. *Lebensläufe nach Aufsteigender Linie, Band 1.* Berlin: Chriftian FriedrichVoß, 1778. http://www.deutschestextarchiv.de/book/view/hippel_lebenslaeufe01_1778/.

Holton, Richard. "Intention and Weakness of Will." *Journal of Philosophy*, vol. 96, no. 5 (1999): 241–262.

Johnson, Andrew. "Kant's Empirical Hedonism." *Pacific Philosophical Quarterly*, vol. 86 (2005): 50–63.

Jopling, David. "Kant and Sartre on Self-Knowledge." *Man and World*, vol. 19 (1986): 73–93.

Katsfanas, Paul. "Kant and Nietzsche on Self-Knowledge." In João Constâncio, Maria João, Mayer Branco, and Bartholomew Ryan (eds.), *Nietzsche and the Problem of Subjectivity* (Berlin: De Gruyter, 2015), 110–130.

Kekes, John. *The Roots of Evil.* Ithaca, NY: Cornell University Press, 2005.

Kerstein, Samuel. *Kant's Search for the Supreme Principle of Morality.* Cambridge: Cambridge University Press, 2002.

Kim, Hyoung Sung. "Function as a Transcendental Term in Kant's Analytic." Paper presented at the 2015 Eastern Study Group of the North American Kant Society.

Kleingeld, Pauline. "Approaching Perpetual Peace: Kant's Defence of a League of States and His Ideal of a World Federation." *European Journal of Philosophy*, vol. 12, no. 3 (2004): 304–325.

Kleingeld, Pauline. "Kant against Situationism." Paper presented in 2012 at the University of Antwerp conference "Kantian Ethics and Moral Life."

Kleingeld, Pauline. "Moral Consciousness and the Fact of Reason." In Jens Timmermann and Andrews Reath (eds.), *Kant's* Critique of Practical Reason: A Critical Guide (Cambridge: Cambridge University Press, 2010), 55–72.

Korsgaard, Christine. "The Right to Lie: Kant on Dealing with Evil." *Philosophy and Public Affairs*, vol. 15, no. 4 (1986): 325–349.

Korsgaard, Christine. *Self-Constitution.* Oxford: Oxford University Press, 2009.

Lichtenberger, Hans Peter. "Über die Unerforschlichkeit des Bösen nach Kant." *Studia philosophica: Jahrbuch der Schweizerischen philosophischen Gesellschaft*, vol. 52, no. 1 (1993): 117–131.

Loncar, Samuel. "Converting the Kantian Self: Radical Evil, Agency, and Conversion in Kant's *Religion within the Boundaries of Mere Reason.*" *Kant-Studien*, vol. 104, no. 3 (2013): 346–366.

Louden, Robert. "Evil Everywhere: The Ordinariness of Kantian Radical Evil." In Pablo Muchnik and Sharon Anderson-Gold (eds.), *Kant's Anatomy of Evil* (Cambridge: Cambridge University Press, 2010), 93–115.

Louden, Robert. *Kant's Human Being: Essays on His Theory of Human Nature.* Oxford: Oxford University Press, 2011.

Louden, Robert. *Kant's Impure Ethics.* Oxford: Oxford University Press, 2002.

MacFarquhar, Larissa. *Strangers Drowning: Grappling with Impossible Idealism, Drastic Choices, and the Overpowering Urge to Help.* New York: Penguin Books, 2015.

Madore, Joël. *Difficult Freedom and Radical Evil in Kant: Deceiving Reason.* London: Continuum Studies in Philosophy, 2011.

Makkreel, Rudolf. *Imagination and Interpretation in Kant: The Hermeneutical Import of the Critique of Judgment.* Chicago: University of Chicago Press, 1990.

Makkreel, Rudolf. "Self-Cognition and Self-Assessment." In Alix Cohen (ed.), *Kant's Lectures on Anthropology: A Critical Guide* (Cambridge: Cambridge University Press, 2014), 18–37.

Mariña, Jacqueline. "Kant on Grace: A Reply to His Critics." *Religious Studies*, vol. 33 (1997): 379–400.

Mariña, Jacqueline. "Transformation and Personal Identity in Kant." *Faith and Philosophy*, vol. 17, no. 4 (2000): 479–497.

McCarty, Richard. "Kant's Incorporation Requirement: Freedom and Character in the Empirical World." *Canadian Journal of Philosophy*, vol. 38, no. 3 (2008): 425–451.

McGinn, Colin. *Evil, Ethics, and Fiction*. Oxford: Clarendon Press, 1997.

McMullin, Irene. "Kant on Radical Evil and the Origin of Moral Responsibility." *Kantian Review*, vol. 18, no. 1 (2013): 49–72.

Meld Shell, Susan. *Kant and the Limits of Autonomy*. Cambridge, MA: Harvard University Press, 2009.

Meld Shell, Susan. "Kant's 'True Economy of Human Nature': Rousseau, Count Verri, and the Problem of Happiness." In Alix Cohen (ed.), *Kant's Lectures on Anthropology: A Critical Guide* (Cambridge: Cambridge University Press, 2014), 194–229.

Melnick, Arthur. *Kant's Theory of the Self*. New York: Routledge, 2009.

Michalson, Gordon. *Fallen Freedom*. Cambridge: Cambridge University Press, 1990.

Miller, Eddis. *Kant's Religion within the Boundaries of Mere Reason: A Reader's Guide*. London: Bloomsbury, 2015.

Moran, Kate. *Community and Progress in Kant's Moral Philosophy*. Washington, DC: Catholic University Press of America, 2012.

Moran, Kate. "Delusions of Virtue: Kant on Self-Conceit." *Kantian Review*, vol. 19, no. 3 (2014): 419–447.

Morgan, Seiriol. "The Missing Formal Proof of Humanity's Radical Evil in Kant's *Religion*." *Philosophical Review*, vol. 114, no. 1 (2005): 63–114.

Morrisson, Iain. "On Kantian Maxims: A Reconciliation of the Incorporation Thesis and Weakness of the Will." *History of Philosophy Quarterly*, vol. 22, no. 1 (2005): 73–89.

Morton, Adam. *On Evil*. New York: Routledge, 2004.

Muchnik, Pablo. "An Alternative Proof of the Universal Propensity to Evil." In Pablo Muchnik and Sharon Anderson-Gold (eds.), *Kant's Anatomy of Evil* (Cambridge: Cambridge University Press, 2010), 116–143.

Muchnik, Pablo. *Kant's Theory of Evil*. Lanham, MD: Lexington Books, 2010.

Munzel, G. Felicitas. *Kant's Conception of Moral Character: The "Critical" Link of Morality, Anthropology, and Reflective Judgment*. Chicago: University of Chicago Press, 1999.

Murdoch, Iris. *The Sovereignty of Good*. New York: Routledge, 1971.

Nielsen, Kai. *Marxism and the Moral Point of View: Morality, Ideology, and Historical Materialism*. Boulder, CO: Westview Press, 1989.

Nozick, Robert. *Anarchy, State, and Utopia*. New York: Basic Books, 1974.

O'Connor, Daniel. "Good and Evil Disposition." *Kant-Studien*, vol. 76 (1985): 288–302.

O'Hagan, Emer. "Moral Self-Knowledge in Kantian Ethics." *Ethical Theory and Moral Practice*, vol. 12, no. 5 (2009): 525–537.

Palmquist, Stephen. *Comprehensive Commentary on Kant's Religion within the Boundaries of Mere Reason*. Oxford: Wiley Blackwell, 2015.

Palmquist, Stephen. "Does Kant Reduce Religion to Morality?" *Kant-Studien*, vol. 83, no. 2 (1992): 129–148.

Palmquist, Stephen. "Kant's Quasi-Transcendental Argument for a Necessary and Universal Evil Propensity in Human Nature." *Southern Journal of Philosophy*, vol. 46, no. 2 (2008): 261–297.

Palmquist, Stephen, and Steven Otterman. "The Implied Standpoint of Kant's *Religion*: An Assessment of Kant's Reply to (and an English Translation of) an Early Book Review of *Religion Within the Bounds of Bare Reason*." *Kantian Review*, vol. 18, no. 1 (2013): 73–97.

Papish, Laura. "Expansionist Interpretations of Radical Evil." In *Natur und Freiheit, Akten des 12. Internationalen Kant-Kongresses*. Berlin: De Gruyter, in press.

Papish, Laura. "Moral Feeling and Moral Conversion in Kant's *Religion*." *Idealistic Studies*, vol. 43, no. 1–2, (2013): 11–26.

Papish, Laura. "Promoting Black (Social) Identity." *Social Theory and Practice*, vol. 41, no. 1 (2015): 1–25.

Pasternack, Lawrence. "Can Self-Deception Explain *Akrasia* in Kant's Theory of Moral Agency?" *Southwest Philosophy Review*, vol. 15, no. 1 (1999): 87–97.

Pasternack, Lawrence. *Routledge Philosophy Guidebook to Kant's* Religion within the Boundaries of Mere Reason. New York: Routledge, 2013.

Patrone, Tatiana. "What Sort of Fact Is Kant's Fact of Reason?" Unpublished manuscript.

Pinheiro Walla, Alice. "Human Nature and the Right to Coerce in Kant." *Archiv für Geschichte der Philosophie*, vol. 96, no. 1 (2014): 126–139.

Potter, Nelson. "Duties to Oneself, Motivational Internalism, and Self-Deception in Kant's Ethics." In Mark Timmons (ed.), *Kant's Metaphysics of Morals: Interpretive Essays* (Oxford: Oxford University Press, 2002), 371–390.

Prauss, Gerold. *Kant über Freiheit als Autonomie*. Frankfurt: Vittorio Klostermann, 1983.

Reath, Andrews. *Agency and Autonomy in Kant's Moral Theory*. Oxford: Oxford University Press, 2006.

Reath, Andrews. "Hedonism, Heteronomy, and Kant's Principle of Happiness." *Pacific Philosophical Quarterly*, vol. 70, no. 1 (1989): 42–72.

Ricken, Friedo. "Die Überwindung des Bösen: Kant über die Aufgabe einer Religiongemeinschaft." *Theologie Und Philosophie*, vol. 19, no. 4 (2009): 499–508.

Ripstein, Arthur. *Force and Freedom: Kant's Legal and Political Philosophy*. Cambridge, MA: Harvard University Press, 2009.

Rossi, Phillip. *The Social Authority of Reason: Kant's Critique, Radical Evil, and the Destiny of Humankind*. Albany: State University of New York Press, 2005.

Rukgaber, Matthew. "Irrationality and Self-Deception within Kant's Grades of Evil." *Kant-Studien*, vol. 106, no. 2 (2015): 234–258.

Sanford, David. "Self-Deception as Rationalization." In Brian P. McLaughlin and Amélie Oksenberg Rorty (eds.), *Perspectives on Self-Deception* (Berkeley: University of California Press, 1988), 157–169.

Schopenhauer, Arthur. *On the Basis of Morality*, translated by E. F. J. Payne. Indianapolis: Hackett, 1995.

Scott-Kakures, Dion. "At Permanent Risk: Reasoning and Self-Knowledge in Self-Deception." *Philosophy and Phenomenological Research*, vol. 65, no. 3 (2002): 576–603.

Shapiro, Tamar. "Kantian Rigorism and Mitigating Circumstances." *Ethics*, vol. 117, no. 1 (2006): 32–57.

Shelby, Tommie. "Ideology, Racism, and Critical Social Theory." *Philosophical Forum*, vol. 34 (2003): 153–188.

Sherman, Nancy. *Making a Necessity of Virtue: Aristotle and Kant on Virtue*. Cambridge: Cambridge University Press, 1997.

Spencer, Tom. "The Root of All Evil: On the Monistic Implications of Kant's *Religion*." *International Philosophical Quarterly*, vol. 56, no. 1 (2016): 23–43.

Stark, Cynthia. "The Rationality of Valuing Oneself: A Critique of Kant on Self-Respect." *Journal of the History of Philosophy*, vol. 35, no. 1 (1997): 65–82.

Sticker, Martin. "Legitimität und Grenzen moralischer Intuitionen bei Kant - Kant über gemeine Menschenvernunft und Vernünfteln." In Alfred Dunshirn, Elisabeth Nemeth, and Gerhard Unterthurner (eds.), *Crossing Borders. Grenzen (über)denken. Thinking (across) Boundaries* (Vienna: Phaidra of the University of Vienna, 2012), 893–904.

Stocker, Michael. "The Schizophrenia of Modern Ethical Theories." *Journal of Philosophy*, vol. 73, no. 14 (1976): 453–466.

Strawson, Galen. "The Impossibility of Moral Responsibility." *Philosophical Studies*, vol. 75, nos. 1–2 (1994): 5–24.

Sussman, David. *The Idea of Humanity: Anthropology and Anthroponomy in Kant's Ethics*. New York: Routledge, 2001.

Sussman, David. "Review of *Kant's Theory of Evil*." https://ndpr.nd.edu/news/24424-kant-s-theory-of-evil-an-essay-on-the-dangers-of-self-love-and-the-aprioricity-of-history/.

Sweet, Kristi. *Kant on Practical Life*. Cambridge: Cambridge University Press, 2013.

Tampio, Nicholas. "Pluralism in the Ethical Community." In Gordon Michalson (ed.), *Kant's Religion Within the Boundaries of Mere Reason: A Critical Guide* (Cambridge: Cambridge University Press, 2014), 175–192.

Taylor, Richard. *Good and Evil*. Amherst, MA: Prometheus Books, 1984.

Timmermann, Jens. "Kant's Puzzling Ethics of Maxims." *Harvard Review of Philosophy*, vol. 8, no. 1 (2000): 39–52.

Timmons, Mark. "Evil and Imputation in Kant's Ethics." *Jahrbuch für Recht und Ethik*, vol. 2 (1994): 113–141.

Tubert, Ariela. "Review of Patrick R. Frierson, *Freedom and Anthropology in Kant's Moral Philosophy*." *Ethics*, vol. 119, no. 4 (2009): 768–773.

Vanden Auweele, Dennis. "Kant on Religious Moral Education." *Kantian Review*, vol. 20, no. 3 (2015): 373–394.

Waldron, Jeremy. "Kant's Theory of the State." In Pauline Kleingeld (ed.), *Toward Perpetual Peace and Other Writings on Politics, Peace, and History* (New Haven, CT: Yale University Press, 2006), 179–200.

Ware, Owen. "The Duty of Self-Knowledge." *Philosophy and Phenomenological Research*, vol. 79, no. 3 (2009): 671–698.

Ware, Owen. "Rethinking Kant's Fact of Reason." *Philosophers' Imprint*, vol. 14, no. 32 (2014): 1–21.

Watson, Gary. *Agency and Answerability*. Oxford: Oxford University Press, 1997.

Williams, Bernard. *Shame and Necessity*. Berkeley: University of California Press, 1993.

Wood, Allen. "The Evil in Human Nature." In Gordon Michalson (ed.), *Kant's Religion Within the Boundaries of Mere Reason: A Critical Guide* (Cambridge: Cambridge University Press, 2014), 31–57.

Wood, Allen. "Kant and the Intelligibility of Evil." In Pablo Muchnik and Sharon Anderson-Gold (eds.), *Kant's Anatomy of Evil* (Cambridge: Cambridge University Press, 2010), 144–172.

Wood, Allen. *Kant's Ethical Thought*. Cambridge: Cambridge University Press, 1999.

Wood, Allen. *Kant's Moral Religion*. Ithaca, NY: Cornell University Press, 1968.

Wood, Allen. *Kantian Ethics*. Cambridge: Cambridge University Press, 2007.

Wood, Allen. "Religion, Ethical Community, and the Struggle Against Evil." *Faith and Philosophy*, vol. 17, no. 4 (2000): 498–511.

Wood, Allen. "Self-Love, Self-Benevolence, and Self-Conceit." In Stephen Engstrom and Jennifer Whiting (eds.), *Aristotle, Kant, and the Stoics: Rethinking Happiness and Duty* (Cambridge: Cambridge University Press, 1998), 141–161.

Zagzebski, Linda. *Virtues of the Mind: An Inquiry into the Nature of Virtue and the Ethical Foundations of Knowledge*. Cambridge: Cambridge University Press, 1996.

Zinkin, Melissa. "Respect for the Law and the Use of Dynamical Terms in Kant's Theory of Moral Motivation." *Archiv für Geschichte der Philosophie*, vol. 88, no. 1 (2006): 31–53.

INDEX

churches, and establishment of ethical community, 223–227

civil society
  and ethical community, 205–209
  and presumption of evil, 214n21

Coble, Kelly, Kant's theory of character, 167n21

cognition
  faculty of, in relation to the faculty of desire, 94, 97, 98–99
  and fantasy, 81
  Kant's theory of, 135n40, 166–167, 236
  in relation to self-deception and rationalization, 72–75
  and sensitivity to evidence, 72–73

cognitive dimensions of evil, 3–4, 98–100

cognitive dimensions of moral progress, 191–197, 224

commitment, and moral conversions, 178, 178n3, 189–191, 191n23, 191n24, 194–195, 195n28

compartmentalization, and self-deception, 75n13

conditional judgments, 63–64, 64n67

conduct, 164, 177, 186, 199–201

constitutivist readings of Kant, 53

contemporary philosophers on Kant's theory of evil, 3–4, 3n9

conversions, moral, 167–168, 177, 178, 183, 184, 186, 187, 189–191, 194–195

Dalferth, Ingolf
  rigorism, 57n54
  subordination of the moral law, 49n35

deception
  vs. dissimulation, 145
  vs. lying, 145

depravity, as stage of evil, 58, 60, 61

diabolical evil
  Kant's rejection of, 41, 54–55, 95–96, 106n26
  in relation to the entrenchment of evil, 106

Dialectic of the *Critique of Pure Reason*, 51, 54

DiCenso, James
  ethical community, inclusivity of, 227n43

ethical community, institutional aspects of, 227n42
  social influences and ethical community, 206, 208

dimes experiment, of Isen and Levin, 32, 32n27

dissemblance. *See* dissimulation

dissimulation
  defined, 144–145
  and general anthropology, 135–136n40
  and human agency, 145, 146, 149
  as an obstacle to self-cognition, 154–156
  and permissible moral illusion, 77
  in relation to self-deception, 147–149
  role in moral reform, 148–149, 148n52
  and universality of evil, 119–120, 136–137, 143–151
  vs. deception, 145
  vs. lying, 145
  and vulnerability to temptation, 151, 234

distraction, rationalization as, 97–102

Doctrine of Virtue, two-stage model of moral reform in, 197–201

Doris, John
  empirical research and ethical theory, 32n27
  moral character, 43–44, 45–46

doxastic flexibility, 76, 77–78, 78n18, 81

Ebels-Duggan, Kyla, 214–215, 214–215n22, 219n33

egoism
  as both motive and principle, 18, 25–26
  divisions of, 16–17, 16n10
  in hedonism and nonmoral psychology, 16–21, 25, 26
  in relation to unsocial sociability, 29

Eichmann, Adolf
  evil and self-deception, 100–101
  and models of nonmoral choice, 33, 33n29
  in relation to evil and self-love, 3, 3n7, 33

empirical action
  and moral reform, 183, 186–187, 194–195, 197

and self-knowledge, 164
  vs. conduct, 199–201, 201n41
entrenchment of evil
  self-conceit and, 108–109
  self-deception and, 7, 88–90, 102–109,
    111, 114
  self-love and, 103–104, 110–112, 114
errors in judgment, 65
ethical community
  and the church, 223–227
  and civil society, 205–209
  duty of humans to form, 204, 204n3,
    227–228, 228n45
  and the ethical state of nature,
    220–227
  and highest good, 204, 219–220,
    219–220n34, 219n33, 230–231
  household as analogous to, 226n41
  inclusivity of, 227–228, 228n46
  independence of thought in,
    225–227
  and international federations,
    207–209
  interpretations of, 203–205
  moral defects addressed by, 203–204,
    204n2, 220–227
  and moral reform, 8–9, 205
ethical state of nature
  analogous with a juridico-civil state of
    nature, 205–209
  in comparison to the state of nature
    among persons, 213–215
  in comparison to the state of nature
    among states, 209–215
  and discordant judgments between
    people, 214–215, 217–218
  in relation to ethical community, 205,
    206–208, 214, 216–222
evidence
  effect on human will of
    acknowledging, 73
  guidance by norms of, 71, 72
evil disposition vs. propensity, 123–126
evil, entrenchment of
  and lack of introspection, 104n23
  root of evil, 7, 87–91
  self-conceit and, 108–109
  self-deception and, 7, 88–90, 102–109,
    111, 114
  self-love and, 103–104, 110–112, 114

evil, Kant's theory of and
  expansionist views, 42–43
  as subordination of moral law,
    40–41, 46
  as overdetermination of the will, 6,
    48–53, 55, 56–57, 61, 62, 64–65
  as prioritization of moral law, 6, 47
evil, necessary conditions of, 7, 89–90,
  90–99, 102
evil, responsibility for, 126–129,
  136–138, 138n41, 146, 150
evil, three senses of rootedness of, 7,
  87–91, 115
evil, three stages of, 58–62

fact of reason, 94–95, 95n15
faith-based community, and ethical
  community, 9, 224–225
fantasy, within faculty of cognition, 81
Firestone, Chris
  ethical community, 228n45
  interpretation of "species," 140n44
Formosa, Paul
  compartmentalization and
    self-deception, 75n13
  universality of evil, 125n11, 127n20
frailty, 58, 59–60, 60n59, 61, 181–182,
  189–192, 196–198
Frankfurt, Harry, 194
freedom
  interpretations of Kant's theory
    of, 114n38
  transcendental freedom and moral
    reform, 113–114, 184–185, 234
Frierson, Patrick
  ethical community, 206, 208n11, 217
  expansionist view of Kant's theory of
    evil, 42, 43, 45
  Kant's empirical theory of human
    action, 186n17
  moral character, 43–45, 52
  moral weakness, 184–185, 195
  in relation to overdetermination, 52
  transcendental freedom, 114n38,
    184–185, 185n15

Garcia, Ernesto, evil vs. immorality, 1n1
God
  belief in, 76
  and highest good, 231

incorporation, of self-love alongside
respect, 47–51, 48n34
incorporation thesis, 40
independence of thought
and churches, 226–227
in ethical community, 225–227
indifferentism, to good and evil, 56
individual character
development of, 139
and rigorism, 56–57
vs. species character, 140–143,
150–151
international federations
and ethical community, 207–209
league of nations, Kant's vision of,
210–212, 213–214
limitations of, 212–213
and potential for conflict,
210–211, 213
interpersonal comparisons,
and establishing one's
happiness, 28–29
introspection, limits of, 162–163,
171–172
Isen, Alice, 32

Jacobs, Nathan
ethical community, 228n45
interpretation of "species," 140n44
Johnson, Andrew, "Kant's Empirical
Hedonism," 13n4, 14n7
Jopling, David, self-knowledge,
188, 188n20
judgment
errors in, 65
objective grounds for, 80
judgments, hypothetical or
conditional, 63–64
Julie, or the New Heloise
(Rousseau), 157

"Kantian Moral Striving," (Biss), 182
"Kant on Religious Moral Education,"
(Vanden Auweele), 204n2
"Kant on the Intelligibility of Evil"
(Wood), 67–68, 68n1
"Kant's Empirical Hedonism" (Johnson),
13n4, 14n7
Kleingeld, Pauline, 44n22, 213n18
Korsgaard, Christine, 53

Lack of Character (Doris), 32n27
lawfulness, as substitute for moral
goodness, 144n47
league of nations, Kant's vision of,
210–212, 213–214
lectures on logic, and self-deception, 72–73
Levin, Paula, 32
logical egoism, 16, 16n10
Louden, Robert
anthropological proof of evil, 131n35
expansionist theory of Kantian evil,
42–43, 45
general anthropology, 135–136n40
significance of humility, 175n34
loving relationships
cognitive demands of, 81–84
and moral reform, 199–201
lying
internal vs. external, 69–71
to oneself vs. others, 70, 71–72
and self-deception and
rationalization, 69–76
vs. deception, 145
vs. dissimulation, 145

MacFarquhar, Larissa, moral
exceptionalism, 199n33, 199n34
Madore, Joël, 70n8, 91
Makkreel, Rudolf,
Kant's account of vitality, 20n17
limits of introspection, 171n27
Mariña, Jacqueline
grace, 9n14
moral weakness, 184–185, 195
transcendental freedom,
184–185, 185n15
maxims
and self-knowledge, 159–160,
174, 174n33
weakness in complying with, 183–185
McCarty, Richard, moral motivation,
49n36, 49n37
McMullin, Irene, proof of radical evil,
126, 127–129, 130n29, 137–138
Meld Shell, Susan, 22n21, 74n11
Melnick, Arthur, knowledge of the self in
experience, 171n28
mental existence, and bodily
experience, 26
Metaphysics (Baumgarten), 17n11

Michalson, Gordon, 37*n*2, 38*n*7, 38*n*9, 40*n*11, 58*n*55
Milgram shock experiments
  conflicted feelings of participants, 45–46
  and overdetermination, 51–52
  in relation to moral character, 43–44, 43*n*19, 46
moral agency, influential critiques of Kant's view of, 34
moral battle, 110–111
moral belief, 76–77
moral conversion, 167–168
  and commitment, 178, 178*n*3, 189–191, 191*n*23, 191*n*24, 194–195, 195*n*28
  reframing, 178–179, 189–197
moral egoism, 16, 17
moral goodness, lawfulness as substitute for, 144*n*47
moral illusion, permissible, 77
moral law
  as fact of reason, 94–95
  and the incentive of respect, 11, 40–41, 62–63
  knowledge of as motivating, 102, 166, 191*n*23
  and self-deception, 67, 84, 99, 105–106
  self-love and positive resistance to, 45
  subordination of, 6, 40–42, 46, 63
moral progress
  cognitive dimensions of, 191–197
  reframing, 178–179, 189–197
  in relation to individual and species character, 138–140
  as requiring ethical community, 203, 220–227
moral reform
  and ethical community, 8–9, 205
  and inscrutability, 5, 172*n*29
  outline of Kant's theory of, 177
  role of dissemblance in, 148–149, 148*n*52
  two-stage model of, 8, 177–201
moral reform, two-stage model of
  cognitive dimensions of moral progress, 191–197
  and conduct, 199–201

conversion as commitment, 178, 178*n*3, 189–191, 194–195
  in *Doctrine of Virtue*, 197–201
empirical character, 177, 182–183, 186–189, 194
good works, 201
importance of finding a moral cause, 199–200
intelligible character, 177, 187
interpretive challenges to, 179–183, 183–185, 185–189
moral conversion *vs.* moral progress, 177–178, 179–182, 189–197
moral progress, 191–197
role of love in, 199–201
strength and virtue in *Doctrine of Virtue*, 197–199
struggles with temptation, 180–181
temporality, significance of, 192–193
transcendental freedom, 184–185, 194–195
moral responsibility, and evil, 126–129, 136–138, 138*n*41, 146, 150
moral rigorism. *See* rigorism
moral strength, 181–184, 192, 196, 197–199
moral weakness, 59–60, 181–185, 189–192, 196–198, 220, 223
Moran, Kate
  ethical community, 204*n*2, 204*n*3, 219
  self-conceit, 84*n*27, 85*n*28, 85*n*29, 85*n*30, 85–86*n*33
Morgan, Seiriol
  "missing" proof for radical evil, 130*n*28, 130*n*29, 132, 144*n*47
  radical evil as a propensity, 125, 126
  root of evil, 87–88
  subordination and moral character, 47, 54–55
motivational dualism, 5, 11–12, 41–42
motives
  in relation to self-cognition, 159, 160
  in relation to self-deception, 70–71
  vs. principles of choice, 17–18
Muchnik, Pablo
  human species and universality of evil, 121*n*4
  interpretation of "species," 140*n*44
  proof of radical evil, 130*n*28, 130*n*29
  propensity to evil, 125–126

subordination and moral character, 47
three stages of evil, 59
Murdoch, Iris, 34, 154, 234

necessary conditions of evil, 7, 89–90,
90–99, 102
nonmoral action
egoism and the self in relation to, 15–19
and hedonistic pleasure, 11–15, 13n3,
14n7, 21, 24–25
nonmoral choice
and interpersonal comparisons, 28–29
sensuality and mental vitality, 26–27
two models of, 22–33
Nozick, Robert, 215

O'Hagan, Emer, challenges to self-
knowledge, 169–170n24
Otterman, Steven, 125n10
overdetermination
and compromises in action,
52–53, 56, 65
and evil, 54–65
and rigorism, 56–58
in scholarship on moral worth, 48n32
and subordination of the moral law,
47–54, 55

pain
alternation with pleasure, 22, 23, 30
need for, 31n26
Palmquist, Stephen
highest good, 219–220n34
Kant's account of conduct, 200n38
Kant's appeals to religion, 225n40
proof of radical evil, 130n28, 130n29
propensity of evil, 125n10, 126n16
passions
and nonmoral choice, 27–28
and self-conceit, 109
and vices, 107–108, 109n31
passivity
and nonmoral choice, 32–33
and self-love, 30–31
Pasternack, Lawrence
Kant's theory of moral reform, 177n2
self-deception and evil, 95–96
physical egoism, 16n10
Pinheiro Walla, Alice, presumption of
evil, 214

pleasure
alternation with pain, 22, 23, 30
definition of, 20, 20n19
and egoism, 20–21, 25, 26
in Kant's theory of motivation,
11–15, 14n7
in relation to vitality, 20–22, 24
and self, 16–21, 25–26
pluralism, 204, 212, 221–223, 226, 228,
230, 231
political conflict, as metaphor for moral
conflict, 111, 111n34
Potter, Nelson, self-deception and
evil, 103n21
pragmatic belief, 77–78, 78n18
Prauss, Gerold, 37n1
presumption of evil, and civil society,
214, 214n21
propensity to evil, 119, 123–129, 125n10,
138, 138n41
purity
in relation to moral progress,
181–182, 181n6
and subordination of the moral
law, 54–56

radical evil
as both propensity and deed, 119,
123–129, 137–138, 138n41
and dissimulation, 117–118, 119–120,
135–136n40, 136–137, 143–151
and human species, 117–118, 120–123,
138–143
interpretations of Kant's account of, 2,
37–39, 122
"missing" proof for, 134, 143, 144n47
a priori vs. empirical proof of, 119,
129–134, 129n27, 130n28, 130n29
in relation to individual character and
moral progress, 125n10, 139–143
and self-deception, 7, 117–118,
147–149, 151
rationalization
and acknowledging evidence, 73–76
in Critique of Pure Reason, 75
defined, 74
as distraction, 97–102
examples of, 74–75, 99–101
indirect quality of, 73–74, 84, 99
instability of, 104